ISLAMIC FINANCE: THEORY AND PRACTICE

Also by John R. Presley

EUROPEAN MONETARY INTEGRATION (*with P. Coffey*)

CURRENCY AREAS: THEORY AND PRACTICE
(*with G. E. J. Dennis*)

ROBERTSONIAN ECONOMICS

PIONEERS OF MODERN ECONOMICS IN BRITAIN (*co-editor and contributor with D. P. O'Brien*)

A GUIDE TO THE SAUDI ARABIAN ECONOMY (*second edition 1989, with A. J. Westaway*)

PIONEERS OF MODERN ECONOMICS IN BRITAIN (Vol.2)
(*co-editor and contributor with D. Greenaway*)

ISLAMIC FINANCIAL INSTITUTIONS (*editor and contributor*)

BANKING IN THE ARAB GULF (*with Rodney Wilson*)

ESSAYS ON ROBERTSONIAN ECONOMICS (*editor and contributor*)

ROBERTSON ON ECONOMIC POLICY (*co-editor with S. R. Dennison*)

Islamic Finance: Theory and Practice

Paul S. Mills
Manager, UK Debt Management Office
HM Treasury
London

and

John R. Presley
Professor of Economics
University of Loughborough
and
Chief Economic Adviser
The Saudi British Bank

332.10917
m65i

First published in Great Britain 1999 by
MACMILLAN PRESS LTD
Houndmills, Basingstoke, Hampshire RG21 6XS and London
Companies and representatives throughout the world

A catalogue record for this book is available from the British Library.

ISBN 0–333–49083–5

First published in the United States of America 1999 by
ST. MARTIN'S PRESS, INC.,
Scholarly and Reference Division,
175 Fifth Avenue, New York, N.Y. 10010

ISBN 0–312–22448–6

Library of Congress Cataloging-in-Publication Data
Mills, Paul S.
Islamic finance : theory and practice / Paul S. Mills, John R.
Presley.
p.   cm.
Includes bibliographical references and index.
ISBN 0–312–22448–6 (cloth)
1. Banks and banking—Islamic countries.   2. Banks and banking–
–Religious aspects—Islam.   I. Presley, John R.   II. Title.
HG3368.A6M55   1999
332.1'0917'671—dc21   99–21092
                                                          CIP

This book is printed on paper suitable for recycling and made from fully managed and
sustained forest sources.

10   9   8   7   6   5   4   3   2   1
08   07   06   05   04   03   02   01   00   99

Printed and bound in Great Britain by
Antony Rowe Ltd, Chippenham, Wiltshire

To my parents, with thanks for their sacrifices

For my first grandchild, Benjamin Ralph

Contents

Preface

The past decade has been one of unprecedented financial turmoil. Banking systems from the US and UK to Scandinavia, East Asia, Russia and now Japan have come under severe strain, if not collapse. Major economies have witnessed asset price bubbles, fuelled by easy credit terms, followed by slumps and credit contractions. Economists have resurrected the 'debt deflation' analysis of the 1930s as Japan suffers a falling price level and negative nominal interest rates are charged in yen deposits. Meanwhile the high level of indebtedness of the world's poorest nations remains largely unresolved.

Each of these financial dislocations have their proposed individual remedies, usually involving large amounts of taxpayers' money to subsidise risk-taking by private sector banks and financiers. It is ironic that when Western government state aid to manufacturing industries has been largely eliminated, the safety net provided to private sector banks goes unchallenged.

This book is motivated by the suspicion that there is another way. In particular, that the critique of interest-bearing debt finance has more economic cogency than is assumed by mainstream economics. This position is of long standing in Judaeo-Christian and early Western economic thought, but is now most clearly developed in the Islamic analysis of banking and finance. Hence, this book begins by setting the Islamic critique of interest and proposals for a non-interest banking system in the context of the Islamic approach to economic analysis. It then develops the theoretical properties of the non-interest model and assesses the recent experience of Islamic banking in practice, before outlining the economic benefits (and costs) of a non-interest financial system.

At a time when the financial headlines continually bear testimony to the recurring problems of our current approach to banking and finance, it is right to consider whether a more fundamental response than the usual palliatives of more bailouts and regulation is needed.

There are many people who have contributed to the publication of this book over several years. We would like to thank John Sessions, in particular, for allowing us to use an adaptation of 'Islamic Economics: the Emergence of a New Paradigm' (*Economic Journal*, 1994, with John Presley) for much of Chapter 4; John Presley would also wish to thank a host of postgraduate students who over the last decade have undertaken research projects into Islamic economics and banking at Loughborough University; these include amongst others Haitham Kabbara, Hussein Sharif Hussein, Bandar Al Hajjar, Tariqullah Khan, Khadija Harery, Mansour Al Fadhli and Jerry Wright. Most especially John Presley wishes to thank his co-author Paul Mills; although the book appears under joint authorship, the vast majority of the work associated with it was undertaken by Paul Mills and, therefore, most of the credit for the book must, as of right, go to him.

Paul Mills' contribution is derived largely from his Ph.D. thesis at Cambridge University. He would like to thank Dr Tony Cramp for his wisdom and advice in supervising the thesis, and Magdalene College, Cambridge, for financial support. He would also like to thank Dr Roy Clements and Dr Michael Schluter for their encouragement and example in applying the Bible to economics.

We wish also to thank the Islamic Foundation for its assistance and, in particular, would acknowledge the support of Professor Khurshid Ahmad, Dr Manazir Ahsan and Dr A. Chachi. John Presley is grateful for continued encouragement and help from Professor Umer Chapra, Professor Fahim Khan, Professor Ziaddin Ahmed, and Dr Munawar Iqbal. Professor Rodney Wilson of Durham University also deserves particular thanks for sharing a research agenda with John Presley for several years, as does, more recently, Humayon Dar.

The authors also wish to express their sincere thanks to Mrs Joyce Tuson, who has typed and helped organise the manuscript with her usual efficiency, and to Barbara Presley for completing the index.

Paul Mills
John Presley
November 1998

1 Islamic Economics and Banking – the Background

METHODOLOGY

Islam is founded upon the notion of *Tawhid* – a total commitment to the will of God, involving submission to the pattern of life disclosed in the expression of His revealed will. The logical conclusion from this premise, that Islam shares with other monotheistic faiths, is that all aspects of life have a spiritual dimension. There is no part of life that can be placed in a secular compartment, devoid of religious and ethical considerations. Islam is a lifestyle and worldview – not just a spiritual opinion about God's character (Abbasi et al., 1989, p. 7).

What distinguishes Islamic thought from Judaism, Christianity and even Muslim pietism is that the jump from individual obedience to the transformation of society is automatic.

> In Islam, there are no concepts of 'mosque' and 'state' as specifically religious and political institutions. Religion and state are believed to be fused together; the state is conceived as the embodiment of religion, and religion as the essence of the state. (Baldwin, 1990, p. 34)

This belief arises from the contents of the Qu'ran – an indivisible mixture of religious teaching, social ethics and law – and Mohammed's establishment of the inaugural Muslim society. This was not an afterthought of the new religion but of a piece with it.

The automatic espousal of theocracy has profound implications for Islamic economic methodology. Most obviously, Islamic law[1] becomes the predominant influence upon, and arbiter of, economic structures. It is highly specific in its proscription of some economic actions (e.g. hoarding), and its prescription of others (e.g. the division of inheritances). Hence, conservative scholars regard 'Islamization' as the embodiment of these provisions in legislation, and the shaping of economic and social policy in accordance with their guiding principles (in the areas where *Shari'ah* is not specific).[2] The role of the Islamic economist is to explore and elucidate the application of *Shari'ah* to

1

economic life, rather than innovating by using ethical precepts of his
or her choosing (e.g. K. Ahmad, 1980, p. xvi).

The organising principle of Islamic social thought is that the spiritual and moral takes precedence over the material and pragmatic,
based on the assumption that human happiness is ultimately to be
found in moral obedience rather than material ease (e.g. Naqvi, 1981,
p. 18). This emphasis is reinforced by the belief that the punishment or
reward of the afterlife will be directly related to the degree of moral
obedience displayed in this, measured against the Qu'ran's standards.
This 'carrot-and-stick' approach is believed to be necessary to ensure
widespread obedience to religious precepts in this life (e.g. Qureshi,
1979, pp. 117–18); and to be useful for the smooth running of
an Islamic economy, by inducing cooperative actions without
needing to resort to costly enforcement mechanisms (Bashir, 1990,
pp. 357–8). Belief in divine judgement also provides paternalistic
justification for restricting economic practices proscribed by *Shari'ah*.
Whilst a wide freedom of contract is admitted, limitations are advoc-
ated to protect individuals from jeopardising their chances of entry
into Paradise.

These features make the framing of a theoretical Islamic model
society *relatively* easy.[3] However, like other theocratic ethical systems,
Islam can diagnose what is currently wrong and describe the 'perfect'
society, but is less certain about what to do if people refuse to conform
to Islamic moral standards. Hence, the role of Islamic economics also
includes the evaluation of the government initiatives and legal reforms
needed to transform current institutions and modes of behaviour
in Muslim societies into those which conform to Islamic norms. It
has the task of building bridges between the 'is' and the 'ought'
(Siddiqi, 1971, p. 33). This leaves ample scope for divergence of
opinion because scant guidance is given in Islamic law on such pragmatic questions.

THE GUIDING PRINCIPLES OF ISLAMIC ECONOMICS

The dominant principle of Islamic economics is that of the responsibility for the stewardship of property, derived from the belief in God
as creator:

> The Almighty Allah is the real Owner of everything. Man is no
> more than His trustee. Man in Islam is Allah's *Khalifa* (vicegerent)

and representative on earth. As His trustee, man is obliged to obey the instructions of the One who appointed him in this capacity. (Presley, 1988, p. 14)

This belief results in the rejection of inalienable private property rights. Since all land and wealth is given in trust by God, *Shari'ah* can govern how property is to be used – it represents the divine terms of the 'loan' arrangement. Hence, property ownership is legitimate only if wealth is not acquired unfairly, hoarded, squandered or denied to the poor.

Islamic writers also agree that the state has a legitimate economic role as the embodiment of God's viceregency on earth, but disagree as to how interventionist this role should be in a Muslim society with little voluntary observance of *Shari'ah*. This degree of flexibility derives from a commitment to both economic freedom and distributive equity. On the one hand, individualised ownership is sanctioned, if not sanctified, by the principle of stewardship (Kalam, 1991, pp. 22ff); there is an appreciable degree of freedom of contract within certain boundaries (Schacht, 1964, p. 144); and free competition is seen as the guarantor of just prices and profits (Choudhury, 1986, p. 34). Conversely, *Shari'ah* emphasises communal responsibility for the relief of poverty; the sanctioning of minimum wage legislation and wealth taxation to fund welfare payments;[4] and the active intervention of the state to combat specific injustices, such as monopoly.

It is a divine duty to work. Social justice is the result of productive labour and equal opportunities such that everyone can use all their abilities to work and gain just reward from that work effort. Justice and equality in Islam means that people should have equal opportunity and does not imply that they should be equal in poverty or in riches (Chapra, 1985). However, it is incumbent on the Islamic state to guarantee a subsistence level to its citizens, that is, a minimum level of food, clothing, shelter, medical care and education (Qu'ran 2:275–9). The major purpose is to moderate social variances within Islamic society, and to enable the poor to lead a normal, spiritual and material life in dignity and contentment.

The scope of economic intervention is broad and can include state interference in many areas of economic activity (Saqr, 1980, p. 59). Such interference can take many forms, including general guidance and regulation by the State, but also might embrace more direct state ownership and direction. The duties assigned to the State under Islam primarily consist of commanding, counselling, controlling and protecting. The Qu'ran orders society to obey God, His Prophet and their rulers (Qu'ran 4:59) (in that order). An Islamic economic system operates on the fundamental principle that the forces of supply and demand should work freely in the determination of prices in all markets. Only in exceptional circumstances is there a justification for state intervention and, even then, the objective of such intervention is not to hinder freedom of trade but to secure more perfect information in the market place or to regulate or organise economic activities so as to protect economic freedom without harming either buyers or sellers.

THE SPECIFIC DETAILS OF *SHARI'AH*

The Islamic economic paradigm also contains detailed institutional structures and rules for individual conduct which must be observed if an economy is to be described as 'Islamic'.

The possession of property imposes obligations. Not only should property be safeguarded against loss or damage, but there is a requirement to enlarge one's possessions of property or wealth. The latter is seen as not only benefiting the property owner but society as a whole. This does not preclude the enjoyment of and benefit from property and wealth, so long as this enjoyment does not embrace extravagance, hoarding, reckless spending or usury nor, for example, indulgence in gambling, alcohol or drug abuse.

The most important of these requirements is the levying of *zakat*, or wealth tax. It is designed to 'purify' wealth from its supposedly inherent tendency to concentrate into fewer and fewer hands in the accumulation process (Abdeen and Shook, 1984, p. 19). The 2.5 per cent annual rate is levied on all marketable wealth, in personal possession for over a year, above specified thresholds. The proceeds are to be spent on the poor, religious causes and the release of debtors amongst other things. Islamic writers believe an additional purpose of *zakat* to be the penalising of hoarding, since the tax is levied on all wealth, including cash holdings, whether invested or not. They strongly believe that such a tax would increase the proportion of wealth held as productive capital and prevent money from being hoarded, following the elimination of risk-free return-bearing assets consequent upon the abolition of interest (e.g. Mannan, 1968, p. 6; Choudhury, 1986, p. 171).

In addition to interest, Islamic law proscribes transactions that involve a particular element of uncertainty (*gharar*) in their contract terms. The Qu'ran forbids gambling on games of chance, and legal opinion developed the principle so as to include within the prohibition all contracts that contain uncertain countervalues in exchange (e.g. the sale of fruit before it has ripened). When applied to modern financial contracts, the prohibition of *gharar* eliminates futures, options and some life assurance contracts (Saleh, 1986, pp. 49–50), in order to protect one party or the other from being disadvantaged by the future course of events, and to restrict speculation.[5]

THE ISLAMIC ECONOMIC SYSTEM – ACHIEVING DIFFERENT OBJECTIVES?

The efficiency of any financial system is determined in part by its ability to help society achieve its accepted economic objectives. At the outset there appears to be no fundamental difference between the accepted economic objectives in the West and those of a truly Islamic economy. The underlying feature of any economy must be the desire to achieve social and economic justice. The key question then becomes the identification of individual macroeconomic objectives and the means of their achievment.

Chapra (1985) identifies the major macroeconomic objectives of an Islamic system as the achievement of full employment and an optimum rate of economic growth combined with a stable value of money. There is nothing debatable here. If there is a difference at all from Western paradigms, it is a question of emphasis. This emphasis relates mainly to the underlying major objective of socio-economic justice and the achievement of an equitable distribution of income and wealth, including what Islamic economists call a just return to all members of society from economic development (Chapra, 1985, pp. 33–45). The Islamic system places the major emphasis upon the dominant need of welfare maximisation for the total Islamic community. In this context all policies in Islam need to be viewed in terms of their relief of suffering and advancement of social welfare. The pursuit of economic growth in some capitalist economies may occur through a redistribution of income and wealth towards better-off members of society, with welfare sacrifices being made by the lower income groups, at least in the short term. This would be unacceptable in Islam. Full employment is to be achieved in an Islamic economy not only because it allows every individual to satisfy basic needs but because it imparts to them dignity within society. Economic growth is only acceptable if it is brought about via a broadly-based development of economic well-being. It is not acceptable in Islam if it is achieved by producing 'non-essential' goods, or by damaging the moral or physical environment (Chapra, pp. 35–6). Much more emphasis therefore in Islam has always been placed upon the type of product and the potential social costs associated with economic growth. Therefore, it appears there is at most a difference of emphasis in the objectives pursued by the Islamic economy – not a significant redirection. There is also nothing in the Islamic paradigm that makes the Islamic economy immune from the problems encountered in the West; conflicts will remain in achieving all macroeconomic objectives simultaneously.

Ultimately, the search in the Islamic economic system is for socioeconomic justice for all members of the Islamic community. This has remained an elusive concept to define. Whether or not it is achieved will be influenced by whether or not people comply with the obligations relating to property or wealth ownership and whether principles of 'tawhid' and brotherhood are adhered to. These dictate how the individual, through his relationship with God, also relates to his fellow man. Whilst social justice appears to promote economic cooperation, it does not involve equality, merely equality of opportunity for all people who are able to work, and a requirement to support all of those in the community who are able to supply work effort.

In Chapter 2 we examine the Islamic critique of interest in terms of textual evidence and the legal, ethical and economic critique of interest. Somewhat surprisingly perhaps there is a great deal of evidence to suggest that historically even in the Western economies and outside of the Islamic faith there has been much opposition to interest; this is the subject of Chapter 8. Chapter 3 is devoted to an outline of the interest-free financial system, focusing upon the partnership principle, the theory of interest-free banks and key issues in the theory of interest-free finance, before discussing the theoretical feasibility and benefits of an interest-free financial system. Chapter 4 presents a theoretical model of *mudarabah* profit and loss as an efficient revelation device.

Practical aspects of Islamic banking are considered in Chapter 5 and this is followed (Chapter 6) by a discussion of the macroeconomic stability in the non-interest economy. Chapter 7 examines some key issues in the Islamic financial system, isolating the more important areas of debate – savings behaviour in a non-interest economy, the allocation of loanable funds, non-interest finance and bank stability, and public finance and government borrowing. The final chapter brings together some of the major themes and conclusions of the book.

2 The Islamic Critique of Interest

THE TEXTUAL EVIDENCE AND SUBSEQUENT CASUISTRY

The Qu'ran disparages the taking of interest (*riba*) in four distinct passages which increase in severity, the later the claim of revelation. Initially, interest is simply described as not counting as true wealth in God's eyes (30:39). The Jews are condemned for not obeying their own Scripture's prohibition of interest[1] (4:161) and reference is made to the contemporary practice of compounding interest and principal upon default:

> O believers, take not doubled and redoubled interest, and fear God so that you may prosper. Fear the fire which has been prepared for those who reject the faith ... (3:130–1)[2]

The final condemnation is the most outspoken and wide-ranging:

> Those who benefit from interest shall be raised like those who have been driven to madness by the touch of the Devil; this is because they say: 'Trade is like interest'. But God has permitted trade and forbidden interest. Hence those who have received the admonition from their Lord and desist, may have what has already passed, their case being entrusted to God; but those who revert shall be the inhabitants of the fire and abide therein forever. ... O believers, fear God, and give up the interest that remains outstanding if you are believers. If you do not do so, then be sure of being at war with God and His Messenger. But, if you repent, you can have your principal. (2:275, 278, 279)

Whilst no financial penalties for usury are outlined, the taking of interest is described as madness, something God wishes to destroy, deserving of a war from God, the antithesis of faith, and something which, if persisted in, deserves a permanent abode in Hell (Uzair, 1980, p. 44). No other act of social injustice receives such severe Qu'ranic censure. In many of the *hadiths*, usury is placed on a par

7

with repeated adultery and deemed more sinful than maternal incest (Chapra, 1985, pp. 236–7).

One might imagine that such forthright condemnation would have been readily accepted by faithful Muslims. Yet casuistical interpretations have arisen within Islam with marked similarities to those within Christianity. (see Chapter 8) Everyone agrees that *'riba'* is prohibited. Interpretation turns on whether the Qu'ran's *riba* is today's 'interest'. For instance, it is alleged that all loans in Mohammed's time were for consumption purposes and so 'interest' then was likely to be exploitative (e.g. Shah, 1959, pp. 34–5). The prohibition does not, therefore, apply to loans to businesses who can protect themselves from exploitation (Kahf, 1978, p. 68), or to modern, competitive banks (Ishfaq, 1991). In addition, the Qu'ran is thought to address only 'usury' in the exploitative sense because of its reference to 'doubled and redoubled *riba*' (3: 130) (Ulgener, 1967, p. 12). Finally, the necessity of a positive rate of interest for economic development is assumed, and so pragmatic considerations justify modifications to the Qu'ran's teaching (Rahman, 1964, p. 7; S. R. Khan, 1987, pp. 20–3).[3]

The rebuttal of these claims also mirrors the Christian debate (see Chapter 8). Evidence is cited to show that Mohammed had intimate knowledge of contemporary trading conditions and that the majority of loans were for productive purposes.[4] Besides, in agrarian economies, it is difficult to differentiate between 'consumption' and 'production' loans (Haque, 1980a, p. 24). Such a distinction is not made in the text, which elsewhere advocates interest-free loans, debt remission or gifts for the aid of the needy (Zaidi, 1986, pp. 34–5). The Qu'ran specifically allows only the return of the loan principal. To permit exceptions would implicitly cast doubt upon the wisdom and universality of *Shari'ah*:

> The Prophet ... did not differentiate between situations where borrowed capitals had relieved borrower distress, or had been invested in some productive enterprise. Had God meant that differentiation, or known that it would be beneficial to mankind, a relevant stipulation would not have been omitted from the Qu'ran. (Al-' Arabi, 1966, p. 10)

This has been the majority opinion of Islamic jurists throughout history. However, it has often been ignored by Muslim governments on grounds of expediency (e.g. for state borrowing). In addition, Islamic legal interpretation has permitted the use of devices to evade the interest ban since a temporal judiciary is only concerned with observance of the letter of *Shari'ah* rather than its spirit[5] (Schacht, 1964, pp. 79–80). It has taken the recent revival of Islamic confidence to prompt the reaffirmation of the usury prohibition.

THE LEGAL CRITIQUE OF INTEREST

The most fundamental Islamic critique of interest rests on the definition of legal exchange. For an exchange of money and/or goods to be legitimate, neither party should receive an advantage without giving an appropriate countervalue. The profitable exchange of goods for money is licit because the excess rewards the provision of a service (e.g. transport, storage or risk-bearing). The exchange of money for money is legal only when no increase (*riba*) occurs since the equivalent countervalue of one monetary sum is exactly the same sum.[6] Hence, 'God has permitted trade and forbidden *riba*' (2: 275).

An analogous argument is that usury involves the illegitimate creation of property rights. In Islamic law, money is a valid claim on property when obtained through work, exchange, gift or inheritance. In monetary loans, which are temporary transfers of property rights, all that can be claimed as repayment are the equivalent property rights and no more, since any excess cannot be justified under any of the legitimate categories. Consequently,

rich become more rich just because

> Interest on money loaned represents an unjustifiable creation of instantaneous property rights. It is unjustifiable because interest is a property right claimed outside the legitimate framework of individual property rights recognised by Islam, and instantaneous because as soon as the contract for lending upon interest is concluded, a right to the borrower's property is created for the lender, regardless of the outcome of the enterprise for which it is used. (Mirakhor, 1988, p. 93)

The return on the loan is contractually separate from the production of value that it might facilitate, and so is illegal.

This argument is underpinned by the legal distinction between loan and rental/hire contracts. The Roman law definitions of *commodatum* (hire) and *mutuum* (loan) find parallels in the Islamic distinction between *'ariya* and *qard*. The former involves a transfer of the use of durable property or goods for a hire charge to cover inherent productivity (of land), risk of ownership and depreciation. The latter entails the loan of a fungible (e.g. money) in which the borrower undertakes to return the exact equivalent of that originally received. A hire charge for the use of money is inappropriate because it can only be spent once. Charging interest on a loan is thus equivalent to selling a loaf of bread for its exchange value and adding a surcharge for its use. Hence, it is a misnomer to claim that interest equates to a rental or hire charge for money, since money is not meant to depreciate systematically and the risks of ownership are transferred to the borrower in a loan.[7] The 'just price' of a loan, therefore, is the exact return of the principal.

THE ETHICAL CRITIQUE OF INTEREST

Islamic economists deploy different ethical arguments against production and consumption interest-bearing loans. The former is deemed to involve an unjust allocation of risk between borrower and lender, because no *real* investment project under competitive conditions can be guaranteed to make a gross profit, let alone automatically cover interest costs. Interest gives the lender immunity from the potential for loss that the borrower faces.[8] This discrimination in favour of loan finance is thought to be unwarranted and a penalty upon entrepreneurial initiative. Business losses act as a socially useful signalling device in the directing of productive activities. The costs of generating such signals should, therefore, be shared between finance and productive capital by profit-and-loss sharing (PLS) arrangements (Siddiqi, 1983a, p. 71, 182; Ahmed et al., 1983a, p. 21).

Interest on consumption loans is conventionally justified on opportunity cost grounds. Islamic economists believe such reasoning to be fallacious because no alternative outlet for funds can guarantee a definite profit (e.g. Qureshi, 1946, pp. 51–2). Besides, interest on consumption loans can be attacked for its own attributes. First, such interest is merely redistributive because it can never represent a claim on extra productive wealth created by the granting of the loan, even though it may increase at a compound rate (Ulgener, 1967, p. 12). Consequently, there is ample scope for the pauperization and enslavement of the borrower, to the advantage of the, probably, wealthy lender. Secondly,

> In the case of consumption loans, [interest] violates the basic function for which God has created wealth, which envisages that the needy be supported by those who have surplus wealth. (Siddiqi, 1981, p. 63)

The genuine need for distress loans should be met from other interest-free sources (such as *zakat* proceeds).

To the ethical critique of interest, Islam adds condemnation of its morally undesirable consequences for society. In a variety of ways, interest is seen as an enemy of social solidarity or 'brotherhood' (S. M. Ahmad, 1947, p. 42). In particular, the existence of interest tends to make the distribution of wealth more unequal. It accrues to generally wealthy net lenders, at the expense of generally poorer net borrowers, and consumers who pay higher prices (Qadri, 1981). Also, larger firms and wealthier borrowers are extended credit on more advantageous terms because they can offer greater security (Chapra, 1991, pp. 22–3). The remuneration of financial capital on a PLS basis would result in lower prices (because producers face less financial risk), and a more equitable distribution of wealth.

The divisiveness of interest is compounded by its nature as unearned income:

> Islam enjoins its followers to strive for their living and not to live on the toils of others. The very spirit of Islam is against living by owning without working. Seen in this light, interest resembles unearned income. (Ariff, 1982b, p. 295)

Although pure rentiers could still exist in an Islamic economy, apologists stress the damage caused by supporting such a class through interest payments. Not only is society deprived of their labour but also the moral characters of those involved are damaged in the process (e.g. Qureshi, 1979, p. 39).

THE ECONOMIC CRITIQUE OF INTEREST[9]

Islamic Definitions of Money and Capital

Islamic economists endorse many conventional attitudes towards money, believing its primary role to be a facilitator of exchange. Differences arise when considering money as a measure and store of value. First, Islamic writers repeat the Medieval scholastic belief that if money is to act as a measure of value, it is paradoxical for it to command a price in terms of itself. Interest acts as the price of money and so makes the measure of value itself an object of exchange. This is believed to impede the effectiveness of money in its role as the means of exchange by assigning it time-dependent values (Uzair, 1978, p. 6; cf. Ballantyre, 1988, p. 5).

Secondly, Islamic economists are suspicious of money acting as a stable store of value due to the Qu'ranic condemnation of hoarding (9:34, 35). Since money was designed primarily to facilitate exchange, it should be spent freely for this function to be performed. The hoarding of cash interrupts the exchange of goods and services, so possibly leading to a deficiency of effective demand (Saud, 1967, p. 13). The root of the problem is the potential for cash to act as a stable store of value, thereby enabling its holders to extort a liquidity premium (interest) for its surrender. Holders of money should not be rewarded, with interest, for releasing it back into circulation via a loan, since this is the purpose for which it is designed.

Islamic disaffection with conventional views on money is complemented by dissension from Western notions of 'capital'. Throughout classical and neo-classical literature, the terms 'profit', 'interest' and 'rent' are often used interchangeably, giving the impression that all income derived from capital is equivalent.[10] This classification is challenged by those who observe that capital would be unproductive without entrepreneurial input,[11] and that profit is only legitimate if effort and/or risk have been involved in its acquisition. Hence, residual profit is the appropriate factor income for the combination of capital and entrepreneurship described as 'enterprise'. Providers of finance can only share justly in this residual profit if they share the risks of a variable return, or even loss. No investment can be guaranteed to be profitable, and so it is unrealistic to assume that finance capital can 'earn' a positive return, irrespective of use:

> There is no justification for obliging the entrepreneur to pay interest if there is no positive return on the money invested. To claim the contrary, as prevalent in the interest-based system, requires that money capital be regarded as essentially productive of value; but this is not so. Value is a market phenomenon and not an intrinsic property of money capital. (Siddiqi, 1983a, p. 72)

Hence, the enjoyment of a return by financial capital is justified only by the service to society provided by sharing the risks inherent in the productive process.[12] Financial instruments that yield a guaranteed *ex ante* return (e.g. interest-bearing loans and some leasing contracts) are consequently deemed illicit.

The Islamic Critique of Mainstream Theories of Interest

The corollary of the economic critique of interest is the rejection of mainstream interest theories. Islamic economists assert that, despite capitalist economies being dominated by the influence of interest, its apologists have failed to provide a convincing justification for its very existence.[13] Traditional explanations of interest are lined up and dispatched in turn (e.g. Siddiqi, 1981, pp. 47–52). The belief that interest is the 'reward' for abstaining from consumption, or acts as the 'price of waiting', is refuted by observing that the hoarding of money involves similar 'sacrifice' without the reward. Besides, the bulk of saving is undertaken by companies and the rich (who cannot claim to have 'sacrificed' anything), and for motives other than achieving a return.[14]

Islamic writers also question the realism of Keynes' 'liquidity preference' explanation of interest. Lenders will (or ought to) calculate their liquidity requirements before deciding to part with their money, since the costs of experiencing a liquidity crisis will far outweigh any marginal benefit derived from interest. Hence, interest does not reward any significant surrendering of liquidity. In addition, modern bank deposits are such that interest is paid on highly liquid assets anyway. Liquidity considerations may help to explain the interest rate structure, but cannot justify the very existence of interest *a priori* (M. Ahmad, 1967, p. 192).[15]

The belief of Böhm-Bawerk and Fisher in the generalised preference for present, as opposed to future, satisfaction is attacked for universalizing a preference that does not apply to all people in all circumstances:

> positive time preference is neither a principle of rationality nor an empirically established predominant tendency among consumers. It is simply one of three patterns of intertemporal choice (the other two being zero and negative time preference), each of which is rational and observable under its own conditions. (Zarqa, 1983a, p. 210)

There can be no automatic assumption, therefore, that positive time preference predominates in all circumstances so as to necessitate a positive rate of interest. Even when this does occur, however, Islamic economists insist that such preferences can and ought to be expressed through profit-related financial instruments or the hire of durables, rather than conventional loans (e.g. Naqvi, 1981, pp. 112–13; M. F. Khan, 1991).

Finally, 'productivity' explanations of interest are rejected. These justify a positive return on money via the opportunity cost argument that present goods can be utilised to produce more goods in the future. The physical possibility of this is not questioned. Rather, the problem comes with requiring a fixed, positive rate of return despite the considerable uncertainties of real capital projects:

> Capital itself is not productive, and it is the application of human efforts to a stock of capital which generates output and income. The reward for capital, then, cannot be legitimately fixed in advance, unlike interest rates, but can only be determined in retrospect ... (Ariff, 1982b, p. 295)

Consequently, productivity theories can only explain why a return on finance capital is justified in some, but not all, circumstances.

The general conclusion of Islamic critics is that mainstream theories of interest are *post hoc* rationalisations of what already exists (e.g. M. Ahmad, 1967, p. 177; Mannan, 1970, pp. 51–2). The ensuing confusion forces practical economists to explain the determination of interest by opportunity cost reasoning – a particular rate of interest being set by the 'pure' rate yielded by riskless government bonds, with inflation, risk, and administrative cost premia added.[16] But there is no watertight justification for the perpetual existence of this 'pure' rate. Interest exists because it is there; it is still held up by its own theoretical bootstraps. The failure of mainstream economics to explain adequately the existence of interest betrays the fact that it is merely a theoretical concept with no true basis in reality. It is a figment of our collective imaginations:

> And so why is there interest? ... Surely there are some phenomena of the mind, the resultants of thoughts and opinions...[which] solely originate in the will of the two parties, not a physical phenomena at all. Surely there are mental phenomena to which the dictum may correctly be applied that there is nothing true but thinking makes it so. (Harrod, 1948, pp. 65–6).

3 The Interest-free Financial System

ISLAMIC PROPOSALS FOR AN INTEREST-FREE FINANCIAL SYSTEM

The devout Muslim with disposable wealth has always faced a dilemma. Qu'ranic opposition to interest is clear, but so too is the condemnation of hoarding and wasteful consumption. The impasse is that of having wealth to save, but few legitimate financial instruments with which to do so. Suspicion of conventional banks, and a dearth of alternative savings outlets, resulted in hoards estimated to be of the order of $80 billion in Muslim countries in the early 1980s (Wöhlers-Scharf, 1983, p. 76). The problem is to devise financial intermediaries that operate without resorting to interest but which still yield a return to depositors, for:

> if a banking structure could be evolved in which the return for the use of financial resources would fluctuate according to actual profits made from such use, the resulting system would be in conformity with Islamic rules and guidelines. (M. S. Khan and Mirakhor, 1987a, p. x)

The achievement of Islamic economists and bankers has been the conception and implementation of such a structure.

Any losses are deducted from the investor's principal. The manager only becomes liable for losses when he or she contravenes any pre-arranged trading instructions or is wilfully negligent. The investor's liability is limited since the manager is only empowered to commit the initial capital outlay to trade – no leveraging of the capital is permitted.

The *musharika* partnership follows similar lines with the significant difference that many partners supply finance, including on occasion the entrepreneur. Profits are again shared between manager and investors on a predetermined basis with residual profits or losses being allocated to investors in proportion to their financial contributions. This contractual form allows some investors to be involved in managerial decision-making and some to remain sleeping partners.[1] Whilst the limited liability corporation does not appear in the classical

15

legal traditions, it has received general approval from Islamic jurists on the grounds of analogy and public interest (Chapra, 1985, p. 255); the major advantage being that shares in limited companies are more easily divisible and transferable than those in partnerships. Although share dividends are paid on a discretionary basis, rather than being a pre-specified proportion of profit, they are acceptable in principle due to their association with profit or loss.

Other Return-bearing Contracts

Islamic theorists emphasise partnership variants to finance commercial investment and the interest-free loan for charitable purposes. Nevertheless, *Shari'ah* contains a range of contractual forms which can be used to derive a return to financial capital without resorting to 'interest'. For instance, Islamic law permits rental charges to be made for property services on the grounds of natural fructibility (of land), the intangible benefits of use (of durables), and the depreciation and maintenance costs incurred by the owner. The only precondition of such *ijara* contracts is that the lessor retains the risks of ownership so that he or she cannot derive a fixed, certain return *ex ante* and remains concerned about the lessee's use of the hired object (e.g. Mannan, 1970, p. 153). The permissibility of rental contracts provides a further return- bearing outlet for financial capital whilst offering firms an alternative source of finance via leasing or hire purchase of equipment. This latter admission has disquieted those Islamic economists who wish to promote profit-related financial contracts, prompting suggestions that rental payments be related to the profitability of use. This is feasible in the case of crop-sharing agreements for agricultural land,[2] but is computationally impractical when trying to associate a firm's rental payments to profits made with leased equipment (Karsten, 1982, pp. 119–22).

The most controversial *Shari'ah* dispensation, however, is that of *murabaha*, or mark-up sale of goods. This contract permits a customer to authorise an agent to purchase a particular good, with repayment being in instalments or a lump-sum at an agreed mark-up. Technically, this is not 'interest' since profit is made in the exchange of money for goods and not money for money (e.g. El-Ashker, 1987, pp. 132–3). The mark-up is justified by the service the agent provides in purchasing advice and negotiation, transport, and the risk that the customer may eventually refuse to purchase on delivery. To be consistent with Islamic law, the agent must make separate contracts with the supplier and customer, take physical possession of the merchandise and not link the mark-up to the period of repayment (e.g. Chapra, 1985, p. 170). However, some Islamic banks are using mark-up contracts to supply trade and import credit in a relatively risk-free manner by not allowing the customer to refuse the good, and not taking physical possession. In addition, Islamic law provides for the levying of service charges (*jo'alah*) in financial transactions, if they are related to incurred costs and not to the size or duration of the transaction, and for the forward purchase of goods yet to be delivered (*bai'salam*). Thus, a wide range of contractual forms is sanctioned under *Shari'ah*, although these are never risk-free and never involve the exchange of money in one time period for more money in another. Consequently, Islamic banks may be prevented from holding interest-bearing assets but are not thereby restricted to purely production-related lending.

The Interest-free Bank in Theory[3]

Islamic bankers and economists have tended to modify the conventional, fractional reserve banking model to non-interest operations. On the liability side, a sharp distinction is made between transactions and investment deposits. Current accounts are characterised by instant access, a guaranteed nominal value and no return. Service charges may be imposed, or waived if a minimum account balance is maintained. Investment accounts are accepted on the basis of limited access (e.g. notice of withdrawal requirements), no guarantee of nominal value and a Profit-and-Loss Sharing (PLS) return derived from the bank's investment portfolio. 'Dividends' are paid out every three, six or twelve months when the overall portfolio's value is assessed (Siddiqi, 1983b, pp. 41–2). The bank can offer a range of risk–return trade-offs by providing higher PLS ratios for deposits of longer maturity, and offering accounts in its general portfolio or in more specialised investments.

On the asset side, an interest-free bank emulates a conventional investment bank. A proportion of current account liabilities are held as cash and highly liquid reserves with the remainder devoted to short-term assets, particularly trade finance. Investment deposits and equity capital are invested in PLS partnerships, property, equities, leasing and mark-up finance. Conventional risk management techniques (such as reserve accumulation, project diversification and maturity matching) are still applicable.

The only major disagreement over this model has been the on-lending of transactions deposits on a fractional reserve basis. Since current depositors do not authorise banks to invest their money in a risk-taking

manner, and instant repayment is guaranteed by the bank, the on-lending of such deposits is thought to violate the ethical principles of contract
law (Anwar, 1987a, p. 300). The ensuing creation of credit, on a fractional reserve basis, is regarded as a bankers' trick to extort the property
of others by using their depositors' funds without permission (Qureshi,
1946, pp. 145–8). Moreover, the private creation of bank credit results
in: money supply volatility, as banks vary their reserve ratios and the
public switch between holding 'inside' and 'outside' money (Presley,
1988, p. 76); the vulnerability of conventional banks to runs and liquidity
crises (M.S. Khan, 1986); and the loss of State seigniorage.

Monetary and banking stability would be more easily achieved
through a 100 per cent reserve system (Al-Jarhi, 1983, pp. 74–5). Also,
the prerogative to benefit from money creation ought to rest with the
State, and be used for the benefit of the whole of society by financing
lower taxation or public welfare projects (e.g. Ahmed et al., 1983b, p. 7;
Anwar, 1987a, p. 295). Consequently, proposals abound whereby the
transactions and investment sides of banking are separated either into
unrelated arms of the same institution or into different institutions.
Transactions deposits would be covered by 100 per cent reserves of
cash or central bank balances, with costs covered by transactions charges
or government subsidy (e.g. M.S. Khan and Mirakhor, 1987c, p. 165).

Much of this case is disputed by Islamic proponents of fractional
reserve banking (e.g. Siddiqi, 1983a, pp. 20–2). If the productive use of
demand deposits is prevented, transactions charges are anticipated to
be prohibitively expensive. In addition, a 100 per cent reserve requirement is not a necessary prerequisite to ensuring that an Islamic central
bank could effectively control the money supply (see below); and it is
the flexibility in the supply of credit, provided by fractional reserve
operations, that enables lenders to respond rapidly to unanticipated
changes in productive activity (Uzair, 1982, p. 227).

This debate has remained entirely theoretical, however, because the
existing private Islamic banks have been competing against conventional, fractional reserve banks and so are unable to afford the 'luxury'
of holding 100 per cent demand deposit reserves.

Issues in the Theory of Interest-free Finance

Trade and Consumer Credit

The prohibition of interest has its most serious impact upon those
forms of finance for which any profit-related return is difficult to

measure or impossible to provide. For instance, short-term trade finance would be difficult to arrange since banks could not charge for overdrafts or profit from the discounting of bills. Interest, being solely time-period dependent, conveniently dispenses with the need to calculate the productivity of the funds provided.

Islamic theorists have responded in two ways. First, they have attempted to devise non-interest, return-bearing forms of trade credit. For instance, Uzair (1980, pp. 51–2) argues that if the actual profitability of the funds' use is incalculable, the firm's average return on capital could be imputed or fixed service charges levied. Secondly, the need for short-term credit is downplayed. Many business borrow perpetually on overdraft as a substitute for raising equity capital. Hence, Islamic banks can provide semi-permanent trade finance via PLS lending or share purchases (e.g. Zarqa, 1983b, pp. 248–9). Also, some claim that such banks need only charge administration costs for overdraft facilities, since they could be financed from interest-free current accounts. If such loans were restricted to a bank's PLS borrowers, it would still benefit from a higher return being made on its return-based assets (e.g. Chapra, 1985, p. 129).

These suggestions parallel those for meeting consumer credit requirements. Non-essential consumer durable purchases could be financed by hire purchase or rental arrangements provided by banks, retailers or employers. Alternatively, banks could provide interest-free overdrafts from their current account funds, rationed to their investment account holders or on a time- multiple basis[4] akin to a credit union.

These proposals are complemented by criticism of consumer lending as practised in developed economies. Consumer credit is blamed for amplifying the business cycle, encouraging materialistic extravagance, producing social problems through indebtedness and 'crowding out' productive investment.[5] Against this background, the ban on interest is not seen as an inconvenience to be side-stepped, but as a necessary check on a socially undesirable practice. Where loans are needed for the purchase of necessities by the poor, however, Islamic writers are unanimous in their advocacy of interest-free loans granted either by state-run loan funds, *zakat* funds or credit cooperatives, due to the Qu'ran's emphasis upon lending freely to the poor (e.g. Mannan, 1968, p. 7).

Government Borrowing and Monetary Policy

Perhaps the most obvious restriction that the prohibition of interest places upon the financial system is that conventional government bond finance is eliminated. State investment projects likely to produce a financial return (e.g. toll roads, power stations) can be funded on a PLS or equity basis. However, for other investment and expenditure requirements, there seem few alternatives to full tax-financing (Chapra, 1982, pp. 226–7).

Once again, some theorists propose alternative methods of non-interest government borrowing, whilst others question the need for deficit financing altogether. The former suggest indexing the nominal value of government bonds to the price level or the nominal growth of GNP, or paying the average of returns on government investment equities.[6] These proposals preserve a zero or uncertain real rate of return on loans, but appear casuistical (Presley, 1988, p. 305). Other suggestions would allow the government to borrow without having to pay any return at all. This could be attempted by exempting interest-free bonds from *zakat*, competing for current accounts by running a transactions system through post offices, or forcing banks to deposit a significant proportion of current account balances with the central bank (Siddiqi, 1983b, pp. 146–50). In wartime emergencies, increased spending could be financed by compulsory, non-interest loans from the private sector (Mannan, 1987).

An alternative would be to dispense with the need for government borrowing by setting a balanced budget target. Islamic theorists make a virtue out of necessity. Deficit finance is blamed for the inflationary propensity of many developing economies, with the resulting negative real rates of return being held responsible for depressing savings and investment (Anwar, 1987b, p. 61). Government's ability to borrow is also charged with imposing unwarranted burdens on future taxpayers, reallocating wealth to a minority of bondholders and giving the state an incentive to inflate the price level so as to reduce the real burden of its debt (e.g. Siddiqi, 1983a, pp. 77–8). Thus:

> The non-availability of debt-financing for (general government expenditure) should prove to be a hidden blessing and help introduce the needed discipline in government spending, the realisation of which is frustrated by easy access to interest-based finance. (Chapra, 1985, p. 192; see also Zaidi, 1986, p. 35)

The absence of an interest rate structure and conventional government bonds has prompted the suggestion that monetary policy would be ineffectual or non-existent in an Islamic economy. Once again, this restriction is portrayed as a blessing in disguise since conventional monetary policy has proved too blunt an instrument (e.g. Ariff, 1982b, pp. 293, 299). However, the non-existence of a definite cost of credit/ discount rate has prompted other Islamic theorists to advocate variants of monetary base or supply control.

Proposals for central bank instruments to control the supply of credit in an interest-free financial system abound.[7] Changes in statutory cash and reserve ratios are deemed flexible enough to act as discretionary policy instruments, and could be reinforced by calls for special supplementary deposits. In addition, bank reserves could be varied directly if the central bank holds investment deposits within the system (Al-Jarhi, 1983, p. 71), or by undertaking open market operations in the equities of state enterprises. A highly interventionist monetary policy could be effected through direct controls on the supply and allocation of credit, usually in the context of bank nationalisation, or the manipulation of maxima and minima for PLS ratios.

When modelled along these lines there is believed to be no fundamental change in the way monetary policy affects macroeconomic variables in an Islamic economy. For instance, the IS-LM model of Khan and Mirakhor (1987c) predicts that an expansionary monetary stance would reduce realised rates of return on finance and increase output in the short run. Hence, confident affirmations of the efficacy of monetary policy in a non-interest system are common:

> Our conclusion must be that, in spite of the prohibition of interest, the Central Bank can discharge all the functions typical of a Central Bank. Even in an interest-free economy, monetary policy is a meaningful idea and it can be made to serve the demands of changing conditions. (Siddiqi, 1983b, p. 124; see also S. Ahmed, 1989)

THE THEORETICAL FEASIBILITY AND BENEFITS OF A NON-INTEREST FINANCIAL SYSTEM

Islamic opposition to interest is primarily inspired by religious adherence to the teachings of the Qu'ran. However, this has not prevented the theoretical analysis and justification of a PLS financial system in order to convince sceptics of the efficacy of *Shari'ah*. In their turn, the sceptics have countered with various theoretical objections that are believed to render a non-interest system impractical or inefficient.

PLS banking is attacked for its impracticality in the light of the principal–agent problems highlighted by contract theory and the likely reaction of savers to the abolition of interest. Islamic proponents deem these accusations to be exaggerated, and offset by the propensity of an interest-based system to misallocate loanable funds, induce financial crises and exaggerate the business cycle.

These arguments will be presented by outlining the theoretical implications of a PLS financial system and assessing its feasibility in the light of conventional economic theory and historical experience. The pragmatic case for the proscription of interest can then be appraised.

PRINCIPAL–AGENT PROBLEMS IN FINANCIAL CONTRACTING

The most frequent argument against PLS banking is that it would be extremely vulnerable to the problems of moral hazard and adverse selection on the lending side of bank operations (e.g. Sharraf, 1984; Pryor, 1985). Such possibilities arise from financial contracts between lenders (principals) and borrowers (agents) being struck in a world of incomplete information and self-seeking. This allegation, and the Islamic response, can be best understood if first, the theoretical debate concerning debt versus equity[8] finance within the principal–agent literature is outlined.

Background

From one strand of the corporate finance literature, the whole question is irrelevant. Within the Miller–Modigliani (M-M) (1958) framework of idealistic assumptions, the value of a firm is independent of its choice of financial structure. No real effects result from varying the debt–equity ratio, and so the supposed advantages of PLS finance over interest-bearing debt (or vice versa) are purely illusory. Hence, the standard textbook descriptions of corporate financial decision-making (e.g. Levy and Sarnat, 1978) focus on where the 'complete markets' assumptions of M-M are broached. For instance, debt finance is advantageous because of its beneficial tax position. This is traded off against the greater risk of incurring bankruptcy costs that higher leveraging involves, and the higher risk premium required by lenders as a result.

The M-M outcome crucially depends on information concerning investment projects being costlessly available to the prospective capital supplier. If this is the case, or if the information can be costlessly shared, or if the two parties' objectives automatically converge, the 'first-best' contractual solution will be reached. Its exact terms will depend upon the willingness and ability of the two sides to bear risk.

Complexity and realism are introduced by acknowledging that information is incomplete and only available after costly monitoring, if at all. Once the capital supplier knows less about the project than the capital user ('asymmetric information'), problems arise in ensuring that the agent will act in the interests of the principal. *Ex ante* asymmetric information can result in adverse selection, whereby the form of contract offered by the principal attracts agents who will not act in the principal's interests, but who cannot be detected beforehand. *Ex post* asymmetric information[9] makes the principal vulnerable to moral hazard concerning the effort that the agent exerts (given that this is not easily observable) and the return that the agent reports (given discretion to under-report profit or over-indulge in personal perquisites).

Such conditions can result in capital suppliers being cheated out of the full financial return they deserve, or realising that they could be cheated, and not wishing to enter into the agreement. Hence, both principal and agent have a reason to devise a formal relationship which overcomes the incompatibility of incentives. Under such second-best conditions, various 'agency costs' will have to be incurred, including direct outlays needed to monitor the agent (e.g. accountancy fees; legal costs in bankruptcy) or a contractual form that allocates risk in a sub-optimal manner (e.g. loan collateral; managerial stock options). In this more realistic world, the benefits of debt versus profit-sharing arrangements can be assessed more adequately.

The Case for Debt Finance with Asymmetric Information

Debt finance plays an important role in minimizing some of the agency costs which arise from imperfect information. First, debt finance enables capital users to expand their operations without damaging incentives for effort.[10] If a proportion of incremental profit resulting from agents' marginal effort automatically goes to the capital supplier (as with PLS), then the agents' incentive to maximize profit will be lessened – assuming that substitution effects outweigh income effects in agents' income/leisure trade off. Conversely, debt contracts leave all profit resulting from marginal effort in the agents' hands as long as bankruptcy is avoided. Such an arrangement is most advantageous where there is great uncertainty as to the final return due to exogenous disturbances, and it is highly costly to monitor agents' level of effort (e.g. agriculture[11]). Debt contracts are a simple way to align incentives (e.g. Jensen and Meckling, 1976, p. 313ff).

Secondly, debt contracts economize on the information required to maintain the contractual relationship. A debt contract specifies a rate of interest per unit time, unrelated to borrower profitability. The lender need only engage in costly monitoring or managerial oversight when the borrower is close to bankruptcy or the value of collateral unexpectedly falls (e.g. Stiglitz, 1985, p. 143). Given the costly nature of auditing and the borrowers' incentive to under-report profits with PLS, the optimal outcome of many financial contracting models is a contract with a flat-rate return and monitoring only in default (e.g. Townsend, 1979; Gale and Hellwig, 1985). The threat of costly bankruptcy attendant upon debt finance also reduces corporations' incentives to over-invest in risky projects that are otherwise encouraged by limited liability (John et al., 1993).

Thirdly, debt acts as a useful signalling device for agents who would otherwise have no credible way of conveying optimistic inside information about a firm's prospects to capital suppliers. Assuming that bankruptcy is costly to managers (through job and equity losses, legal fees and damaged reputations), then capital suppliers will believe that they will not willingly incur a significant risk of bankruptcy. Therefore, if agents amass high levels of debt voluntarily, it is interpreted as a signal of managerial confidence in their firm's future profitability. Hence, the choice of debt–equity ratio overcomes *ex ante* information asymmetries that would otherwise lead to an inefficient allocation, and higher cost, of financial capital (Ross, 1977; Narayanan, 1988, pp. 46–8).

Finally, debt circumscribes the autonomy of managers who are inadequately monitored by the existing corporate governance structure. In particular, managers of mature, cash-rich companies have an opportunity to retain financial assets unnecessarily, or over-invest in their own company, rather than pay out higher dividends. Easy access to liquid funds (retentions) enables managers to avoid examination by capital suppliers, whilst company growth benefits managers through greater salaries, perquisites and prestige. Managers have such latitude because dividend pay-outs are discretionary, the supervisory board rarely monitors them closely enough and institutional shareholders cannot afford to do so. The result is over-large, inefficiently run companies. However, by substituting debt for equity (e.g. in a leveraged buy-out), managers bond themselves to pay out future cash-flows in interest rather than use them inefficiently internally. The threat of bankruptcy makes this a far more credible promise than a commitment to raise dividends, and explains why the value of a firm invariably rises when debt is issued to retire equity (Grossman and Hart, 1982; Jensen, 1986). Leveraged buy-outs were expected to succeed precisely because they gave managers little discretion (Jensen, 1989).[12]

The Limitations of Debt Finance with Asymmetric Information

Despite economizing on some agency costs, the countervailing drawbacks of debt ensure that firms are rarely entirely debt financed. Its most important shortcoming is its inadequate treatment of uncertainty. Profits are variable and somewhat unpredictable. Consequently, any commitment to pay a non-contingent return to capital suppliers significantly increases the probability of bankruptcy. This would not be problematic if principals and agents were risk neutral, and/or bankruptcy was costless. However, the more realistic assumptions are that bankruptcy is costly and that the contracting parties are risk averse.[13]

In an economy with secondary financial asset markets, the capital user is likely to have less opportunity to reduce exposure to risk than the capital supplier. Hence, the agent is usually exposed to more risk than the principal. A fundamental tenet of efficient risk allocation is that it is beneficial for both parties if most risk is borne by the least risk averse[14] (Arrow, 1971, pp. 136ff). Consequently, variable-return liabilities (e.g. shares) exist to permit businesses to raise finance whilst laying off some of the risk of failure onto capital suppliers, who can bear it more easily. They are, effectively, insurance against difficult trading conditions, which the firm pays for through high dividends in good trading conditions (Hicks, 1982, p. 14). If only debt-finance were available, the risk aversion of capital users would severely curtail investment, particularly in those activities with a volatile earnings stream.[15] Also, the increased probability of bankruptcy would produce a more fragile economic system, as firm collapses impose negative externalities on customers and suppliers. Hence, an all-debt financial system would yield an economy with inadequate risk-taking and a more volatile business cycle.

In addition to sub-optimal risk-sharing, debt finance imposes its own forms of agency cost in a world of asymmetric information (e.g. Jensen and Meckling, 1976, pp. 333ff). First, debt finance might economise on informational requirements, but the capital supplier must still monitor the borrower. Bankruptcy is not only administratively costly for lenders, but may also involve capital losses through the borrower's assets being protected by limited liability or court orders, or because collateral may have been overvalued. Hence, lenders must still ensure that borrowers do not incur excessive bankruptcy risk.

Secondly, debt finance produces perverse incentive effects when combined with equity in a borrowing firm's capital structure. On the one hand, managers of leveraged companies could be acting in their shareholders' interest by under-investing in potentially profitable projects – the whole of the cost will be borne by shareholders (in forgone dividends and capital gains) whilst some of the benefit accrues to existing bondholders, in the form of a lower probability of bankruptcy and more valuable liquidation-sale assets (Myers, 1977). On the other, it is in the interests of shareholders if managers adopt projects that are riskier than creditors would wish. Shareholders will receive 100 per cent of the residual return from riskier projects whilst only being liable for the potential loss of a fraction of the necessary capital.[16]

These considerations induce lenders to reduce their exposure to risk by adapting the standard debt contract to include clauses restricting borrowers' freedom of action. For instance, primary creditors are given favoured status in bankruptcy via specific collateral requirements and floating charges on a borrower's assets. In addition, bondholders' permission may need to be sought before managers are allowed to invest in projects, or lenders can insist on borrowers using inputs with a high resale value (for collateral purposes). Such preconditions result in productive inefficiencies.[17] Hence, debt finance also imposes agency costs in a world of incomplete information.

Implications for Interest-free Banking and Finance

From the perspective of this corporate finance literature, the obvious advantage of PLS banking is its greater ability to allocate risk optimally through the sharing of project returns between capital supplier and user. Conventional banks are often reluctant to, (and prevented from), holding variable-return assets because their fixed-return liabilities (interest-bearing deposits) leave them exposed to insolvency risk. PLS banks avoid the problem by only issuing variable-return liabilities (investment accounts), so freeing them to invest in riskier assets (cf. unit trusts). In theory, therefore, a PLS bank should be able to lend on a longer-term basis to projects with a higher risk–return profile than a conventional equivalent, and its borrowers should be more willing to undertake such projects because the PLS contract reduces their risk exposure. There is some evidence that this theoretical prediction has been borne out with Egyptian PLS banks (El-Ashker, 1987, ch. 11).

Despite its risk-sharing benefits, PLS banking faces severe principal–agent problems arising from asymmetric information and costly monitoring. First, such a bank would face difficulties resulting from *ex ante* information limitations concerning project quality. Borrowers have inside information about their personal abilities and projects' likelihood of success that cannot be credibly signalled to the bank because every PLS applicant will claim to be of the highest quality. The banks' difficulty in determining the quality of loan applicants produces various adverse selection problems – especially when debt finance is available from competing sources. Those borrowers who expect their projects to supply high non-monetary benefits but low realised profits will choose PLS financing because they will enjoy high total returns at an artificially low cost of capital (Pryor, 1985).[18] Similarly, PLS banks will attract applicants with inside knowledge that their project is highly risky, and borrowers who will inflate their declared profit expectations in the hope of being quoted a lower profit-share ratio by the bank (Nienhaus, 1983). Consequently, the bank would have to undertake costly project appraisal (further increasing the borrower's cost of capital) and sacrifice some of its risk-sharing benefits by insisting on collateral and managerial share-holdings.

Secondly, *ex post* information asymmetry leads to a moral hazard problem between PLS bank and borrower. Relating the bank's return to declared profit automatically gives the borrower an incentive to under-report or artificially reduce declared profit. This might take the form of blatant fraud – made easier by an unsophisticated legal, tax and auditing system – but need not. Borrowers could legally reduce reported profits by increasing non-pecuniary rewards (e.g. through excessive perquisites or extra leisure) or by resorting to accounting subterfuges. Hence, a non-interest bank would have to engage in costly monitoring to ascertain whether declared profit was a true reflection of reality, and yet still be unsure of borrower competence and motivation.

The preliminary verdict of corporate finance theory upon non-interest banking is, therefore, dismissive. Risk-sharing benefits would be offset by additional dead-weight costs in information gathering and project appraisal, reduced work incentives for entrepreneurs and higher production costs (e.g. Goodhart, 1987, p. 86). A PLS bank's susceptibility to moral hazard and adverse selection would probably make it uncompetitive with conventional rivals.

The Defence of Non-interest Banking

This charge of impracticality can be answered in a number of ways. To some degree, the risk-sharing benefits of non-interest banking outweigh the increased monitoring costs that ensue.[19] In any case, monitoring need not be prohibitively costly – due to standardized accounting procedures, random inspection of borrowers' accounts, bank representation on a borrowing firm's board and handling of the borrower's transactions[20] – and may prove to be of benefit through the provision of expert managerial advice to borrowers.[21]

Some Islamic proponents, however, resort to the assumption that commercial standards of morality would improve once society is 'Islamized' along with the financial system. Greater belief in Allah's ultimate judgement, and regard for the interests of others, would reduce the system's propensity to foster moral hazard, and need for legal enforcement methods (Siddiqi, 1983b, p. 13). Indeed, some regard observation of higher ethical standards as a prerequisite for the introduction of PLS banking since:

> an interest-free system can successfully function and really prove to be fruitful only subject to the condition that simultaneously with its introduction strenuous efforts are made on a wide front to inculcate in society such basic virtues as fear of God, honesty, trustworthiness, sense of duty and patriotism. (CII, 1983, p. 18; also Abdallah, 1987)

This reliance upon greater moral uprightness to make PLS banking workable prompts the charge of utopianism.

Relationship Finance

A more robust defence of non-interest banking is to set financial contracting within a multiperiod context as a means of reducing agency costs.[22] Corporate finance models yield the standard debt contract as the optimal arrangement between lender and borrower not only because they assume a risk neutral agent, but also because they are frequently set in a one- or two-period framework (e.g. Gale and Hellwig, 1985). Over a limited period, the agent's incentive to cheat is maximized because there are no future penalties incurred. Hence, the debt contract is optimal because it is less vulnerable to moral hazard than profit-sharing arrangements (Bashir, 1983).

A well-established result of game theory is that a one-shot, two-player game will produce an inefficient, non-cooperative Nash equilibrium when both players have an incentive to cheat, given the likelihood that the other will cheat too (e.g. Hart and Holmstrom, 1987, pp. 97–8). A cooperative, efficient outcome is more likely to arise from repeated plays of the game when future punishments result from current cheating. Similarly, problems of adverse selection and moral hazard in financial contracting can be attenuated by multiperiod considerations being brought into play.[23] Repeated interactions, and the development of beneficial reputations, overcome the uncertainties arising from asymmetric information by revealing the agent's attributes and actions more clearly.[24]

Given that a PLS financial system is likely to be more prone to adverse selection and moral hazard, then such banks should attempt to encourage borrowers to undertake long-term implicit or explicit contracts so as to curtail misrepresentation and under-reporting of profit. Hence, banks are likely to offer new borrowers the prospect of a lower PLS ratio for finance in later periods if satisfactory returns are reported initially. Alternatively, if unsatisfactory returns are reported for no good reason, the bank will retain the threat to withdraw funding, or to increase its costs (Parigi, 1992). As with conventional banking, information on deliberate defaulters could be shared with a credit reference register to dissuade cheating (Qureshi, 1979, p. 43). Multiperiod relationships will not solve all the problems of non-interest banking, but they offer grounds for believing that such a system does not require the moral transformation of society in order to be feasible (Bashir, 1990).[25]

Long-standing bank–borrower relationships would improve the efficiency of PLS banking in other ways. For instance, repeated interactions will reduce monitoring costs as the bank becomes familiar with a borrower's auditing systems, and handles their transactions over an extended period. It should then be able to develop a more accurate opinion of borrower performance relative to other firms in similar circumstances and so be better able to tell whether a low reported return is the result of borrower inefficiency, cheating or a sectoral downturn (Levinthal, 1988; Haubrich, 1989).

However, the greatest potential benefit of long-term bank–borrower relations, combined with a risk-sharing contract, is that of enabling borrowers to undertake long-term investment projects safe in the knowledge that the bank has a direct interest in ensuring their success. The point is illustrated by Japanese firms' commitment to long-term investment being ascribed to the implicit risk-sharing contract that a corporate borrower has with its 'lead' bank. During periods of prosperity, this bank closely monitors the borrower, lends long term, holds its equities and receives excessive rates of return on loans through reciprocal deposits. In times of distress, however, the lead bank will reschedule loans at soft rates of interest, coordinate other creditors to postpone foreclosure and replace managers if it deems the borrowing firm to be viable.[26] Such behaviour has prompted the comment that, in Japan,

> banks provide precisely the functions that one would expect of a risk sharer: the willingness to sustain current losses, in the expectation of future compensation – essentially equity-type services. What is formally described as debt in Japan has all the characteristics of equity finance. (Mayer, 1988, p. 1181)

Notwithstanding the parallels that such arrangements have with PLS banking, where risk-sharing is explicit, the important point is that Japanese banks and borrowers have overcome the moral hazard problem that arises from investment in long-term projects in an interest-based economy. The problem exists because, even though a long-term project may be expected to yield a greater total discounted profit eventually, it may show a poor short-term return. Without credible inside information, shareholders will interpret temporarily poor performance as inefficiency, so depressing the value of the firm, raising its cost of capital and leaving it vulnerable to takeover. For their part, lenders will believe the firm to be a greater risk and either call in their loans or require a greater risk premium. Either way, the firm is penalised for investing long-term in an environment that offers a real return on short-term loan finance.

A long-standing, risk-sharing bank–borrower relationship, however, should give the firm sufficient confidence to invest long-term and enable the bank to distinguish between poor performance and long-term investment (Hellwig, 1991, p. 47). If such an arrangement is maintained, the puzzle is why the borrower does not ditch the bank in the good times in favour of another lender who does not expect compensation for seeing the firm through its lean period? The Japanese system avoids the problem through interlocking directorships, bank shareholdings and the cultural importance given to reputation.[27] The PLS system copes with this time-inconsistency problem explicitly by including profit-sharing in the bank–borrower contract. The bank can be sure of its long-term future return, if it takes a short-term loss, since the borrower is pre-committed to sharing profits as well as losses for the duration of the contract (Barroux, 1988, p. 1189).

Localized Financial Intermediaries

Many Islamic writers have recognized that a non-interest financial system will need to rely on long-term lending relationships and reputations if moral hazard is to be overcome. However, they have failed to draw the further corollary that such relationships, and consequent ease of monitoring, will be more readily sustained within a decentralized, regional banking system.[28]

There are two stages to the argument. First, there are benefits in decentralizing the lending decision-making process, particularly when the borrowers are idiosyncratic small firms. For instance, Holland (1994) found that banking relationships work best when contact is long-standing, close, applied over a range of banking services, and on a roughly equal basis – so that neither side can easily exploit the other. Crucially, non-contractual commitments to share relevant information develop best within the context of informal personal and social contacts (ibid., p. 375; see also Petersen and Rajan, 1994). These conditions are more likely to be met when loan officers work and live in the vicinity of their borrowers, enabling them to guage their reputation and inspect operations more easily. These are the standard reasons why small business loans are originated at a local/branch level. Conventional branch banking is an attempt to minimize the informational asymmetries that result from distance (Porteous, 1993a, p. 238).

Secondly, a multi-branch, national bank will allocate credit differently than a comparable collection of independent regional banks. For instance, a national bank may impose looser credit restrictions in the locality of its head office or regional decision-making centres due to the lower information-gathering and monitoring costs (e.g. Chick and Dow, 1988, p. 238).[29] Loan officers in a national bank will move location more frequently, so making it difficult to establish the long-term relationships and local knowledge necessary to make informed lending decisions. Also, loan officers in peripheral areas are likely to be more junior, and so risk averse, due to the reputational damage of high default rates. Crucially, a regionally undiversified bank, with a local deposit base, will reap more of the externality benefits flowing from the funding of successful local businesses, and so should impose fewer restrictions on lending as a result. These considerations suggest that decisions to lend to small-and medium-sized firms will be made more effectively by regional banks than their national, multi-branch equivalents.[30] They have prompted calls for the regional dismemberment of the UK clearers (Duncan, 1993).

The two prongs of this argument suggest that PLS banking will be more successful in reducing information asymmetries and monitoring costs if lending to small firms is conducted by regionally-based banks seeking to curb moral hazard through long-standing relationships and reputation. Larger corporations could be serviced and monitored by national banks and institutional shareholders.[31]

ASSESSMENT

The initial judgement of financial contract theory is that any proposed economic system which attempts to eliminate interest-bearing debt contracts is unworkable. Non-contingent debt contracts limit the adverse selection of borrowers, reduce monitoring costs, discipline borrowers and are simple. Indeed, the perceived theoretical advantages of debt contracts are now so numerous that some confess difficulty in explaining the very existence of equity (e.g. Dowd, 1992, p. 157). This case is strengthened by the difficulties faced by Islamic banks in achieving a high proportion of profit-sharing assets on their balance sheets in practice.

However, the case against a non-interest financial system is far from overwhelming. In practice, debt finance copes inadequately with risk-sharing in an uncertain world and imposes its own significant agency costs. Also, the practical difficulties associated with non-interest finance are not insuperable. Monitoring costs can be reduced by randomized checking and the handling of borrowers' transactions,[32] whilst their incentive to cheat can be restrained by intertemporal contracts which tie lower PLS ratios in the future to satisfactory performance in the present. In particular, financial contract theory and conventional banking experience suggest that PLS finance will be far more feasible if placed within the context of long-term banking relationships (e.g. Cobham, 1992, p. 18). For small business borrowers in particular, monitoring and discipline will be best carried out by localized financial intermediaries.

The purpose of this discussion is not to claim that, when judged by the costs of intermediation, a non-interest banking system would be superior to its conventional alternative. Indeed, in many circumstances, debt-based intermediation would be far less costly. Rather, the question is one of the feasibility of a PLS banking system, since the contention is that an interest-based financial system economizes on the costs of intermediation by imposing other externality costs on the rest of the economy. By stressing the intertemporal nature of the financial terms on offer, an non-interest banking system should at least prove workable.

4 Modelling Profit-and-Loss Sharing

INTRODUCTION: PROFIT-SHARING – THE WEITZMAN ANALOGY

The theoretical benefits and limitations of a non-interest financial system bear a close resemblance to those of Weitzman's (1983, 1984, 1985, 1987) proposal to replace flat-rate wages with profit- or revenue-sharing labour remuneration arrangements. He assumes monopolistically competitive firms and long-run full employment equilibrium, but 'sticky' wages and prices due to implicit contracts with 'insider' workers (e.g. 1984, p. 34ff). Wage contracts allocate labour efficiently in equilibrium but can yield prolonged stagflation following an aggregate demand shock (ibid., p. 42ff). By replacing wages with a profit-sharing system, Weitzman believes that the marginal cost of employing an extra worker to the firm will always be less than their marginal revenue product, even at full employment levels (ibid., pp. 85–7).[1]

Weitzman claims startling macroeconomic properties for this manipulation of contractual terms. Firms will always desire to increase employment because this will increase net profitability (e.g. 1985, p. 948); adjustment to aggregate demand shocks will occur automatically as lower revenues result in lower wage costs, rather than wage rigidity, lay-offs and bankruptcies (e.g. 1984, p. 107); firms will have less incentive to raise prices as this will increase labour costs; workers will have a direct incentive to increase productivity; and the authorities can afford to tighten monetary control because a deflationary policy will not permanently raise unemployment (ibid., p. 111f). Weitzman predicts a robust economy with a cycle of diminished amplitude and a tendency to full employment (e.g. 1985, p. 949). He cites the Japanese bonus payment system as evidence of the stabilizing consequences of introducing flexibility into the labour remuneration mechanism (1984, pp. 74–6).

The theoretical similarities with a PLS financial system are obvious. By changing a contract from one with a non-contingent pay-off (interest) to a contingent one (PLS or equity), similar macroeconomic benefits are predicted. For instance, a sharing-rule supposedly confronts borrowers with an anticipated marginal cost of capital less than the expected marginal efficiency of investment at full employment levels. Consequently, firms are believed to have an automatic desire to invest because it will always be profitable for them to do so (e.g. Siddiqi and Zaman, 1989).[2] But most significantly, a non-interest economy is theoretically characterized by greater macrostability, as revenue shocks are shared and diffused rather than concentrated upon a few productive units to generate bankruptcies and output reductions. Ironically, Mayer (1988, p. 1182) believes that Weitzman exaggerated the stabilizing properties of the Japanese bonus wage system, and neglected the profit-sharing attributes of the banking system.

Unsurprisingly, a profit-sharing rule produces comparable incentive problems. With highly profit-sensitive pay, existing workers may resist the expansion of employment and change jobs when they expect profits to fall (Ali, 1983, p. 259). Profit-share pay might also adversely select low productivity workers who wish to free-ride on the efforts of others, whilst workers will be subject to moral hazard in that it firms under-represent profit, labour costs fall. Similarly, PLS banking faces incentive problems due to asymmetric information and costly monitoring. In both instances, the high agency costs may be allayed by multiperiod contracting in a competitive environment. In addition, both systems have stability 'externalities' that cannot be appropriated by individual agents and which give them incentives to 'free-ride' once a sharing scheme is widely operative.[3] Consequently, each may only be robust if the state imposes tax penalties upon non-sharing contracts – especially in an economy open to high labour and capital mobility. It is no coincidence that profit-share firms and banks have been established and enjoy efficiency gains,[4] but that no economy has truly converted to a complete profit-share system of either variety.

MUDARABAH PROFIT-AND-LOSS SHARING AS AN EFFICIENT REVELATION DEVICE

There have been several attempts in the literature to investigate the impact of profit-and-loss sharing upon the economic system. In this chapter a theoretical model developed by J. Sessions with one of the authors (Presley and Sessions, 1994) is presented.[5] This model examines the situations where capital is financed through *riba* and *mudarabah* based contracts respectively, and shows that, under certain conditions, the latter will act to raise the level of capital investment in the project. In so doing, the model demonstrates that *mudarabah* has an ability to act as an efficient revelation device.

The model focuses on the example of a single project undertaken by a single manager, the outcome of which is determined by the level of capital investment, the level of managerial effort, and the state of nature, which are envisaged in terms of some random shock to demand or technology. The key assumption is asymmetric information. The manager is assumed to have superior information to investors in two respects: first, having signed a contract with investors the manager is able to observe the demand or productivity conditions affecting the project before committing to production decisions; and second, he alone observes his personal level of effort. Such an asymmetry is not unusual and, indeed, rationalises the manager's involvement in the project. But whilst the manager's relative informational expertise suggests that he should be delegated some authority over production decisions, the exploitation of this expertise is problematic. Since effort is private information, the manager cannot be compensated directly for its provision. A revelation problem therefore arises with the manager's preferences over productive inputs only coinciding with those of investors if he personally bears the entire risk of adverse shocks.

If the manager is risk averse then such a policy, whilst productively efficient, is sub-optimal (see Holmstrom and Weiss, 1985). Furthermore, a policy of paying the manager a fixed return independent of outcome is also inefficient because there is no incentive for him to supply more effort when its marginal revenue product is high.

One way out of the dilemma is to design an incentive-compatible contract which ensures that the cost of misinformation by the manager is sufficiently high to make honesty his best policy. To obtain such incentive compatibility with minimum loss in efficiency requires the contract to specify inefficiently low levels of productive inputs in particular states of the world (see Hart, 1983; Hart and Holmstrom, 1987).

In what follows two states of nature only, 'good' and 'bad', are assumed; and a production technology such that both total and marginal revenue products are higher in the good state than in the bad state. Under these assumptions an incentive-compatible *riba* contract implies that capital investment in the bad state is set below the full information, productively efficient level, whilst in the good state it is set at the productively efficient level. These results arise from the manager's temptation under a *riba* contract to substitute capital for effort and thereby reduce effort cost, which is not public knowledge. Intuitively, a reduction in investment in the bad state has only a second-order effect on the return from the project, but nevertheless imposes a first-order cost on the good-state manager should he choose to misinform investors as to the demand or productivity conditions affecting the project. This permits the compensation differential between the two states to be reduced whilst maintaining incentive compatibility.

Under a *mudarabah* profit-and-loss sharing contract it is managerial effort which picks up the role of policing the contract. A *riba* contract creates an explicit mapping between the input and remuneration of capital. Under a standard incentive-compatible *riba* loan contract the manager is left free to chose the individually optimal level of effort in each state contingent on the specified level of investment. A *mudarabah* contract, in contrast, creates an explicit mapping between the remuneration of capital and the outcome of the project, the prohibition of interest implying that compensation cannot be tied directly to the level of capital investment.

Mudarabah therefore allows the contract to control directly the manager's incentive to exert effort, since this effort affects the relationship between capital investment and the outcome of the project. Under a *mudarabah* contract the manager is left free to choose the individually optimal level of investment in each state contingent on his contractually specified level of effort. It is shown that these individually optimal levels correspond to the full information, productively efficient levels such that a mean-variance improvement in capital investment is obtained – average investment is increased whilst inefficiently large fluctuations around this level are reduced.

A number of assumptions are made in the model.[6] There is a large number of such projects available in the economy, the return to each of which requires capital investment and managerial effort. Individuals differ in terms of their attributes and are endowed with either managerial ability or capital. Capitalists are risk neutral and individually or collectively search for potential investment opportunities.[7] Once such an opportunity has been spotted they hire a single, risk averse manager to co-ordinate the project.

The contract negotiated between the manager and the syndicate provides for the former to retain the value of the project net of an agreed return to the latter. The outcome of a project is assumed to be stochastic, depending on the state of nature.[8] Thus the return to the syndicate will also be state dependent.

Production

The outcome of a project depends upon managerial effort, e, capital investment I, and a random shock representing the state of nature, Θ. For simplicity only two states of nature are assumed: 'bad', denoted by Θ_1 and assumed to occur with probability $(1 - \phi)$ and 'good', denoted by Θ_2, and assumed to occur with probability ϕ. Project outcome in state i is denoted:

$$Z_i = f^i(I, e) \tag{1}$$

$\forall_i = 1, 2$. Managerial effort is essential for a successful (i.e. positive) outcome and this effort implies a cost. Grossman and Hart (1981) are followed with regard to this cost in terms of an opportunity cost for alternative income rather than as an opportunity cost for leisure. This permits the cost to be measured in monetary terms independent of the manager's level of income.

Measuring both effort and investment in terms of their costs implies a profit function of the form:

$$\Pi_i = f^i(I, e) - I - e \tag{2}$$

The following assumptions regarding production technology are made:

Assumption 1

For $i = 1, 2$,

(a) $f^i(I, e)$ is strictly increasing, twice continuously differentiable and strictly concave,
(b) $f^i_{Ie}(I, e) \geq 0$,
(c) $f^i_I(I, e), f^i_e(I, e) < 1$ for sufficiently large I, e,
(d) $f^i(I, 0) = 0, \forall i.$[9]

Assumption 2

For all $(I, e) > 0$,

(a) $f^2(I, e) > f^1(I, e)$,
(b) $f^2_I(I, e) > f^1_I(I, e)$,
(c) $f^2_e(I, e) \geq f^1_e(I, e)$.

These assumptions follow Holmstrom and Weiss (1985) (hereafter HW). Assumption 1 is relatively standard. Part (c) assures that input levels will be finite and part (d) implies that effort is necessary for any output. Assumption 2 states that both the total and marginal revenue of each input is higher in the 'good' state (i.e. $\Theta = \Theta_2$).

The return from the project net of investment costs in state i is denoted:

$$y_i = f^i(I, e) - I \tag{3}$$

Similarly, the effort required on the part of the manager to ensure a return of y with investment I in state i is denoted $e^i(x)$, where $x = (I, y)$ and which is defined implicitly through:

$$y = f^i[I, e^i(x)] - I \tag{4}$$

which implies a value added profit function for the project in terms of I and y:

$$\pi^i(x) = y - e^i(x) \tag{5}$$

Information and Contracts

The central feature of what follows is the asymmetry of information between managers and capitalists. The manager is assumed to have superior information on two accounts: first, he alone can observe the value of e; and second, having signed his contract with the syndicate, he is able to observe the realisation of Θ before committing himself to production decisions. The syndicate observes neither e nor Θ. All other variables are common knowledge.

The information superiority of the manager rationalises his presence within the project – since he alone knows factor productivities, it is efficient for him to be delegated some control over production decisions. However, problems arise because his preferences for production decisions do not coincide with those of capitalists. The manager has an incentive to substitute effort for investment in an attempt to reduce the cost of supplying effort which is not publicly observable.

This problem is dealt with by the design of an incentive-compatible contract which provides the manager with a return as a function of the publicly observed variables y and/or I. An alternative, but equivalent, approach is to regard the contract as specifying how much the manager should pay the syndicate as a function of y and/or I. The latter interpretation is adopted and defines (I, y) as a contingent payment schedule from the manager to the syndicate. Since there are only two states of nature it follows that the manager will chose at most the pairs (I_1, y_1) when $\Theta = \Theta_1$ and (I_2, y_2) when $\Theta = \Theta_2$.

A *riba* contract between the manager and the syndicate will consist of a schedule relating s to the amount invested in the project, I.[10] Note that this will leave the manager free to choose the individually optimal level of π, via e, given the state of nature, Θ, and the level of capital input, I. Since $\Theta_i \in [\Theta_1, \Theta_2]$, such a contract may be described by:

$$\delta^r = \{(I_1, s_1), (I_2, s_2)\} \qquad (6)$$

Thus the *riba* contract leaves the manager free to chose the optimal level of y in each state. If managerial utility is defined through the concavely increasing function $u(c_i)$, where $c_i = \pi^i(x_i) - s_i$ denotes net managerial return in state i, then a *riba* contract implies:

$$u'(c_i)[1 - e^i_{yi}(x_i)] = 0 \qquad (7)$$

for all $i = 1, 2$. Since the manager observes Θ before choosing e and I he can always ensure a particular relationship between y and I by choosing e appropriately. The freedom to set y optimally in each state thus implies a freedom to set e optimally in each state.[11]

With a *mudarabah* contract, capital remuneration in the form of interest is prohibited. Instead capitalists are induced to invest in the project by being offered a share in the outcome of the project. It is assumed that a *mudarabah* contract consists of a schedule relating s to the net outcome of the project, y, and that it may be described by:[12]

$$\delta^m = \{(y_1, s_1), (y_2, s_2)\} \qquad (8)$$

The *mudarabah* contract, whilst restricting the manager's optimal choice of y through e, permits the manager freedom over I so that:

$$u'(c_i)e^i_{I_i}(x_i) = 0 \qquad (9)$$

for all $i = 1, 2$.[13]

Asymmetric Information

The manager's unique ability to observe Θ (after contracting but before committing to production decisions) lends him an incentive to misinform investors as to its true value. To characterise the optimal asymmetric information contracts under both *riba* and *mudarabah* financing, it is necessary to impose the following incentive compatibility constraints:

$$\pi^1(x_1) - s_1 \geq \pi^1(x_2) - s_2 \tag{10.1}$$

$$\pi^2(x_2) - s_2 \geq \pi^2(x_1) - s_1 \tag{10.2}$$

Constraints (10.1) and (10.2) simply ensure that the manager will report $\Theta = \Theta_i$ when state i occurs (see Dasgupta et al., 1979; and Myerson, 1979).

Optimal Contracts

It is assumed that at the time of contracting all parties share the same information about Θ and therefore hold the same beliefs regarding ϕ. The optimal contract is the one which chooses an *ex ante* efficient contract subject to the appropriate incentive constraints. The problem may be written formally as:

$$\max_\delta U = (1 - \phi)u(c_1) + \phi u(c_2) \tag{11}$$

subject to:

$$\pi^1(x_1) - s_1 \geq \pi^1(x_2) - s_2 \tag{11.1}$$

$$\pi^2(x_2) - s_2 \geq \pi^2(x_1) - s_1 \tag{11.2}$$

$$(1 - \phi)s_1 + \phi s_2 \geq 0 \tag{11.3}$$

where $\delta \in (\delta^r, \delta^m)$ and (11.3) is a zero profit constraint for the syndicate. Recalling the definition of the characteristics of the *riba* and *mudarabah* contracts it is apparent that the desire of the manager to maximise his return on the project will imply further constraints depending on the nature of the contract. To be sure, if the contract is *riba* financed then, from (7), there are two further constraints specifying that the manager chooses the optimal level of y in each state:

$$u'(c_1)[1 - e^1_{y_1}(x_1)] = 0 \tag{11.4}$$

$$u'(c_2)[1 - e^2_{y_2}(x_2)] = 0 \tag{11.5}$$

Table 4.1   Optimal contracts and information

Information	Contract Type	
	Riba	*Mudarabah*
Symmetric information	$\max_{\delta^r} (11)$ subject to (11.3), (11.4), (11.5)	$\max_{\delta^m} (11)$ subject to (11.3), (11.6), (11.7)
Asymmetric information	$\max_{\delta^r} (11)$ subject to (11.1), (11.2), (11.3), (11.4), (11.5)	$\max_{\delta^m} (11)$ subject to (11.1), (11.2), (11.3), (11.6), (11.7)

Alternatively, under *mudarabah* financing, equation (9) applies and we have the additional constraints that the manager chooses the optimal level of investment in each state:

$$u'(c_1)e^1_{I_1}(x_1) = 0 \qquad (11.6)$$

$$u'(c_2)e^2_{I_2}(x_2) = 0 \qquad (11.7)$$

Finally, for future reference, note that the term λ_j, $j = 1, 2, \ldots, 7$, is used to refer to the appropriate Kuhn–Tucker multiplier applying to the particular constraint (11.*j*). For ease of reference the characteristics of the optimal contract with *riba* and *mudarabah* financing, under both symmetric and asymmetric information, are set out in Table 4.1.

The solution to (11) under asymmetric information is termed the *second best*. Before looking in detail at the characteristics of such a solution what a *first best* solution would look like is considered.

First Best

The *first best* solves (11) without imposing the incentive compatibility constraints (11.1) and (11.2). It differs from the second best, therefore, in that $\lambda_1 = \lambda_2 = 0$. The *first best* solution is denoted (s^*_i, x^*_i) and its full characteristics are detailed in Appendix A, at the end of this chapter.

The *first best* solution $\delta^* = \{s^*_i, x^*_i\}$, $i = 1, 2$, is independent of contract design and is characterised by:

$$c^*_1 = c^*_2 \qquad (13)$$

$$e^i_{I_i}(x^*_i) = 0 \qquad (14)$$

$$e^i_{y_i}(x^*_i) = 1 \qquad (15)$$

From Assumption 2 it follows that $\pi^*_2 > \pi^*_1$ such that $s^*_2 > s^*_1$. Moreover Assumption 1 implies that $I^*_2 > I^*_1$, $y^*_2 > y^*_1$ and $e^*_2 > e^*_1$.

It is apparent, then, that when information is symmetric the optimal contract with either *riba* or *mudarabah* financing yields identical levels of investment, syndicate return, and project outcome. Although the syndicates' reservation constraint (11.3) forces the manager to bear some risk (see (A1.1) and (A2.1) below), it does not of itself create an explicit role for *mudarabah*. Under symmetric information, the contract is able to specify efficient production choices directly. Syndicate remuneration need not play an allocative role and can be based purely on risk-sharing considerations.

Second, it is apparent that the value of ϕ, whilst, of course, affecting the value of the manager's return from the project, does not affect the value of production decisions x^*_i. This is in contrast to the world of *second best*, where there is asymmetric information between managers and investors.

Second Best

The characterisation of the *second best* solution under *riba* and *mudarabah* financing is detailed in Appendix B, again at the end of this chapter.

The first point to note is that the first best solution is unobtainable under either *riba* or *mudarabah* financing. This follows from HW's observation that constraint (11.2) can be written as $c_2 \geq c_1 + \Delta(x_1)$, where $\Delta(x_1) = \pi^2(x_1) - \pi^1(x_1) = e^1(x_1) - e^2(x_1) > 0$, $\forall x > 0$, implying that it must be the case that $c_2 > c_1$. The *first best* full insurance solution is therefore not possible. Intuitively, if such a solution were obtainable then the good-state manager would have an incentive to claim falsely that he was operating within the bad state of nature. To ensure truthful reporting by the manager in the good state some risk sharing advantages have to be compromised, and the *second best* solution is characterised by this trade-off between reduced risk sharing and increased efficiency in production. Since $c_2 = c_1 + \Delta(x_1)$ – because (11.2) will obviously bind at the optimum (see Hart and Holmstrom, 1987) – the trade-off boils down to the choice of $\Delta(x_1)$. It is apparent that $\Delta(x_1) > \Delta(x^*_1)$ is not optimal, since, by increasing the gap between c_2 and c_1, it would imply losses in both productive and allocative efficiency. It must be the case then that $\Delta(x_1) < \Delta(x_1^*)$, which implies that (11.1) is not an effective constraint such that $x_2 = x_2^*$.

Second Best: *Riba*

The optimal *second best* solution under *riba* financing, $\delta^r = \{s_i^r, I_i^r\}$, is detailed in Appendix 1. The salient features are summarised in the following proposition:

Proposition 1: Under Assumptions 1 and 2 the optimal *second best* solution under *riba* financing is characterised by:

$$c_2^r > c_1^r \tag{P1.1}$$

$$s_2^r > 0 > s_1^r \tag{P1.2}$$

$$\pi^2(x_2^r) - s_2^r = \pi^2(x_1^r) - s_1^r \tag{P1.3}$$

$$(1 - \phi)s_1^r + \phi s_2^r = 0 \tag{P1.4}$$

$$I_1^r < I_1^* \tag{P1.5}$$

$$I_2^r = I_2^* \tag{P1.6}$$

$$y_i^r = y_i^* \tag{P1.7}$$

for all $i = 1, 2$. With a *riba* contract the project manager sets effort at the individually optimal level in each state of the world. Informational asymmetries are countered by capital investment which is required to be set at an inefficiently low level in bad states of the world.

Second Best: *Mudarabah*

The optimal *second best* solution under *mudarabah* financing, $\delta^m = \{s_i^m, y_i^m\}$, is detailed in Appendix B, section 1, at the end of this chapter. The sailent features are summarised in the following proposition:

Proposition 2:   Under Assumptions 1 and 2 the optimal *second best* under *mudarabah* financing is characterised by:

$$c_2^m > c_1^m \tag{P2.1}$$

$$s_2^m > 0 > s_1^m \qquad (P2.2)$$

$$\pi^2(x_2^m) - s_2^m = \pi^2(x_1^m) - s_1^m \qquad (P2.3)$$

$$(1 - \phi)s_1^m + \phi s_2^m = 0 \qquad (P2.4)$$

$$y_1^m < y_1^* \qquad (P2.5)$$

$$y_2^m = y_2^* \qquad (P2.6)$$

$$I_i^m = I_i^* \qquad (P2.7)$$

for all $i = 1, 2$. With a *mudarabah* contract the project manager sets capital investment at the individually optimal level in each state of the world, being restricted by the terms of the contract as to the level of effort he is permitted to exert in each state. Informational asymmetries under *mudarabah* are countered by restrictions on managerial effort, which must be set at an inefficiently low level in bad states of nature.

Riba and *Mudarabah* Contracts Compared

A *riba* contract creates an explicit mapping between the compensation and the input of capital. Incentive compatibility requires the manager to set inefficiently low levels of capital investment in bad states of the world, whilst leaving him free to set effort at the individually optimal *first best* level in all states. If *riba* is prohibited then the return to investors cannot be tied to the level of their capital investment and alternative compensatory arrangements will be required. The prevalent method of *mudarabah* financing ties compensation to the outcome of the project. Mudarabah therefore allows the contract to control directly the manager's incentive to exert effort, since this effort affects the relationship between capital investment and the outcome of the project. Under a *mudarabah* contract the manager is left free to choose the individually optimal level of investment in each state contingent on his contractually specified level of effort. Such a contract permits a mean-variance improvement in capital investment – average investment is increased whilst inefficiently large fluctuations around this level are reduced.

SUPPLEMENTARY THEORETICAL ISSUES

Two of the many other ramifications of non-interest finance will be merely indicated. First, conventional economics has neglected the role interest plays in fostering wealth inequalities. This obviously occurs when an uncompetitive credit supply enables lenders to charge extortionate rates (e.g. Cassel, 1903, pp. 180–1), but is less apparent in a mature economy where the recipients of interest include small-scale savers and pensioners. Nevertheless, some radicals continue to believe that interest flows significantly exacerbate wealth inequalities.[14] A non-interest financial system would retain substantial scope for inegalitarian flows of property income, but these should be lessened by the absence of compound interest and the widespread sharing of profits and losses with savers.

Secondly, the quest to find workable (and beneficial) alternatives to interest has strong implications for agricultural finance, particularly in developing economies. The potential for rural moneylenders to exploit and enslave smallholders through high rates of interest and input prices is well-documented (e.g. Lewis, 1955, p. 127; Bhadhuri, 1977). Consequently, there is great scope for PLS development banks specializing in agricultural finance and input supply (e.g. S.M. Ahmad, 1947; W.M. Khan, 1985).

APPENDIX A: FIRST BEST

1. Riba

$$(1 - \phi)[\lambda_3 - u'(c_1^*)] = 0 \tag{A1.1}$$

$$\phi[\lambda_3 - u'(c_2^*)] = 0 \tag{A1.2}$$

$$(1 - \phi)s_1^* + \phi s_2^* = 0 \tag{A1.3}$$

$$-(1 - \phi)u'(c_1^*)e_{I_1}^1(x_1^*) = 0 \tag{A1.4}$$

$$-\phi u'(c_2^*)e_{I_2}^2(x_2^*) = 0 \tag{A1.5}$$

$$u'(c_i^*)[1 - e_{y_i}^i(x_i^*)] = 0 \tag{A1.6}$$

$$\forall i = 1, \ 2.$$

2. Mudarabah

$$(1 - \phi)[\lambda_3 - u'(c_1^*)] = 0 \tag{A2.1}$$

$$\phi[\lambda_3 - u'(c_2^*)] = 0 \tag{A2.2}$$

$$(1 - \phi)s_1^* + \phi s_2^* = 0 \tag{A2.3}$$

$$(1 - \phi)u'(c_1^*)[1 - e_{y_1}^1(x_1^*)] = 0 \tag{A2.4}$$

$$\phi u'(c_2^*)[1 - e_{y_2}^2(x_2^*)] = 0 \tag{A2.5}$$

$$u'(c_i^*)e_{I_i}^i(x_i^*) = 0 \tag{A2.6}$$

$$\forall i = 1, \ 2.$$

APPENDIX B: SECOND BEST

1. Riba

$$(1 - \phi)[\lambda_3 - u'(c_1^r)] + \lambda_2 = 0 \qquad (B1.1)$$

$$\phi[\lambda_3 - u'(c_2^r)] - \lambda_2 = 0 \qquad (B1.2)$$

$$(1 - \phi)s_1^r + \phi s_2^r = 0 \qquad (B1.3)$$

$$-(1 - \phi)u'(c_1^r)e_{I_1}^1(x_1^r) + \lambda_2 e_{I_1}^2(x_1^r) = 0 \qquad (B1.4)$$

$$-e_{I_2}^2(x_2^r)[\phi u'(c_2^r) + \lambda_2] = 0 \qquad (B1.5)$$

$$u'(c_i^r)[1 - e_{y_i}^i(x_i^r)] = 0 \qquad (B1.6)$$

$$\forall i = 1, \ 2.$$

2. Mudarabah

$$(1 - \phi)[\lambda_3 - u'(c_1^m)] + \lambda_2 = 0 \qquad (B2.1)$$

$$\phi[\lambda_3 - u'(c_2^m)] - \lambda_2 = 0 \qquad (B2.2)$$

$$(1 - \phi)s_1^m + \phi s_2^m = 0 \qquad (B2.3)$$

$$(1 - \phi)u'(c_1^m)[1 - e_{y_1}^1(x_1^m)] - \lambda_2[1 - e_{y_1}^2(x_1^m)] = 0 \qquad (B2.4)$$

$$[1 - e_{y_2}^2(x_2^m)][\phi u'(c_2^m) + \lambda_2] = 0 \qquad (B2.5)$$

$$u'(c_i^m)e_{I_i}^i(x_i^m) = 0 \qquad (B2.6)$$

$$\forall i = 1, \ 2.$$

5 Non-interest Banking in Practice

The history of the interest prohibition in Muslim experience is strikingly similar to that of 'Christian' societies (see Chapter 8). The proscription was adhered to during and immediately after Mohammed's lifetime, and was subsequently upheld by the Caliphate. Commercial investment was legally financed through partnership arrangements, with beneficial consequences for Arab prosperity (Udovitch, 1970). Interest-based lending was usually confined to non-Muslim minorities, particularly the Jews. But the interest prohibition became increasingly inconvenient, and was circumvented more and more. Lenders began to use forms of contract within the letter of the law but which, in effect, yielded a risk-free return. Rulers came to see *Shari'ah* as applicable to individual conscience but not to social legislation, whilst accommodating theologians questioned the contemporary relevance of the Qu'ranic prohibition, particularly with regard to commercial loans (Rodinson, 1978, p. 149). Paradoxically, the outcome has been that short-term returns and security have been emphasised by Arab banks, to the detriment of equity or partnership investment. A high propensity to hoard amongst pious Muslims and very shallow share markets have resulted (Abdul-Hadi, 1988).[1]

THE EXPERIENCE OF PRIVATE ISLAMIC BANKS

The establishment of Islamic banks[2] has accompanied the development of PLS banking theory. After initial Pakistani experiments with non-interest agricultural credit cooperatives in the 1950s, the seminal influence on Islamic banking was the establishment of the Mit Ghamr Savings Bank in Egypt in 1963. This was designed as a non-interest community savings bank, enabling local farmers and craftsmen to avoid exploitation by moneylenders. It offered deposit and investment accounts and acquired assets through interest-free consumption loans, PLS partnerships and equity investments. The bank enjoyed rapid expansion and a low default ration due to the moral and social pressure on local borrowers to repay. Its very success proved to be the bank's downfall, however, because of the ensuing hostility of other local banks and the lack of personnel to fill new branches. The Mit Ghamr was nationalised in 1967 and converted to conventional operations, losing much of its customer loyalty and deposit base in the process. It was reconverted to non-interest operations in 1971, as the Nasser Social Bank, and has continued as a non-commercial undertaking (Wilson, 1983a, pp. 75–7).

The enthusiastic response the Mit Ghamr received from ordinary Muslims provided the spark that initiated the Islamic banking movement. It was subsequently fanned into flame by the rise of Arab nationalism, Islamic fundamentalism and inflated oil revenues, resulting in the establishment of over 50 non-interest banks in more than 20 countries. Their operating practices tend to be variations of the fractional reserve model outlined previously.[3] Rather than describe the histories of individual banks, we shall outline general trends and themes.

Liabilities

The common experience of Islamic banks is of rapid initial deposit growth, particularly if they are the first to offer interest-free services in a Muslim country.[4] Growth rates abate as the novelty of non-interest accounts wears off, but tend to exceed those of the interest-based competition, resulting in Islamic banks that account for significant proportions of domestic deposits.[5] This impressive performance has ensured that Islamic banks will remain a permanent feature of Muslim financial organisation. The, as yet, unanswered question is whether they will stagnate in maturity by just serving their niche market or continue to attract deposits away from conventional banks by offering competitive returns.

Although religious sentiment has played a part in attracting deposits, Islamic banks have nevertheless offered competitive returns on investment deposits. Not only do they face competition for funds from other non-interest investment outlets (e.g. property) and other Islamic financial institutions, but they wish to attract the deposits of less zealous Muslims seeking a competitive return. The result has been strong pressure to provide returns at least commensurate with the conventional competition. This goal has generally been achieved,[6] but at the expense of skewing investment policy towards short-term, secure and quick-returning outlets (see below).

The deposit performance of Islamic banks thus far shows that they are, at least, a valuable complement to conventional banks in attracting deposits that would otherwise be hoarded or invested unproductively.[7] However, the most obvious developmental contribution that Islamic banks could make would be to establish a rural branch network to channel local savings back into agricultural projects (Karsten, 1982, pp. 122–3). This role is largely ignored by interest-based banks due to the risks involved and greater rural suspicion of interest. With the exception of the Sudanese banks, however, this task has been neglected. In their understandable desire to achieve a large deposit base quickly and maintain reasonably safe returns, non-interest banks have concentrated on opening branches in large population centres (Nienhaus, 1986, pp. 6–7).

Assets

The theoretical literature envisages Islamic banks as predominantly risk-taking institutions committed to long-term productive investment on a partnership or equity basis. A less risk averse bank investment strategy ought to flow from depositors sharing risk through accepting profit-share returns. Thus far, the practice of non-interest banks has failed to conform on two counts.

First, Islamic banks have tended to experience excess liquidity. Deposit growth has rarely been matched by the demand for PLS finance, resulting in reserve ratios well in excess of regulatory requirements. Whilst pious Muslims have been eager to make deposits, businesses have been more cautious in requesting unfamiliar forms of Islamic partnership, which may involve a greater degree of bank supervision than is deemed welcome. When this is combined with poorly developed equity markets, Islamic banks have been forced to hold more cash than their interest-based counterparts.[8] The problem is exacerbated by denial of access to the interbank and government bond markets, which provide conventional competitors with return-bearing outlets for excess liquidity. Hence, Islamic banks have even attempted to slow down investment deposit growth on occasion, or sought non-productive outlets (e.g. property) for liquidity (Khouri, 1987, p. 148; Karim and Ali, 1988, p. 63).

Excessive liquidity levels have subsided with the maturing of Islamic banks. However, the investment outlets found tend not to be the long-term, profit-share, manufacturing and agricultural projects of Islamic theory, but the relatively safe, short-term, trade and leasing arrangements that are permissible under *Shari'ah* but which ignore the spirit of the usury prohibition.[9] The result is a preponderance of trade mark-up finance in the portfolios of Islamic banks,[10] with the remainder of assets tending to be *musharika* partnerships, equities, property and leased equipment. *Mudarabah* arrangements with farmers and small manufacturers have been relatively neglected. The concentration on trade finance has ensured that the majority of Islamic funds has been devoted to the importing of consumer durables, commodities and production equipment rather than fostering internal economic development.

Practical Difficulties Faced

The over-concentration on short-term, trade finance is the most frequent criticism of the current operation of Islamic banks.[11] It has arisen partly from the preferences of the banks themselves (in seeking to protect the reputation of non-interest finance by offering safe, adequate returns straightaway), but largely from the commercial environment in which they operate. Islamic banks have been competing against government bonds and conventional banks for funds, and so have had to offer equivalent returns to retain their deposits. This has ensured that Islamic banks have had to take a 'short-termist' perspective, to the detriment of long-term project finance.

In addition, conventional banks have various advantages that result from the favourable treatment afforded to them by most Muslim governments and the status quo. First, the corporate tax systems of most countries discriminate against non-interest finance by giving tax relief on interest but not profit-shares and dividends (e.g. O. Ahmed, 1990, p. 98). Secondly, conventional banks are often underwritten by state-organised deposit insurance schemes which cannot embrace non-interest banks. Thirdly, Islamic banks are usually excluded from access to lender-of-last-resort facilities due to an unsympathetic or overly cautious central bank, or difficulty in devising a return-related loan arrangement. Finally, government bills and bonds serve as return-bearing liquid assets for conventional banks, but are barred to Islamic banks.[12] Hence, seemingly at every turn, their operating environment prompts non-interest banks to be risk averse and avoid PLS investment when, theoretically, they were meant to do just the opposite.

The concentration on mark-up finance is also explained by transitional problems with partnership investment. Not only is the concept novel to potential business customers, but it may involve more bank supervision of accounts and management decisions than entrepreneurs are willing to consider. In addition, ensuring that a firm's cost of finance does not rise on the transfer of business from a conventional to an Islamic bank is more easily accomplished when using mark-up, rather then PLS, instruments (Iqbal and Mirakhor, 1987, p. 21). For the banks' part, partnership financing may have been neglected due to inexperience in, and cost of, project assessment, and the perception of low levels of business morality when declaring profits, resulting in moral hazard and adverse selection.[13]

The consensus of Islamic theorists thus far is that the experiment has demonstrated the attraction of non-interest banking for the Muslim public, and the potential it contains for significantly contributing to development.[14] This promise, however, remains largely unfulfilled. Theorists distinguish 'interest-free' from 'Islamic' banking (e.g. Mirakhor, 1987a, p. 185ff). The former has been achieved by relying on mark-up trade finance. The latter will not be achieved until partnership and equity finances predominate in the banks' asset portfolios. This can only come with the maturing of the institutions themselves, and changes in their operating environment.

THE EXPERIENCE OF ISLAMIC BANKING SYSTEMS

Some of the problems of Islamic banks have resulted from their operating in a 'hostile', interest-based economy, at an artificial disadvantage to conventional banks. In order to assess fully the feasibility of Islamic banking, the experiences of those societies that have recently prohibited interest outright need to be described.

Pakistan

A gradual conversion of Pakistan's nationalised financial system to non-interest operation was instituted from 1979 onwards. Interest-free counters were opened in the state-run banks in the transitional phases, with interest being finally phased out in 1985.[15] By then the five nationalised banks, the state-owned development corporations and foreign-owned commercial banks could only accept and invest domestic currency deposits on a non-interest basis.

The conversion of deposits to a PLS basis was relatively simple and widely accepted. By 1985, 27.6 per cent of all bank deposits had been voluntarily converted to PLS investment accounts, by depositors motivated by religious sentiment, adequate returns and government guarantees (Khan and Mirakhor, 1990, p. 365). After conversion, 61.6 per cent of funds were held in PLS accounts, with the remainder being demand deposits. The trend growth of bank liabilities seemed little affected by the transition, suggesting neither a strong, popular adverse reaction nor the significant attraction of hoards from pious Muslims. Average deposit returns were initially competitive, but have suffered a general decline since 1982 (Zaidi, 1991, p. 43ff). This has been blamed on the lack of demand for Islamic forms of finance and extension of the range of quality of business that banks now lend to (S. R. Khan, 1987, p. 144).

The asset side of Pakistan's interest-free banks mirrors that of Islamic banks elsewhere. Approximately 80–90 per cent of return-bearing assets have been devoted to trade-related mark-up techniques, with some participation in equity investment and *musharika* partnerships. The mark-up contracts used bear striking resemblance to interest-bearing trade credit:

> The banks were thus able to continue on a broad basis their previous security-oriented allocation of credit rather than bearing the additional risks Islamic banking would necessarily bring about. Changes made to the old system have actually been limited to the minimum. (Gieraths, 1990, p. 183)

This concentration on mark-up finance has resulted from a combination of pressures. Businesses have shunned partnerships because their contractual forms under Pakistani law give too much power to the financier, whilst mark-up operations make it easier to ensure that the cost of finance does not rise. The banks have been happy to collaborate due to their high level of risk aversion. This results from the opacity of Pakistani commercial accounts (leaving banks vulnerable to the under-reporting of profit by partners and the need to incur high monitoring costs); the low level of penalties, set by tribunal, to be paid by defaulting debtors (instead of interest); and the banks' lack of experience in venture capital project appraisal.

These problems are compounded by the State Bank regulating the banks' profit-share ratios and setting uniform deposit rates of return. This was intended to protect borrowers and forestall potentially destabilising deposit shifts. But such regulation not only eliminates much of the rationale of PLS banking but also suppresses the one monetary signal that bank executives could use to demonstrate their relative efficiency, and so attract deposits. With the banks gaining no benefit from successful risk-taking, the rational course is to become risk averse, by concentrating on mark-up credit (Khan and Mirakhor,

1990, p. 371). The danger is that the market for mark-up finance will become oversupplied, resulting in declining returns for the banks, whilst profit-share finance is neglected.

The allocative benefits of theoretical non-interest banks have not materialised. The State Bank has continued to plan the sectoral allocation of credit to be made by the state-controlled banks,[16] and has supplied additional finance to the system at the rate each bank pays on its savings or six-monthly investment accounts (Presley, 1988, pp. 266–7). A continuing problem is the necessity of funding the central government's fiscal deficit. Since no satisfactory non-interest alternative has been devised, non-inflationary deficits must still be covered by bond sales to the public, at interest rates that exceed the returns paid on bank deposits. This policy causes disintermediation from the banks, and sets a floor to the returns expected from equities and PLS deposits (S. R. Khan, 1987, p. 151). Again, the attainment of the theoretical results of a PLS system is thwarted.

The Pakistani experiment may have instituted 'interest-free' banking, but little has changed as a result. The inertia is parly due to the architects of the reforms being bankers and economists, rather than more radical Islamic scholars (Gieraths, 1990, p. 194).

Iran

The Iranian experiment with Islamic banking differs from that of Pakistan in two major respects. First, it has been undertaken in an avowedly theocratic context following the Islamic revolution of 1978–9. Thus *Shi'ite* Islamic Law is operative and the state displays little compunction in directing the economy in its desired development path. One of the first actions of the Revolutionary Council was to nationalise the banking system due to its poor developmental record, precarious financial position and ability to facilitate capital flight. Secondly, the bank Islamization process was more abrupt than in Pakistan. After an interim phase, when interest was changed in name only to 'service charges', the Law for *Riba*-free Banking was passed in August 1983. It required all bank deposits to conform to *Shari'ah* law within one year, and all bank assets to convert in three.

Following Islamization, Iranian banks offer interest-free current accounts, whose nominal value is guaranteed by the central bank; and short-and long-term investment accounts that have minimum duration and balance requirements specified. A return is paid on a profit-share basis, but the authorities guarantee that no loss will be passed onto depositors. These arrangements produced a smooth transition to interest-free banking, with a rapid growth in deposits, and of investment relative to current accounts (Aryan, 1990, pp. 165–6). The expansion of deposits was assisted by growing public acceptance of the concept of interest-free banking, and the authorities' commitment to extend the branch network to rural areas (Khan and Mirakhor, 1990, p. 362).[17]

Iran has had more success than most in converting bank assets to PLS instruments. Banks have 14 return-bearing asset types available, including partnerships, direct investment, instalment sales of equipment at mark-up, hire purchase and crop-sharing (Shirazi, 1990). However, regulations require that no finance is granted for the importing or purchase of luxuries, and that preference be shown to agricultural and industrial projects. Interest-free loans must also be given to finance low-cost housing construction and purchase. This regulatory framework has ensured that a relatively high proportion of bank assets are held as profit-related instruments (38 per cent in 1985), with another 10.4 per cent held as interest-free loans (Iqbal and Mirakhor, 1987, p. 13). A significant share, however, is devoted to instalment and hire purchase credit, and there is little hope that the share of PLS lending will increase significantly. A collection of familiar factors is responsible.[18] Banks and private businesses have remained relatively risk averse and 'short-termist' due to great uncertainty within the Iranian economy due to the Iran–Iraq war, sanctions, and the ever-present threat of business nationalisation. Deposit-taking banks have been hampered by their lack of experienced personnel, particularly those trained in project appraisal. Finally, nationalised banks still lend to one another at interest, whilst the government's fiscal deficit is financed by loans from the banking system at 6 per cent interest.

Again, the Iranian experience shows that the concept of non-interest banking is not entirely impractical, but the predictions of Islamic theorists have not been fully tested. The Iranian regime has ensured that its banking system has made a greater contribution to development projects, but through direct fiat. Private decision-making has not been allowed to determine resource allocation, resulting in the subsidising of 'socially beneficial' projects by bank depositors.

ASSESSMENT

Pakistan and Iran may have 'Islamized' their financial systems in different ways and circumstances, but the results have been remarkably similar.[19] Both examples demonstrate that Muslim depositors are not frightened off by the notion of interest-free banking, and that monetary policy is not rendered impotent thereby. However, neither country's central bank has attempted to implement PLS banking in full or permitted depositors any price signal with which to judge bank competitiveness or efficiency. Both banking systems are prone to risk averse investment strategies due to the high monitoring costs of partnerships, administrative confusion and uncertainty, the lack of appropriate staff skills, and deficit financing still being conducted on a conventional basis.

These experiences demonstrate that various preconditions exist for PLS banking to be practicable. Clearer definition of property rights is required if entrepreneurs are to be confident enough to undertake long-term investment projects, and banks are to be sure of recourse through the courts if default occurs. Government fiscal stringency is needed to eliminate the need for new borrowing at interest,[20] and to reduce marginal rates of corporation tax. Finally, PLS banking will not be implemented unless an improvement occurs in the 'organisational infrastructure' of business – including a uniform accounting system, the training of bank experts in project appraisal and an improvement in ethical standards.

The introduction of interest-free banking has not caused the collapse of the Pakistani and Iranian financial systems. Deposit mobilisation has been successful;

> But at the same time, because government policies in Iran and Pakistan strongly influence the asset acquisition behaviour of the banking system, it is far more difficult to judge the efficiency of Islamic banking in allocating the mobilised resources... (Khan and Mirakhor, 1990, p. 374)

The jury is still out on the economic potential of PLS banking because both countries have abolished 'interest' without committing themselves to a full-blown PLS system. They remain open to the charge that non-interest banking has been instituted merely to salve the consciences of pious depositors rather than to make a radical impact on how the financial system operates.

6 Non-interest Finance and Macroeconomic Stability

The most frequently posited advantage of profit-and-loss sharing (PLS) is its contribution to the stability of the non-interest economy. Whereas conventional finance supposedly amplifies the business cycle, PLS finance is predicted to dampen it. The case will be examined by setting out the supportive 'monetary' and financial theories of the cycle and the ways in which non-interest banking would alter matters.

'MONETARY' THEORIES OF THE CYCLE

Although fashionable in the 1930s, 'financial' explanations of the business cycle have since been neglected due to their abrogation of the neo-classical 'real-money' dichotomy, and the absence of rigorous microfoundations (Gertler, 1988). The former aspect has never been an insuperable problem, but the latter has only recently been addressed by the introduction of asymmetric information considerations into financial modelling.

Wicksell

Wicksell (1935, 1936) developed a business cycle theory which held the prevailing interest rate structure responsible for cyclical fluctuations.[1] The 'natural' rate of interest (r) is determined by the supply and demand for 'real' capital and, as such, dependent upon the expected profitability of new investment and the propensity to save. r would prevail if money did not exist, equating savings and investment *ex ante* and ensuring output and price stability.

That such stability is not experienced is attributable to the existence of money and the prevalence of fractional reserve banks in the monetary supply mechanism, ensuring that the money rate of interest (i) need not coincide with r at all. Divergences arise because banks cannot easily identify when r has changed. For instance, if $r > i$, planned investment will exceed planned savings. The price level will rise as excess demand is financed by dishoarding or the creation of bank credit, with the process sustained by extrapolative expectations of price increases. Inflation and output expansion continue whilst $r > i$.

A turning point is reached either when the banks realise they have over-lent, reserves become scarce, the monetary authorities become fearful of inflation, or the dictates of a monetary system (e.g. the Gold Standard) enforce a tightening. Temporarily, $i > r$ as profit expectations are reduced, money is sterilized in hoards, credit is withdrawn and the price level falls. The process stabilizes at the original price level, when $i = r$ again.

This system displays a long-period equilibrium of full employment and price stability when $i = r$; whilst the monetary system reflects the 'real' economy, there is a tendency to move smoothly towards equilibrium. It is only when the monetary system operates independently of 'real' forces that cycles in output and prices arise. Hence, Wicksell could maintain the orthodox dichotomy, whilst claiming that monetary forces had a significant cyclical impact by driving a wedge between the natural and market rates of interest.

Hayek

Wicksell's analysis formed the foundation of many subsequent 'monetary over-investment' cycle theories, such as that of Hayek (1933). He believed in the efficacy of the price mechanism to regulate the supply and demand for 'real capital', but that:

> Only when we come to consider the second group of prices (those paid for borrowed capital or, in other words, interest) is it conceivable that disturbance might creep in since, in this case, price formation does not act directly, by equalising the marginal demand for any supply of capital goods, but indirectly, through its effect on money capital, whose supply need not correspond to that of real capital. (ibid., p. 77)

The root of the monetary contribution to instability is that the price of loans (i) does not, and cannot, reflect perfectly the fluctuating profit expectations of investors in 'real' capital projects.

Hayek regards an elastic money supply, resulting from fractional reserve banking, as the 'necessary and sufficient' condition for the exaggeration of perturbations in the productive economy into a full-blown cycle (ibid., p. 141). The artificially low i, that results from easy credit expansion, leads to over-investment and an excessive expansion of the capital goods sector (ibid., p. 128). When the expansion ceases, for whatever reason, much of the existing capital stock is revealed to be unnecessary (ibid., p. 176).

The villain of the piece is a banking *system* that can increase the supply of loanable funds at the prevailing i without experiencing an increase in the savings that would validate such an expansion. 'Real' factors may initiate a disturbance but the failure to adjust smoothly to the next equilibrium is the responsibility of the credit mechanism. Fractional reserve banking provides a flexible credit supply, but:

> So long as we make use of bank credit as a means of furthering economic development we shall have to put up with the resulting trade cycles. (ibid., p. 189)

'Monetary' theories cogently explain some of the recurring features of business cycles (e.g. procyclical credit growth; exaggerated volatility in capital goods demand). However, they rely upon a high interest elasticity of investment, which empirical studies have usually failed to discover.

THE 'FINANCIAL INSTABILITY HYPOTHESIS'

Fisher

The 'financial instability hypothesis' marries an analysis of conventional banking, stressing the procyclical nature of lending policies, with an examination of the vulnerability of an economy when investment is financed by issuing liabilities which have a fixed nominal value (i.e. interest-bearing debt). These considerations were raised by Veblen (1904) and Keynes (1931), but found their most influential spokesman in Fisher (1933a, b; 1935).

Fisher gives little explanation of why 'over-indebtedness' occurs during the upswing, but focuses on its role in exacerbating the downswing. Once profit and asset price rises begin to decelerate, for whatever reason, highly leveraged firms and speculators find themselves with debt servicing commitments that place too high a burden on available cash-flows. This initiates a general movement to liquidate assets to meet and relieve debt-service commitments. This has two distinct results. First, distress selling reduces asset values, leading to a loss of confidence (due to declining personal net wealth), the hoarding of currency and the elimination of debt-financed speculation (e.g. 1933b, p. 14; 1935, p. 111). Falling asset prices also lower collateral values, making banks wary of rolling over loans. Secondly, the repayment or defaulting of bank loans, and the hoarding of cash, leads to a multiplied contraction in the money supply due to the fractional reserve system, resulting in declining profits and prices. Consequently, real interest rates may rise, despite nominal base rates falling.[2] The process ('debt-deflation') is self-reinforcing as higher levels of real debt induce further bankruptcies and distress asset sales, depressing prices even more. Thus, individually rational acts of foreclosure and distress selling yield a collectively detrimental result (the 'Fisher Paradox').[3]

For Fisher, the primary problem was the combination of debt contracts fixed in nominal value, and a falling price level. The main task of the monetary authorities was to stabilize prices, through monetary injections, so that real interest rates did not exceed nominal ones (e.g. 1933b, p. 39). Bond contracts should be indexed to the price level and open to renegotiation by the borrower when repayment falls due in a depression (1933b, p. 118). Although Fisher's analysis was simplistic in automatically linking changes in the money stock to those in the price level, there is validity in the proposition that debt finance is potentially destabilizing (Haberler, 1937, pp. 115–16, 331–6).

Minsky

Minsky's analysis[4] amplifies Fisher's insights into a full financial ex-planation of the cycle by explaining initial overindebtedness. Whereas Fisher highlighted the difficulties arising from falling prices, Minsky emphasises the inherent fragility that results from pledging anticipated but uncertain profits to service debts. Problems will not arise when investment finance comes from retained earnings and equity flotations ('hedge' finance), since bankruptcy risk is not increased thereby. It is when debts are incurred and the avoidance of default is dependent upon interest rates remaining low relative to profits ('speculative' finance), or the continuation of asset price inflation ('Ponzi' finance), that fragility is introduced.[5] The greater the proportion of speculative and Ponzi finance, the more vulnerable is a financial system to real interest rate rises.

This much is not controversial. What is, is Minsky's belief that a debt-based economy has an inherent tendency to transform a safe financial structure into a vulnerable one (e.g. 1982, p. 24). Given a 'real' shock that improves profit expectations, producers will retain more profit by borrowing to fund new investment than by selling new equity. Also, when asset values are appreciating faster than interest costs, profits are maximized by leveraging purchases as much as possible. Banks and bond-holders are able and willing to supply credit, possibly at declining real interest rates, as risk premia are reduced when collateral values are appreciating. As investment expands and prices rise, profit expectations will be validated and further investment encouraged.

Eventually, however, nominal interest rates will be forced up either endogenously, to attract reserves into the banking system, or exogenously by the monetary authorities. This rise may, however, be delayed until after many borrowers have committed themselves to 'Ponzi' schemes. Rising real interest rates must eventually prompt the failure of most of these (e.g. Minsky, 1982, pp. 32–3). Once profit expectations begin to deteriorate, profit and price rises decelerate, and bankruptcies spread, a Fisherian debt-deflation process *might* begin. However, given the current downward inflexibility of prices, Minsky places greater emphasis upon declining profits failing to meet debt-service commitments, with banks rationing credit more severely, in order to explain increased bankruptcies and depressed aggregate demand. The ensuing recession eventually transforms the financial system from a state of fragility to one of robustness as real interest rates fall and 'hedge' finance becomes predominant.

Minsky cites the series of limited US post-war financial booms and busts as confirmation of his hypothesis, attributing the absence of major collapses to large government expenditures (e.g. 1982, p. 28) and the leniency shown by the monetary authorities to pre-empt crises. The price has been persistent inflation[6] and an ever-expanding stock of government debt needed to ward off debt-deflationary processes. Indeed, the US only avoided full-blown debt deflation in 1990–1 by the state honouring the liabilities of bankrupt financial institutions and acting as 'borrower of last resort' (Minsky, 1993, p. 34).

Orthodox economics has difficulty in accepting the Fisher–Minsky analysis for a number of reasons. For instance, it requires that borrowers and lenders behave 'irrationally'. They regard a temporary rise in profits or asset values as a sustained favourable shift in their operating environment, (and increased leverage), rather than as a transient run of good fortune (e.g. Sinai, 1977; Fleming, 1982, p. 40). This objection hardly seems valid given the numerous incidents in which seemingly well-informed agents have speculated 'irrationally' (Kindleberger, 1989, ch. 3). More seriously, the 'financial instability hypothesis' breaches the neo-classical dichotomy by maintaining that changes in the price level and financial structure do have 'real' effects on output. Rigorous microfoundations for this assertion are now being provided by considering the impact of asymmetric information on financial interactions.

FINANCIAL CYCLE THEORIES DEPENDENT ON ASYMMETRIC INFORMATION

The Equity-rationing Approach

Greenwald and Stiglitz (1988a, b, 1990) have produced a macromodel with such rigorous underlying assumptions but which manifests a financial structure that amplifies shocks into cyclical disturbances. The key feature is that firms are constrained in the amount of equity finance they can issue; that is, if more shares are issued to finance new investment, the value of existing equities falls significantly. This phenomenon is well-established empirically (e.g. Asquith and Mullins, 1986; Korajczyk et al., 1990) and is explicable through various problems caused by asymmetric information.[7] Whatever the exact reason, firms act 'as if' they were equity-rationed (Stiglitz, 1988, pp. 313–14).

The observation of equity rationing is then married to the plausible assumptions that output decisions are risky (since complete futures markets do not exist and therefore final sales and prices are uncertain), and managers are risk averse (due to the career and financial penalties of bankruptcy). A model of the productive economy then emerges in which firms increase output if their equity base is enlarged, so as to diversify bankruptcy risk (since expected bankruptcy costs increase with output). Due to equity rationing, this can only happen slowly through the retention of profit. Shocks to the firm's cash-flow (e.g. from real interest rate rises), and the stability of its operating environment, then have multiplied effects on desired output and investment. Firms do not want to borrow to finance new investment during recessions because they cannot diversify away the additional bankruptcy risk.

Although equity-rationed models are difficult to test directly, they do yield predictions that are consistent with a number of facets of cyclical behaviour. For instance, they generate a cash-flow–investment accelerator to drive a cycle, following an exogenous shock that alters corporate cash-flow or managers' perceptions of uncertainty. This conforms to recent empirical findings of investment being heavily influenced by firms' current cash-flow.[8] The theoretical prediction of relevance in the present context is that if firms were better able to diversify production risks through easier access to equity (or PLS) finance, longer term investment plans would become feasible and cyclical fluctuations dampened. Increasing the ability of risk averse firms to share production risks with their suppliers of finance would reduce the expected bankruptcy costs for any given level of production, so shifting the aggregate supply curve to the right (Stiglitz, 1992, pp. 280–2).

The Agency Cost Approach

A related means of providing microfoundations to the Fisher–Minsky analysis is to focus on the agency costs of a commercial borrower–lender relationship beset by incomplete information (e.g. Bernanke, 1983; Bernanke and Gertler, 1989, 1990). In such circumstances, agency costs are reduced by high collateralizable borrower net worth (bnw), used as loan security. Its existence will reduce borrower incentives to self-select adversely and to incur high bankruptcy risk against the lender's wishes, resulting in lower risk premia and less restrictive loan conditions. Hence, particularly for small entrepreneurs, the cost of capital will vary inversely with bnw.[9]

This immediately raises the potential for credit conditions to amplify the cycle, since bnw will increase with rising asset values in a boom and be reduced in a slump. Lender agency and monitoring costs will move counter-cyclically, so exaggerating the output cycle. Indeed, asset price shocks to bnw can become an independent source of real fluctuations.[10] If bnw declines sufficiently, lenders may find it impossible to devise a loan contract which has a positive expected return. Even borrowers with high quality projects could be completely denied credit through being insufficiently creditworthy, and a collapse in the supply of new investment loans could ensue (e.g. Bernanke and Gertler, 1990, p. 99; cf. Mankiw, 1986).

Although this approach is limited in its focus on small firms (Sheffrin, 1989, p. 132), it provides a way in which variations in asset prices can have 'real' output effects without resorting to the assumption of 'money illusion'. Asset price fluctuations raise and lower the cost of capital to some borrowers without penalising or benefiting non-asset-holders. For instance, a collapse in collateral values may ration many borrowers out of the market whilst only benefiting those who have no desire to enter business (Bernanke, 1983, p. 267; cf. Kindleberger, 1989, p. 14).

NON-INTEREST CONTRIBUTIONS TO CYCLICAL DAMPENING

Given this theoretical background, the potential for interest-based finance to exacerbate the cycle, and for PLS finance to contribute to macroeconomic stability, can be explored.

Destabilizing Movements in the Cost of Capital

The purely monetary theories of the cycle focused on the potential for the money rate of interest to destabilize the 'real' economy by not reflecting the 'true' cost of capital. Although it abstracts from expectations, there is a kernel of truth in the analysis. For whatever reason (e.g. endogenous bank credit, the dictates of monetary or exchange rate policy, government borrowing), real and nominal interest rates can move in ways that destabilize aggregate demand. In a pure PLS economy, with no interest-bearing assets, this should not occur because the *ex post* return to financial capital must reflect the return made on real capital.[11] Hence, potential capital-users cannot face a situation where *ex ante* expected profits and capital costs are moving in opposite directions (e.g. Uzair, 1978, p. 105). A non-interest banking system will be even more conducive to macrostability if market-determined PLS ratios move procyclically, as envisaged by Siddiqi (1983c, pp. 171–6).

Fractional Reserve Banks and Credit Volatility

An essential element of monetary and financial theories of the cycle is the propensity of the conventional banking system to expand and contract credit supply procyclically. This systemically 'irrational' phenomenon results from the aggregation of 'rational' bank decision-making. During an upswing, the increasing confidence of borrowers is translated into banker confidence as rising profits, incomes and collateral values make *all* loan proposals seem less risky. The cost of capital falls as risk premia decline and lenders compete for assets. This, in turn, encourages greater demand and higher prices (e.g. Stiglitz, 1988, pp. 312–13). Banks have some discretion to satisfy extra loan demand, without having to raise interest rates to attract reserves and deposits, due to the combination of fractional reserve operations and liability management. The process is further exaggerated by banks operating on lower reserve and capital ratios to maximize profits, justified by lower default rates, and the potential of loan officers to be infected with 'herd instinct' (see the next chapter).

During a downswing, the increasing incidence of defaults and falling collateral values forces banks to conserve reserves and raise margins to rebuild their depleted capital.[12] Hence, at a time when borrowers require easier terms, their loan risk premia rise and banks switch their portfolios into high-quality assets. The result is a self-reinforcing mood of caution and conservatism – loan propositions considered safe during normal conditions are dismissed for being excessively risky (Keynes, 1931, pp. 171–3; cf. Llewellyn, 1991).

The maturity mismatch that fractional reserve banks face adds a further dimension to the procyclical lending cycle. In the upswing, depositors are less likely to be risk averse and will make net deposits, whereas loan applicant cash-flow is strong, encouraging banks to 'overlend'. In the downswing, depositors are likely to make net withdrawals to compensate for cash-flow deficiencies whilst borrowers' cash-flows are depressed. Banks will then be forced to tighten credit conditions (Dymski, 1988).[13]

These considerations have provoked numerous allegations that a fractional reserve, conventional banking system acts to amplify and propagate the output cycle.[14] This propensity *should* be reduced by a combination of 100 per cent reserve transactions deposits and PLS investment accounts. Reserve operations of 100 per cent would restrict the ability of the banking system to expand and contract the transactions medium whilst affording greater effectiveness to the monetary authorities' attempts to dampen the cycle. PLS lending ought to make banks more concerned about the longer-term profitability of borrowers rather than the short-term safety of cash-flow and collateral.[15] Such banks should be more circumspect when lending in the upswing and less willing to withdraw funding when macroeconomic conditions are tight. In addition, the safety of the transactions mechanism, and greater ability of banks to share portfolio risks with depositors, ought to reduce the pressure to withdraw funding from worthwhile projects in the downswing.

Bank Failures in Depression

The failure, and risk of failure, of conventional banks in a downswing can have strongly deflationary ramifications. Such failures not only lead to the disruption of the payments mechanism and reduction of depositor real wealth, but also entails the destruction of valuable information-capital acquired through bank–borrower relationships (e.g. Bernanke, 1983; Guttentag and Herring, 1987, p. 158ff). When a bank fails, borrowers must repay loans that they may have expected to be rolled over, and search for alternative credit sources. However, high-quality borrowers cannot credibly convey their attributes to new banks easily, and may face higher costs of capital or be rationed-out of the market entirely (cf. Sharpe, 1990, pp. 1084–5). Hence, irrespective of 'contagion effects' and their ramifications for the money supply, bank collapses can have an impact on the 'real' economy.[16]

Risk of failure encourages banks to be highly conservative during downswings by raising margins and reserve ratios, and switching to liquid, safe assets (e.g. B. M. Friedman, 1991). The major benefit of 100 per cent reserve and PLS operations is that a non-interest bank need not fear insolvency and, if its investment portfolio collapses in value, transactions deposits are unaffected.[17] As a result, non-interest banks should be less risk-averse in downswings and there will be less of a macroeconomic impact if financial intermediation collapses.

Speculative Lending and Borrowing

Interest-based finance can also be destabilizing by facilitating borrowing for speculative asset purchases (e.g. highly leveraged mortgages or takeovers). The problem lies in the lender's return being unrelated to the realised capital gain, with security often being provided by the asset that the loan is used to purchase. In an upswing, when assets begin to appreciate at a rate higher than the nominal rate of interest, borrowers maximize their capital gain by leveraging themselves as much as possible. Lenders acquiesce because collateral values are rising. Consequently, initial price rises can be transformed into a 'bubble' as more credit-financed purchases are made of assets in inelastic supply and prices bear little relation to 'fundamentals' (cf. Blanchard and Watson, 1982). (Assets also become more liquid, and so more valuable, simply because they can be used as collateral.) Asset appreciation may eventually only be sustained by credit-financed purchases, so that loans are viable only if more loans are made (cf. Beckman, 1988, p. 223). The process is reversed by some shock, or rise in real interest rates, that shakes lender confidence or places borrower cash-flows under pressure. Asset price falls are exacerbated by distress selling and repossessions. Easy access to credit makes such asset price 'bubbles' far more likely, and of greater potential magnitude, than would be the case with a 'cash-only' market (Bach, 1977, p. 182).[18]

Asset price swings would still occur in a non-interest economy. However, the amplitude of such movements should be reduced by the absence of interest-bearing credit. *If* finance were available from a PLS bank for speculative purchases,[19] the lender would have to contract for a share of realised capital gains. Immediately, this reduces the expected return for the borrower, and forces the lender to share in the risks of price volatility. Hence, both parties are dissuaded from entering into the arrangement relative to the conventional case. In addition, the absence of fixed debt service commitments should ensure that borrowers are not forced to sell on a falling market. Consequently, a non-interest economy should be characterised by less asset price volatility.

Non-contingent Liabilities and Debt Deflation

The feature of interest-based finance that contributes most to macro-instability, however, is the non-contingency of liabilities incurred by borrowers and banks. It is central to the Fisher–Minsky analysis. This predicts that measures of credit growth and financial fragility (e.g. income gearing ratios) will move procyclically and tend to lead output measures. The higher the levels of leverage and gearing, the more vulnerable an economy will be to real interest rate rises. If the unanticipated price and asset value falls occur, the predicted consequences of debt deflation ensue (increased insolvencies, tighter credit rationing and reduced investment, consumption and output).

Objection: The debt-deflation scenario broaches the orthodox tenet of money neutrality by maintaining that changes in the price level *do* affect the real level of output. In particular, it denies that the downward flexibility of prices and wages will automatically return aggregate demand to its full employment level. Rather, it posits that changes in real output can result from the symmetric redistribution of wealth from debtors to creditors caused by an unexpectedly low price level. Why doesn't the increase in consumption of creditors offset the decline in consumption of debtors ('the Pigou effect') as conventionally supposed?

Response: The standard reply has been that the marginal propensity to consume from wealth of debtors is, by definition, higher than that of creditors. A redistribution of wealth from the former to the latter automatically reduces consumption (e.g. Tobin, 1980). However, this assumption is neither theoretically justified nor empirically obvious, since many creditors are retail savers whilst some debtors are the largest corporations.[20]

A more cogent explanation relies on capital market imperfections to achieve output effects from *ex post* wealth redistributions (Fazzari and Caskey, 1989; Jefferson, 1994). For instance, with unexpectedly low inflation, debtors curtail expenditure in response to increased bankruptcy risk, yet the default risk for creditors has also increased, making their assets less secure. Also, a debt deflation simultaneously increases borrowers' need for external finance whilst making them less creditworthy. Given that these are also the people likely to have special knowledge and access to new investment projects, a debt deflation reduces investment by reducing their access to credit (Bernanke, 1992/3, p. 62).

Empirical Evidence: Supporting evidence has been derived from a re-examination of the US Great Depression. For instance, Mishkin (1978) found that rising consumer indebtedness, resulting from falling incomes and prices, induced a significant fall in durable and housing demand. Also, Bernanke (1983) found that small business and personal insolvencies *were* major contributors to bank instability, with the absence of indexed debt contracts ensuring that disinflation had a severe impact.[21] Large corporations fared best because their expansion in the 1920s had been financed by equity sales (Fisher, 1933b, p. 72ff).

Further evidence is provided by post-war experience. Many studies have found that the supply of credit has been a better predictor of output than money supply aggregates. In particular, Eckstein and Sinai (1986) discovered that financial events and contractions were influential in almost every post-war US recession, with the high elasticity of credit supply being a significant initiator and sustainer of expansions.[22] More recently, the credit boom and bust in English-speaking economies and Japan has provided ample proof of the ability of debt to foster output expansion and contraction. Corporate indebtedness became fashionable as a way to improve managerial disciplines. The boom in debt-financed equity buy-backs, takeovers and LBOs resulted in the capitalized value of US equities actually falling. The debt net worth ratio for non-financial US corporations rose from 32 per cent (1982) to 55 per cent (1989) (Simpson, 1992, p. 71). Such high levels of debt leave firms more vulnerable to real interest rises or demand downturns.[23] Recent record bankrupticies have been associated with high levels of debt in the UK (Joyce and Lomax, 1991;

Sargent, 1991), the US (Simpson, 1992) and France (Bordes and Melitz, 1989). King (1994) found a positive correlation between the shortfall in consumption in 1989–92, relative to trend, and the preceding growth in the ratio of household debt to GDP (1984–8) across ten major Western economies.

The potential for heavy reliance upon non-contingent debt liabilities to contribute to economic instability and fragility has prompted numerous warnings of the dangers of excessive leveraging,[24] and advocacy of greater reliance on indexed or contingent bonds, or equities.[25] Such fears are automatically addressed by a financial system that uses equity and PLS funds solely to finance investment projects. When profits and incomes are expected to increase, the anticipated cost of capital rises *pari passu*, dampening investment demand and widely spreading the benefits of higher profits to shareholders and bank depositors. Conversely, the expected cost of finance falls when profits are declining, and the number of bankruptcies are reduced since firms are not committed to debt service payments (cf. Goodhart, 1993, p. 283).

An interest-based economy allocates systemic risk in an irrational manner (Siddiqi, 1983c, p. 183). Rather than concentrating risk-bearing on firms (which can suffer costly bankruptcies) and banks (which threaten 'runs' and contagion), a PLS system shares risk with equity-holders and bank depositors. Consequently, declining profits would tend to produce widespread downward adjustments in household real wealth. Dynamic stability is the predicted outcome.[26]

ASSESSMENT AND IMPLICATIONS

Debt finance has long been accused of contributing to cyclical instability. Although financial instability theories have their limitations – there is no explanation of the initiation of cycles – there is common-sense appeal in the notion that financial structure amplifies the cycle. However, this is one of the commonsense propositions that economics has delighted in contradicting.

Two subsequent developments have given the proposition far greater credence. First, the application of asymmetric information considerations to financial relationships has shown ways in which financial structure can have an effect on the real economy. Secondly, the increase in private sector indebtedness in the 1980s, resulted in financial fragility and contributed to the length and depth of the subsequent recession.[27] Two implications can be drawn.

Over-indebtedness and the Tax System

Corporations have an inherent tendency to borrow excessively. Limited liability ensures that shareholders do not bear the full costs of bankruptcy. In addition, there are substantial indirect costs of bankruptcy that cannot be reflected in the risk premium paid on debt.[28] Consequently, there is an externality case for curbing corporate indebtedness (Summers, 1986, p. 165) in addition to considerations of macroeconomic instability. Firms will borrow more than is economically optimal.

Hence, it is illogical that the corporate tax systems of developed economies invariably favour debt over equity finance. Interest payments are tax deductible whilst dividends and retentions are considered as taxable profit. This reduces the cost of debt finance, relative to the equity equivalent, by a company's marginal tax rate. This bias needs to be eliminated not only on efficiency grounds (e.g. IFS, 1991; OECD, 1991), but also to encourage greater resilience to financial shocks (e.g. Wallich, 1977; Gertler and Hubbard, 1993). Indeed, the externality costs of debt financing indicate that the tax incentive should be reversed rather than eliminated (Bernanke et al., 1990, p. 275; cf. Chapra, 1985, p. 89).

Debt and Inflationary Bias

The growth of aggregate demand in Anglo-Saxon economies is now closely tied to the private sector's willingness and ability to borrow (Bell, 1976; Cameron, 1993). That such debts are rarely indexed introduces an inflationary bias to the output: inflation trade-off facing the monetary policy-maker, particularly on the downswing of the cycle:

> Entrepreneurs' willingness to incur debt denominated in nominal terms is intimately related to their anticipations of future monetary and real shocks. This realisation necessarily places restrictions on the monetary authority. The costs of delivering lower than anticipated inflation rates...are high. Output falls, defaults rise, and society bears more of the deadweight loss associated with bankruptcy when there is unanticipated deflation (or disinflation). On the other hand, unanticipated inflation appears to be beneficial...To the extent that the monetary authority attempts to 'fine tune' the economy,...errors on the downside tend to unleash Fisher's debt deflation phenomenon. (Jefferson, 1994, p. 52; see also B. M. Friedman, 1990)

This inflationary bias is reinforced by the imperative for policy-makers to avoid widespread bank failures during periods of financial fragility. However, in addition to increasing real long-term interest rates, the perpetual accommodation of debtors through unexpected inflation engenders moral hazard – the private sector will continue to leverage up in the expectation that it will be bailed out (Davis, 1992, p. 103). These considerations partly explain why the UK's price level has risen 20 times in the post-war period. Given the UK private sector's relatively high level of indebtedness, sterling's exit from the European Exchange Rate Mechanism appears inevitable in hindsight.

The purpose of this discussion has not been to claim that interest-based finance is the only cause of instability within capitalist economies, nor that a non-interest economy would be without cycles. Rather it has demonstrated that recent theoretical developments and experience support the contention that a non-interest economy would be more stable than its debt-financed counterpart. The benefits, in terms of a lower cost of capital and a more advantageous output: inflation trade-off would be considerable.

7 Key Issues in the Islamic Financial System

INTRODUCTION

The implications of complete Islamic economic and financial systems are all embracing; in a book of this kind it is impossible to discuss every ramification of such a system. In this chapter some important topics are examined from the perspective of a non-interest economy, but it cannot be pretended that these are necessarily the most important topics nor that the coverage of these is totally comprehensive. For example, the question of equity in Islam is worthy of a book in itself, but here it gains only a passing and superficial treatment.[1] The four topics chosen – savings behaviour; the allocation of loanable funds; bank stability and public finance; and government borrowing – if anything, are selected because they reflect the interests of the authors – no more and no less.

SAVINGS BEHAVIOUR IN A NON-INTEREST ECONOMY

A potential theoretical weakness of proposals for a non-interest financial system that is often alleged is their possible impact upon savings behaviour. If the supply of savings is highly interest elastic, and savers will not refrain from consumption without the expectation of a positive real reward for their 'abstinence' (e.g. Santoni and Stone, 1981), then the concept of a non-interest market economy appears untenable. However, careful weighing of the arguments suggests that the introduction of a profit-and-loss sharing (PLS) banking system would have an indeterminate effect on aggregate savings behaviour, and might even raise the average propensity to save and the bank-intermediated supply of loanable funds. There are several strands in the argument.

The Insignificance of Return-related Savings

The first response to the savings 'pessimists' is that the proportion of saving dependent upon the expectation of a real return may be insignificant. Keynes (1936, p. 107) proposed seven motives for saving, in addition to the desire to enjoy 'a large real consumption at a later date'. Even if marginal savings were to attract no real return, many other motives would remain (e.g. for old age).[2] A low interest elasticity of savings could come from the predominance of income over substitution effects in the consumption/saving trade-off as the rate of return varies.

The Reaction of Savers to Greater Return Variance

Such discussions may have relevance for a socialist or capital-abundant society in which savings do not attract a real return, but do not necessarily apply to a PLS financial system. A real return should continue to be paid to investment account holders, it is just that it will be directly linked to the profitability of the banks' portfolio of assets, and so theoretically liable to incur nominal losses in value. The pertinent question, therefore, is how will savers react to the abolition of return-bearing 'risk-free' assets, and their replacement by PLS investment accounts with supposedly greater capital risk and return variance.

   Two issues need to be distinguished when considering the reaction of savers to increased risk. It has been traditionally assumed that when risk averse agents face greater *income* risk, their preferred savings rate rises as they attempt to achieve the same expected target level of real wealth (e.g. Fisher, 1930; Boulding, 1966, pp. 534–5).[3] However, when risk averse savers are confronted with greater *capital* risk – that is, expected asset returns remain constant but their variance increases – the usual prediction is that desired savings levels will decline due to the enhanced attractiveness of current consumption relative to more uncertain future consumption (e.g. Marshall, 1930, p. 226). This expectation is reinforced by standard mean-variance portfolio choice theory,[4] which predicts that the elimination of risk-free interest-bearing loan opportunities will reduce the size of the desired portfolio of a risk-averse investor and will render a Pareto optimal outcome unattainable. Consequently, Pryor (1985) believes that a PLS financial system would induce a lower average savings propensity.

   When the savings decision under increased capital risk has been modelled, however, it has been found to be highly sensitive to particular assumptions concerning the form of risk aversion, the measurement of utility and the relative strengths of income and substitution effects within the agent's utility function.[5] Consequently, the theoretical models provide no determinate prediction of changes in savings behaviour that would result from greater capital risk.[6] The intuitive explanation is that if capital risk increases, risk averse agents will feel less inclined to expose their resources to the greater possibility of loss (substitution effect), but will also believe that greater risk makes it necessary to save more to be confident of achieving a target level of future consumption (income effect). There being no *a priori* theoretical prediction as to which effect will predominate, it becomes an empirical matter as to whether aggregate savings would rise or fall upon the introduction of a PLS financial system, notwithstanding its effect on average savings returns (Iqbal and Mirakhor, 1987, p. 6; Haque and Mirakhor, 1989).

The Riskiness of PLS Deposits

The elimination of risk-free, return-bearing assets would necessarily reduce aggregate savings. However, the *ex post* variance of real PLS account returns might not be greater than that of their interest-bearing equivalents after all. First, a non-interest bank can still use standard techniques to reduce deposit return variability. These include bank asset diversification and the accumulation of liquid reserves (Siddiqi, 1983a, pp. 23–4). In addition, nominal return variance could be diminished by the inclusion of non-PLS assets (e.g. rentshare property) in the bank's portfolio, and its ability to pay its shareholders a residual dividend of even greater variance. Consequently, investment account holders should suffer a significant reduction in *ex post* returns only when there is an economy-wide fall in profitability (Siddiqi, 1983c, p. 182).

Secondly, the riskiness of conventional bank deposits, and the variance of their real returns, is far from insignificant. Notwithstanding the greater potential for an interest-based bank to become insolvent (see below), conventional bank depositors face considerable uncertainty concerning their real rate of interest. Not only can nominal floating rates alter unexpectedly, but there also need be no necessary connection with the prevailing inflation rate (Ahmed et al., 1983b, p. 20). Consequently, conventional depositors (and bondholders) are exposed to the risk of unexpectedly low *ex post* real returns, with the consequent windfall gains for borrowers. With a PLS bank, however, the return on the bank's portfolio will be indexed to the price level to the extent that average profits and rents are related to price movements. Although not perfect, this correlation should be sufficiently strong to provide some reduction in the real rate of return variance experienced by PLS depositors (Karsten, 1982, pp. 131–3; S. R. Khan, 1987, p. 157).[7]

Hence, it is hazardous to make *a priori* predictions concerning aggregate savings levels in an interest-free economy. If savers are offered assets of the same expected return but with a greater variance, it is uncertain whether savings propensities would rise or fall. However, it is possible that real PLS deposit returns could be higher and/or be characterised by less *ex post* variation in any case.

Related Issues

A possible consequence of the proscription of interest is that highly risk averse savers might prefer to hold guaranteed current accounts or cash (when inflation is low), and durables or precious metals (when inflation is high). A reduction in the supply of loanable funds intermediated through the banking system may result thereby. Within the Islamic system, such tendencies to hoard unproductively are counteracted by the levying of *zakat* on holdings of idle wealth (S. R. Khan, 1987, p. 102). Consequently, Saud (1980, pp. 80–1) can envisage the introduction of explicitly depreciating money if cash is hoarded excessively (cf. Gesell, 1890). Mannan (1970, pp. 220–1) even advocates the taxing of current account holdings if they are favoured excessively *vis-à-vis* bank investment deposits (cf. Kennedy, 1988, pp. 27–30).

A final problem for savers in a PLS economy would be that of having to monitor banks more closely (e.g. *Economist*, 1992a). Conventional depositors ought to monitor the insolvency risk of their bank,[8] but will receive almost uniform rates of interest whichever bank they chose. However, PLS depositors need to examine their bank's investment strategy, the quality of its management and dividend pay-outs to shareholders, since their returns are directly dependent on these variables. A theoretical concern about a bank that issues variable-value deposit liabilities is that the management may be tempted to use the leeway granted in order to follow their own interests, rather than maximize deposit values (Goodhart, 1987, p. 87).

These potential problems can be reduced by ensuring that a non-interest bank operates within a suitable environment. Depositors' monitoring costs can be significantly reduced by central bank inspection of the probity of the bank's accounting standards, and regulation to prevent excessive risk-taking (e.g. as with conventional banks, PLS banks could be prevented from concentrating their general portfolio in the assets of one borrower or sector). More importantly, banks within a non-interest economy must remain competitive,[9] particularly with regard to deposit returns. This provides price signals to depositors, enabling them to switch funds to the most efficient intermediaries, thereby reducing the vulnerability of the system to moral hazard.[10] Critics retort that deposit instability would then ensue as funds are rapidly transferred to banks that have just announced high returns. This tendency, however, would be offset by the transactions costs and withdrawal periods involved. Besides, unit trusts operate upon a similar basis, and it is theoretically desirable that deposits are placed with the most efficient intermediaries.

THE ALLOCATION OF LOANABLE FUNDS IN A NON-INTEREST ECONOMY

A fundamental concern of critics of a PLS financial system is that the elimination of interest removes the one price signal that efficiently allocates loanable funds between competing demands, and the equilibration of planned saving and investment. An inefficient allocation of loanable funds and lower productivity are predicted. This outcome relies on the assumptions that there is no alternative to the rate of interest as an allocator of loanable funds, and that it does the job efficiently at present.[11] Both assumptions are open to dispute.

Debt Finance as an Inefficient Allocator of Finance

In a hypothetical economy in which markets and information are complete, the 'first-best' allocation of loanable funds is achievable. All investment projects whose returns exceed the prevailing market rate of interest would receive funding.[12] If the supply of loanable funds increases, the rate of interest falls and more projects become feasible. Once risk is introduced, the first-best allocation would involve the funding of those projects with the highest expected profit. The role of financial intermediaries in such an economy is to transfer, and concentrate, resources from those agents with wealth allocations but no viable projects, to those firms and entrepreneurs with the projects with the highest expected returns (Goldsmith, 1969, pp. 392–3). Economic growth is furthered by the process.

There are numerous reasons for doubting the likelihood of such an outcome in a debt-financed economic system. They revolve around the features of the standard debt contract – a non-contingent return (interest), collateral requirements and detailed monitoring only in insolvent states. Each of these contribute to the belief that debt financing *cannot* achieve an approximation to the first-best allocation.[13]

First, the fact that lenders do not receive any share of net profit from borrowers with successful projects, but can make losses from financing unsuccessful ones, ensures that lenders will be biased against funding risky projects even though they may have higher anticipated returns. In effect, because lenders do not gain from gambling successfully, but lose from gambling unsuccessfully, they tend not to gamble at all, even though it may be socially optimal for them to do so.[14] Hence, banks tend not to finance projects with the highest expected returns, after accounting for risk, but those with the most stable cash-flow. This outcome departs substantially from the first-best allocation.[15]

Secondly, debt finance establishes a set pattern of interest and amortization obligations into the future. This disciplines the borrower to ensure that sufficient cash-flow is available at intermediate periods, so reducing monitoring costs. However, this biases the provision of debt finance towards projects with early and stable cash-flows and contributes to the procyclicality of bank lending – since firms' cash-flow, and access to credit, varies positively with output growth (e.g. Webb, 1993). However, these projects are not necessarily those with the highest net present value. Debt finance can therefore contribute to 'short-termist' project selection when equity finance is unavailable (e.g. Jacobs, 1991, p. 129).[16]

Thirdly, the emphasis upon the provision of collateral as a usual precondition for funding ensures that finance is not necessarily provided to those projects with the highest expected returns, but to those with the best security (e.g. Siddiqi, 1983a, p. 71). This is the rational response of lenders who receive little direct reward for financing risky, successful projects. Collateral also acts as a substitute for active monitoring by the lender. Consequently, those entrepreneurs who have highly promising project proposals, but inadequate collateralizable personal wealth, will be deprived of finance at reasonable terms,[17] in favour of well-established, large firms and wealthy entrepreneurs. Hence, debt-financing tends to entrench the market positions of existing producers by excluding potentially more competitive entrants (Galbraith, 1975b, pp. 186–7, 297).

Finally, their non-contingent returns and collateral ensure that lenders have little need or incentive to discriminate against non-productive loan applications, or to monitor borrowers' actions outside bankruptcy (Stiglitz, 1985, p. 143). This may result in a lower cost of capital, but can lead to a sub-optimal allocation and use of loanable funds. For instance, banks have no need to bias their lending against uses for which there appears to be little social benefit (e.g. consumer credit or speculation), provided there is sufficient likelihood of debt service payments being maintained (S. M. Ahmed, 1947). Furthermore, the bank has little incentive to ensure that the borrower maximizes profit. Financial intermediaries ought to be a valuable source of managerial advice and expertise for their commercial borrowers, due to their opportunities for specialisation in the relevant skills and close monitoring of borrower actions. That this does not *automatically* occur is the result of the standard debt contract giving lenders no direct reward for ensuring the efficient use of loaned resources. Hence, conventional banks are the creditors, and not the partners, of their commercial borrowers (Anwar, 1987b, p. 83). It is ironic that debt finance is designed to economize on monitoring costs, but that insufficient monitoring can then occur.

An Illustration: Developing Country Debt

Perhaps the most obvious recent example of the misallocation of loanable funds attributable to interest-based finance has been the boom and bust in sovereign lending to developing countries (DCs) by Western commercial banks since the mid-1970s. Despite exhaustive analysis, few have recognised the underlying root cause of the débâcle to be the illogicality of allocating finance capital to DCs using interest-bearing debt, rather than contracts with explicitly contingent returns.[18]

The immediate causes of the crisis are well-known (e.g. Congdon, 1988, chs 4–5). Banks lent and DCs borrowed petro-dollars heavily at a time of low or negative real interest rates and rapidly increasing commodity prices. In the early 1980s, the rise in world interest rates coincided with a collapse in the terms of trade of many heavily indebted DCs, ensuring that effective real interest rates on much of the debt rose dramatically (e.g. Eichengreen and Portes, 1987, p. 41). In order to maintain debt service payments and qualify for multilateral agency loans, most DCs have been forced to increase exports dramatically, and submit to austere IMF 'structural adjustment programmes'. The results have included the widespread degradation of the world's environment as debtor countries have struggled to produce cash crops for export (George, 1988, ch. 10); the net transfer of resources from developing to developed countries, notwithstanding aid and further loans;[19] and significant cuts in the real incomes of many of the world's poorest populaces, to pay for loans from which they derived little benefit. The lives of millions have been lost as a result, and the health and education of millions more have been blighted (Jolly, 1989).

Responsibility for this tragedy must be shared. Commercial banks lent huge sums, at minimal risk premia, without adequately considering the possibility of changing economic circumstances, the uses to which the loans were put and the lending practices of other banks which contributed to the systemic risk. DC governments oversaw the misuse of borrowed resources in the funding of public deficits, capital flight, luxury goods and arms imports, and 'white elephant' development projects.[20] That such errors were possible, however, can fundamentally be attributed to the cost of borrowed capital being unrelated to the profitability of its use. Borrowers were tempted to overcommit themselves by an artificially low real cost of capital. If a reasonable profit-related return had been specified, loan demand would have been tempered prudentially. However, overborrowing was also,

> the result of lenders, because of fixed interest charges, not seeing themselves as fully sharing the risks of project failure and therefore not devoting sufficient energy to assessing risk. Had the banking system been more rigorous in its approach to risk assessment and taken much more responsibility in terms of an efficient and profitable utilisation of funds, many of the current problems of international debt may well have been avoided. (Presley, 1988, p. 61)[21]

Consequently, non-interest financial intermediation should have allocated funds in a far more prudent and efficient manner, *ex ante*, by restricting finance to those projects with a reasonable expectation of making a realisable return. *Ex post*, if the projects proved unsuccessful, the borrowing economies would not have been burdened with unsustainable servicing payments.[22]

It is no surprise, therefore, that debt–equity swaps have been canvassed as a way of linking the cost of capital to the ability to pay of DC borrowers, despite their risks and drawbacks.[23] Neither is it surprising that the global banking system was able to survive the crisis only by being subsidised and underwritten by Western governments,[24] whilst doing untold harm to the world's population, environment and economy in the process. With hindsight, commercial bankers are able to acknowledge the mistakes of the past.[25] Unfortunately, the lessons learnt in the sovereign debt crisis of the 1930s had been forgotten:

The criterion for economic international loan transactions should be that the proceeds of the loan should be so employed as to increase both the national income and the transfer capacity of the country by an amount at least equal to the total service of the loan during the whole period of its currency. When the proceeds are employed on non-profit earning undertakings, the most rudimentary elements for applying this criterion are lacking, and the world is likely rather to gain than to lose if changes in financial organisation make the raising of such loans more difficult. (Loveday, 1933, p. 418)

The Allocative Properties of PLS Finance

Given these theoretical considerations, and the practical experience of conventional bank decision-making, it is possible that non-interest intermediation would be characterised by a more efficient allocation of loanable funds. Merely by making banks residual claimants of borrowers' profit, bank–borrower relations ought to be transformed in a number of ways.

First, banks will have a direct incentive to identify and fund those projects with the highest expected risk-adjusted returns – thereby maximizing bank share and deposit values. Indeed, competition to attract investment deposits should force PLS banks to seek the most productive outlets for loanable funds, rather than those with the most secure cash-flow.[26] The receipt of a contingent return will involve the bank in more rigorous project appraisal *ex ante*, but this should improve project selection (e.g. Karsten, 1982, pp. 111–12; Siddiqi, 1983a, p. 54).

Secondly, the emphasis on expected profitability should ensure that PLS banks are less concerned about security requirements. If an entrepreneur has a first-class project proposal but little collateralizable wealth, a PLS bank ought to look more favourably on the application for funds than a conventional counterpart.[27] Consequently, a non-interest system would more readily fund small firms with risk capital, and be more innovative and competitive as a result (e.g. Gieraths, 1990, pp. 180–1). Lending on the basis of project quality rather than collateralizable assets ought also to lead to a more even distribution of income and wealth (Abdouli, 1991).

Thirdly, since they are residual profit recipients, non-interest banks will monitor borrower actions more closely. This raises the agency costs of equity funding, given the direct costs involved and resentment of bank scrutiny by borrowers. However, they will be offset by a more disciplined and informed use of capital (as banks provide management and consultancy services to borrowers),[28] and greater likelihood of borrower survival in periods of recession (as banks will have an incentive to accommodate their borrowers rather than withdraw funding at the first sign of trouble). PLS contracting encourages capital-suppliers and users to play a cooperative, rather than a zero-sum, game.

Finally, careful project appraisal and monitoring, and the residual profit-share of PLS banks, should deter speculative and excessively risky project proposals. Whereas interest-based lenders are, to some extent, shielded from project risk by collateral requirements and a non-contingent return (and so seem willing to finance the speculative acquisition of property and companies), PLS banks will share the risks and rewards of such ventures, and so ought to be more circumspect. In addition, because PLS borrowers will only receive a proportion of the reward for incurring high risks, some will be dissuaded from applying for such funds. Hence, a PLS financial system ought to be less susceptible to asset price booms and slumps by restricting credit for leveraged, speculative ventures.

Thus, there are theoretical grounds for believing that the short-term agency costs of non-interest finance ought to be offset by greater efficiency gains in the longer term (e.g. Chapra, 1985, p. 218). Having compared the 'equity-type' arrangements of German and Japanese banks with the debt emphases of British and US banks, Frankel and Montgomery conclude:

> There are theoretical reasons for believing that allowing banks to hold equity shares may improve the incentives for banks to make good financing decisions. Equity claims make the bank more of a residual claimant... If the bank has a close enough relationship with its customer to have substantial private information on the customer's business and also to have some control over the decisions that the customer makes, then equity holdings will give the bank a better incentive to make value-increasing decisions. (1991, p. 293)

Similar considerations prompted *The Economist* to speculate that:

> Islamic banking is not merely consistent with capitalism (i.e. with a market driven allocation of capital, labour and resources), but in certain respects may be better suited to it than Western banking. (1992a, p. 76)

Macroeconomic Equilibrium in a Non-interest Economy

The final issue concerning the allocative properties of a non-interest system is establishing an equilibrium in the market for loanable funds. Sceptics claim that the elimination of interest would remove the one price signal that equilibrates *ex ante* savings and investment via the market for financial capital. It would necessitate the state allocating investible funds in accordance with its own estimation of social priorities.

Notwithstanding the involved debate concerning what role the rate of interest plays in an open, monetary economy, it should be clear that a PLS system would retain price signals to allocate loanable funds.[29] In the property and equity markets, financial capital would continue to be allocated by rent and dividend expectations. In the market for PLS funds, two price signals would exist to equilibrate demand and supply. Not only would profit expectations in the productive economy influence the demand for finance and the supply of deposits, but also the profit-share ratios offered to new depositors and borrowers[30] would fluctuate in accordance with an excess supply of, or demand for, bank finance. For instance, given the level of expected profits,[31] an upward-sloping supply curve of investment deposits with a rising PLS ratio offered by the banks can be formulated. That is, bank deposit supply should be positively related to the expected deposit return – itself a function of expected bank portfolio profit and the PLS ratio offered to depositors. Conversely, a downward-sloping demand curve for bank finance is anticipated, with less demand resulting from a higher PLS ratio, *ceteris paribus*.[32]

Therefore, if PLS banks are competitive pure intermediaries, without the discretion to alter their margins at will, excess demand and supply for PLS funds should be eliminated by competitive movements in the PLS ratios offered to new depositors and borrowers. This result admits exercises in comparative statics which demonstrate the equilibrium properties of such a market,[33] and leads to the prediction of the equalization of risk-adjusted rates of return across a non-interest economy (Ariff, 1982a, p. 7). Consequently, profit expectations make a perfectly feasible allocative signal, rendering the rate of interest entirely dispensable for the purpose of forming a macroeconomic equilibrium (Siddiqi, 1983c, pp. 180–1).

Unfortunately, the case against interest has been exaggerated somewhat when the role of interest in establishing the level of activity is considered. Some Islamic authors seize upon Keynes' result, that the money rate of interest can stick at too high a level to ensure full employment, to claim that the existence of interest-bearing loan capital 'virtually perpetuates underemployment equilibrium' (M. Ahmad, 1967, p. 180; cf. Mannan, 1970, p. 169). This is too simplistic a conclusion. Keynes' analysis requires heavy qualification to be theoretically tenable (Mills, 1989), and experience has cast doubt upon the practical impact of interest rate fluctuations on real activity.[34]

However, there is intuitive appeal in the idea. Interest is the price of credit. It is not *automatically* related to the expected profitability of productive activity. Consequently, there will be occasions when the real rate of interest is high and rising, the expected real return on productive investment is low and falling, and the rate of interest moves in an inappropriate direction for the maintenance of employment and economic activity.[35] This possibility is strengthened by the anticipation that a rising real rate of interest will reduce consumer demand, and hence profit expectations, and make leveraged investment even more risky. Thus, adverse movements in interest rates could induce large, contractionary *shifts* in the interest–investment function even though it may not be highly interest elastic (e.g. S. M. Ahmed, 1969, p. 23 ff). Such a scenario could not be played out in a non-interest economy since the cost of capital to producers is linked automatically to realised profit.

Assessment

The allocative efficiency of the rate of interest is taken as axiomatic within orthodox economics. Outside the credit-rationing literature, there are few dissenters to the textbook assertion that movements in the rate of interest ration the supply of loanable funds to their most efficient uses. Yet intermediating finance through interest-bearing contracts biases the supply to borrowers and projects with collateral and secure cash-flow. There can be no presumption that these projects have the highest net present value of those on offer. The resulting allocation of credit discriminates against small firms with little capital, entrenches the status quo and increases the amplitude of the lending cycle (Zhou, 1992).

Interest-based finance circumscribes short-term agency and monitoring costs, leading to a lower cost of capital. These advantages are offset by longer-term inefficiencies in project selection and inappropriate risk-taking (cf. DC debt). Insufficient monitoring of borrowers may result.

Few non-interest proponents claim that their system would achieve the 'first-best' allocation of investible resources, and macroeconomic equilibrium at a high level of activity in theory, let alone in practice. However, there are sufficient grounds for questioning the allocative efficiency of the rate of interest as a price signal, and for claiming that a profit-related allocator may do better.

NON-INTEREST FINANCE AND BANK STABILITY

Banks and other deposit-taking financial intermediaries exist to transform the maturity and liquidity of financial assets. Yet, by issuing interest-bearing liabilities, whose nominal (par) value is guaranteed and potentially recallable on demand, conventional banks pretend that they are *not* transforming asset maturity and liquidity. In effect, they gamble that the 'law of large numbers' and depositor confidence hold, in order to remain solvent and liquid. Early banking history is littered with occasions when they did not, and the 'emperor was found to be without any clothes'. Hence governmental regulation and underwriting of banks is a universal phenomenon, and yet bank collapses and runs are still with us. The fundamental problem cannot be solved by treating its symptoms with better regulatory medicine because the ultimate cause of bank instability lies in contracting on an interest basis.

Why are Banks Unstable?

Individual bank vulnerability is rooted in the primary function of commercial banking – taking deposits and issuing promises to repay, which circulate as substitutes for commodity or fiat monies. Banks profit from depositor confidence in the redeemability of their deposits, and the independence of deposit withdrawals in stable conditions, by holding only fractional reserves and acquiring return-bearing assets with the remainder.

Fractional reserve banking is motivated by the desire to appropriate the seigniorage that accrues to a money-issuing authority when its liabilities are given an exchange value in excess of their intrinsic worth, by virtue of their acceptance as 'money' (e.g. Wilson, 1978, p. xxiii). With non-interest-bearing deposits, this seigniorage constitutes the return on loans of bank money created by fractional reserve operations.[36] However, when deposits attract interest and banking is competitive, seigniorage is shared between depositors, borrowers, shareholders and the state (via bank reserve requirements). The 'historical accident' of the marriage of transactions and intermediary bank functions is explained by the desire to appropriate seigniorage rents.

The liquidity transformation, and risk, entailed by fractional reserve banking is a necessary but not sufficient condition for instability. It must be accompanied by characteristics of bank operations that arise from uncertainty and incomplete information. On the liability side, depositors require a return-bearing asset recallable on demand or at short notice,[37] so banks are forced to incur maturity mismatches between assets and liabilities.[38] Since the bank cannot predict the demand for deposit withdrawal in extreme circumstances, there is a risk that reserves, asset sales and loan repayments could be insufficient to meet withdrawal demand. Hence, a solvent bank may be unable to honour its commitments by being locked-in to longer-term assets. If this is anticipated, rational depositors will 'run' to avoid repayment delay.

On the asset side, the bank's very existence can be ascribed to uncertainty and asymmetric information. Banks specialise in lending to individuals and firms who would otherwise be unable to obtain credit by issuing bonds, due to high monitoring and transactions costs (e.g. Guttentag and Herring, 1987, pp. 152–3). The bank's rationale can, however, be its downfall. Since a high proportion of its loans are information intensive and 'idiosyncratic', they cannot always be securitized and sold to other lenders if reserves need to be acquired quickly, due to a 'lemons' problem (e.g. Berger et al., 1991, pp. 755–7). Add to this the uncertainty surrounding future default probabilities and asset values, and all banks face considerable portfolio risk. The current value of bank assets is thus difficult for insiders to assess, let alone regulators and depositors. This uncertainty is sufficient to prompt a 'run' because only a rumour of a large loan default could produce suspicions of bank insolvency that cannot be easily allayed.[39]

Fractional reserves, maturity mismatch and portfolio risk combine to produce a volatile concoction with the potential to induce bank failure (e.g. Guttentag and Herring, 1982, pp. 101–2). However, the catalyst that gives this mixture explosive potential is the issuing of fixed par value deposits. Irrespective of the current value of its assets, the bank promises to repay its depositors – often on demand – to the full value of their original deposit plus agreed interest. Unfortunately, this undertaking gives depositors an incentive to withdraw immediately, if they suspect that the bank cannot meet all its commitments, to pre-empt withdrawals by other creditors.[40] Once a bank's illiquidity or insolvency is rumoured, so triggering withdrawals, it can become a self-fulfilling prophecy as the bank is forced to sell assets quickly at low prices, or acquire reserves at high prices, to meet depositor withdrawals. This 'run equilibrium' exists because the bank has issued fixed-value claims against a variable value portfolio.[41] If the bank issued equity-type liabilities (as with a unit trust or mutual fund), then depositors would have no 'insolvency' incentive to 'run' because the value of their deposits would fluctuate automatically with that of the underlying portfolio (Bryant, 1981, p. 459; Freedman, 1987, p. 189). Such a bank may face liquidity difficulties but *cannot* become insolvent, because its losses are passed on to its depositors. The urgency to withdraw is thereby significantly reduced.

Hence, the combination of fractional reserves, illiquid assets and nominally guaranteed deposits makes any bank vulnerable to collapse, no matter how prudent. Its continued operation depends upon depositor confidence. It is difficult to conceive of a less logical basis on which to run an economy's transactions mechanism.[42]

Why are Banking Systems Unstable?

Many of the aspects of interest-based banking that contribute to the instability of individual banks then have harmful consequences for other banks. Banking systems can thus be destabilised by competition and 'contagion'.

Historically, bank deposit interest rates have been regulated in the belief that competition for deposits tends to raise rates to levels sustainable only by the banks incurring ever greater portfolio risk. Whilst some theoretical evidence gives support to this belief (e.g. Bhattacharya, 1982; Smith, 1984), it is the competition to expand banks' asset portfolios that is the more obvious *ex ante* destabilising element. For instance, competitive pressures ensure that prudent banks will be disadvantaged for taking precautions against unforeseen events, so inducing 'disaster myopia' (Guttentag and Herring, 1986); whilst high levels of capital, reserves or maturity matching involve a loss of shareholder value relative to those banks willing to take greater risks (Holland, 1985, pp. 3–4; Davis, 1992, p. 138). Prudence is also eroded by loan officers, with high job mobility, being paid on the basis of current asset growth (Goodhart, 1989).

Competitive pressures also seem to induce a 'herd instinct' (some would say 'lemming-like' quality) in the banking psyche which increases the potential for crisis. It has been demonstrated of late in the propensity of Anglo-Saxon banks to invest in DC loans, property, junk bonds and LBOs (e.g. Frazer, 1991). It is explicable by 'reputation effects' in the labour market for loan officers[43] and the greater likelihood of government bailout if all banks are in the same type of trouble (e.g. Wojnilower, 1977). In addition, because banks do not share in the profits of their borrowers via equity-type arrangements, bank profitability is dictated by the expansion of the loan portfolio, particularly into innovative areas that competitors and regulators have thus far neglected, where margins are consequently higher. Other banks follow to maintain market share, and because the liquidity of novel assets increases with the development of an interbank secondary market. Over-leveraging of borrowers then occurs due to bank confidence in the continued supply of credit by others to that sector, and appreciating asset values being used as collateral for further borrowing. Consequent high debt commitments make borrowers vulnerable to falls in cash-flow. When a downturn occurs, the banking system finds itself over-exposed and liable to sustain default losses. In protecting themselves from further risk, banks collectively switch to other sectors, so completing the 'herding' cycle.

A banking system can also be vulnerable, *ex post*, to the failure of one of its members. Such 'contagion' is transmitted in three ways. First, banks hold similar types of asset, and accept similar forms of collateral, since a liquid secondary market is available for the sale of bonds, securitized loans or seized collateral when a bank needs reserves. However, during an economy-wide shock, the liquidity of such markets disappears, as many banks may be forced to sell simultaneously to acquire reserves. Falling asset prices raise doubts concerning the solvency of banks exposed to those sectors (Schwartz, 1986, p. 21). The system as a whole cannot turn assets into reserves, and individual attempts to do so produce a collectively detrimental result (Kindleberger, 1989, p. 125).

Secondly, a single bank 'run' can be made system-wide by the close pyramiding of inter-bank deposits. A bank requiring reserves will call in its loans to other banks, and take up negotiated credit lines, so spreading the demand for reserves. Such a crisis can become systemic because the system as a whole can haemorrhage reserves – deposits can be switched to other countries, into cash or other securities. Besides, solvent banks are often reluctant to lend excess reserves to banks suspected of insolvency (Saunders, 1987, p. 206).

Thirdly, the payment clearance mechanism ensures that if a bank is declared insolvent, it could be left owing significant balances to other banks simply through their acceptance of its customers' cheques.

The lack of information that depositors possess about the quality of their bank's portfolio ensures that the failure of one bank casts doubt upon the solvency of others holding similar assets or interlocking deposits. Such suspicions can switch demand depositors from a 'stable' to a 'run' equilibrium. Perfectly sound banks can thus be dragged down by the failure of imprudent competitors.

Regulatory Responses

In order to forestall 'runs' and insolvencies, governments and central banks effectively underwrite the losses that may be suffered by the creditors of regulated banks via 'lender of last resort' (LLR) facilities and state deposit insurance (DI). Such guarantees are rarely extended to other sectors of the private economy. Reasons for this favoured status include the potential for runs to bankrupt solvent but illiquid banks, and for the productive economy to suffer severe repercussions from the collapse of a bank due to the destruction of information capital entailed (e.g. Bernanke, 1983). More importantly, banks hold the payments system as a hostage against being allowed to fail. The widespread economic disruption that would result from significant bank failures means that governments are implicitly blackmailed into guaranteeing banks (Karekan, 1985, pp. 62–3).

LLR and DI are similar. Both operations attempt to ensure that depositors have no incentive to 'run' by bolstering bank liquidity or guaranteeing the value of deposits. When a bank is insolvent, both operations attempt to forestall a run to allow for the planned disposal of the bank's remaining assets, so maximizing their value. Both try to ensure that a single bank failure does not initiate a contagion. Given the scarcity of bank runs in developed economies, these operations have avoided successfully the instability that interest-based, fractional reserve banking threatens. However, there are less obvious costs to such interventions.

The 'Lender of Last Resort' Function

The traditional goal of the LLR is to protect the transactions mechanism and forestall bank contagions without sheltering banks from errors of judgement. This is meant to be achieved by following the 'Bagehot rule' – emergency loans should only be made to solvent but illiquid banks at penal rates (Bagehot, 1873).

The LLR's difficulties fall into two categories. First, Bagehot's advice cannot be applied as a 'rule'. It is difficult to judge whether a bank is insolvent or merely illiquid in the time available, particularly when the distinction varies with asset price fluctuations.[44] Consequently, LLRs have lent to insolvent banks (e.g. Johnson Matthey) through ignorance and the desire to pre-empt a wider panic. LLRs invariably opt for short-term stability benefits at the expense of longer-term banking moral hazard.[45] Similarly, a 'penal rate' is troublesome to charge. If a bank cannot find refinancing in the private market, a penalty rate could induce bankruptcy. Yet a soft rate will encourage excessive risk-taking by other banks. Consequently, LLRs have preferred to retain discretion over whether and how they will aid a troubled bank, because the penal rate is not a credible threat.

Secondly, the very existence of an LLR allows banks to take greater risks, hold fewer reserves and maintain less equity, whilst depositors have fewer incentives to monitor their bank's portfolio. The gains from risk-taking are enjoyed by bank borrowers and shareholders, whilst the risk is shared with the monetary authority and taxpayers. The provision of a safety net may forestall present crises, but increases the likelihood of future ones (Kindleberger, 1989, p. 163) whilst protecting inefficient banks from the consequences of their actions (Schwartz, 1986, p. 27). The vagueness that LLRs maintain to counter bank moral hazard, in turn makes 'runs' more likely whilst distorting bank competition. If it is anticipated that the LLR will only lend to some banks but not others, large institutions will attract deposits at lower cost since they pose a greater threat to economic prosperity and will be more likely to receive any aid going (Mayer, 1975). Truly, LLRs are 'damned if they do, and damned if they don't' (Hirsch, 1977, p. 252).

Deposit Insurance

LLR coverage is often supplemented by government DI schemes. Private schemes have been tried but tend to be found wanting when faced by a system-wide contagion. Credible assurances can only come from the tax-raising or money-creating authority. The aims of DI are to protect minimum wealth-holdings of small depositors and forestall bank runs by making depositors' fears of non-repayment irrelevant (McCarthy, 1980). Insured banks contribute a flat-rate premium per unit value of their deposits.

Like the LLR, the DI agency faces an inherent dilemma. Runs will be forestalled only if 100 per cent coverage of deposits is given. Unfortunately, this represents a government loan guarantee to depositors, giving them little incentive to monitor their bank, so encouraging excessive risk-taking. To combat this moral hazard problem, DI agencies often resort to some form of coinsurance by limiting the sums guaranteed. This, however, has caused problems in the US because the absence of cover for large deposits and CDs has prompted corporate depositors and other banks to initiate 'runs' against suspect banks. Consequently, in the cases of Continental Illinois (1984) and First Republic Bank of Dallas (1988), the Federal Deposit Insurance Corporation (FDIC) extended DI coverage to 100 per cent of wholesale deposits to forestall a run. These precedents, and frequent subsidising of the mergers of vulnerable banks, effectively extended DI coverage in the US to 100 per cent, and gave banks an artificial incentive to grow in order to enjoy the DI risk-taking subsidy (Boyd and Gertler, 1993, p. 7).[46]

DI is now blamed for much of the fragility of the US banking system, particularly in the Savings and Loan (S&L) sector. Flat-rate premia ensured that taxpayers and conservative banks subsidised the gambling of risk-taking banks,[47] permitted banks to run down their capital ratios (Peltzman, 1970) and encouraged troubled S&Ls and banks to try to speculate their way out of difficulty (Merton, 1978, p. 448; Berlin et al., 1991, p. 739). In addition, DI distorts the competition for savings in favour of banks (and against equities, etc.), whilst the ambivalence as to which banks will receive minimum or 100 per cent coverage again biases competition in favour of larger institutions which are more likely to receive the full coverage.[48]

These perverse effects cannot be eliminated by charging risk-related DI premia. It is impossible to set actuarially-fair premia for events, such as loan defaults, that are not stochastic and independent, and difficult to assess the riskiness of new forms of bank business, non-marketable loans or off balance sheet commitments. Besides, once the premia are paid, banks can quickly alter their portfolio risk at little cost (Berlin et al., 1991, p. 744), and will act to substitute LLR support for the more expensive DI (Karekan, 1985, pp. 70–1). There seems no 'quick fix' for the dilemma of the deposit insurer.

The threat of bank collapse and contagion has forced monetary authorities to intervene to prevent the possibility of widespread instability. Rather than reform bank structure to ensure immunity to contagion, the authorities have chosen to underwrite banks via LLR and DI facilities, thereby guaranteeing a significant proportion of private debt obligations (Wojnilower, 1985, p. 356). In so doing, they demonstrate their willingness to shift the losses caused by bank errors from depositors to taxpayers, or the rest of the economy in terms of higher inflation. Meanwhile, tough supervision and capital adequacy requirements are needed to restrain the excessive risk-taking that would otherwise occur (Davis, 1992, p. 239).

Notwithstanding the injustice of the situation, the guarantees represented by DI and the LLR, and the unwillingness to allow large banks to suffer the consequences of their own mistakes, contribute to the inflationary bias of Western economies (Schwartz, 1986) and distort competition by giving advantages to bank deposits over other savings media and large banks over small. These problems associated with conventional, fractional reserve banks, and the unavoidable dilemma of the LLR and DI agencies, have prompted a wide range of reform proposals. The remainder of this chapter will examine the feasibility of reforms implied by non-interest banking – 100 per cent reserve accounts and non-par-value deposits.[49]

100 Per Cent Reserve Transactions Deposits

The danger that fractional reserve banking places the payments mechanism in has prompted a range of proposals to separate transactions and savings deposits into two funds or institutional types, so as to prevent cross-subsidization and infection.[50] The most radical of these proposals[51] involves a 100 per cent reserve requirement for all liquid deposits that can be used as 'money' – that is, can be withdrawn on demand and transferred via cheque or plastic. Permitted reserves would be cash holdings or balances at the central bank.

The primary advantage of 100 per cent reserves is that there is no reason for demand depositors ever to 'run' because the nominal value of their assets is entirely safe. Immediate benefits ensue. Banks and monetary authorities are saved the expense and distortionary consequences of DI, whilst banks *can* be allowed to suffer the consequences of their lending errors because the transactions mechanism is immune to bank failure. Not only would banks be permitted to fail, but they would necessitate less regulation as to the riskiness of the portfolio they hold on the intermediation side. Depositors would be offered a choice of an entirely safe demand deposit with no return, or deposits with a variety of risk–return combinations. Hence, *caveat emptor* would become as explicit in the choice of bank deposit as it is with unit trusts or pensions. In addition, banks would be freer to engage in the longer-term lending of time deposits because they would no longer need to cater for demand deposit redemption (e.g. Fisher, 1935b, p. 17, 138).

Reserve requirements of 100 per cent would also reassign monetary seigniorage to the state. By permitting only state-issued currency, or deposits backed by it, to act as 'money', the state regains control over the money supply process and becomes its sole beneficiary. Given a growing economy, and the goal of price stability, 100 per cent reserve advocates envisage real money supply expansion of 2–3 per cent p.a. The significant levels of seigniorage generated could be used to lower taxes or gradually repay the government's debt (e.g. Currie, 1934, pp. 153–4; Fisher, 1935b, pp. 189–90). Thus, seigniorage would benefit the whole of society.

However, this seigniorage could not be conjured out of thin air. The likely losers would be demand depositors who would be expected to cover the costs of running the transactions system. Users would then bear the full opportunity cost of the service enjoyed, so reducing wasteful over-provision.[52] If the running of the payments system has sufficient 'public good' elements to justify subsidy, this could be supplied through explicit grant, interest on balances at the central bank, or permitting gilts and T-bills to qualify as reserves, as in conventional 'narrow banking' (Simons, 1948, p. 235).

The greatest claims made for 100 per cent reserves, however, are that they facilitate governmental control over money stock growth, and prevent credit provision from amplifying the business cycle. Fisher (1935b), Friedman (1948, p. 247) and Simons (1948, p. 170) saw the 100 per cent reserve requirement as a way of eliminating the discretion of banks to alter the money stock, or thwart the intention of open-market operations, by their lending decisions. Price stability would result from reducing the bank money multiplier ratio to unity, so making the money stock entirely exogenous.

No less controversial is the claim that 100 per cent reserves would contribute to macrostability by divorcing the creation of money from the supply of investible funds (e.g. Currie, 1934, p. 152). Fisher attributed the shrinkage of US money supply in 1929–33, and accompanying depression, to a fractional reserve system whose supply of the monetary medium was dependent on loan demand, itself reliant on something as fickle as borrower confidence. Such a monetary system seems purpose-built to amplify cyclical fluctuations. This will

be our predicament so long as we have a system under which our circulating medium is a by-product of private debt. The time when nobody wants to go into debt is the very time when we most need money and so most hope that somebody will kindly accommodate us by going into debt. (Fisher, 1935b, p. 94; cf. Soddy, 1926, p. 258)

100 per cent reserves would de-couple the money supply process from loan demand.

Despite receiving some Congressional support in 1934, the benefits claimed for 100 per cent reserves were exaggerated. For instance, if banks charged heavily for operating the payments mechanism, then fringe operators would offer money substitutes that evaded the reserve requirements, whilst banks would offer time deposits with monetary features (e.g. Angell, 1935, p. 14). Also, the monetary authorities would have to monitor banks closely to ensure that demand deposits were not on-lent, would have little control over changes in velocity of circulation and would need to exercise discretion over fiscal policy and open market operations skilfully if price stability was to be achieved. 100 per cent reserves are not, therefore, *the* simple solution to monetary control problems (Hart and Walker, 1934/5; Allen, 1993, p. 716).

However, the major drawback of a 100 per cent reserve system, (and other 'narrow banking' proposals for that matter), is that alone it does not yield a 'run-free' banking system. It may insulate the payments mechanism against bank vulnerability, but the intermediation side will still be subject to runs (e.g. Goodhart, 1987, p. 85). LLR and DI facilities, and portfolio regulations, will still be necessary if the collapse of large financial intermediaries is too costly to risk. Consequently, the separation of transactions and intermediary functions is insufficient to produce an invulnerable banking system. This was realised by some 100 per cent reserve advocates who implicitly (Fisher, 1935b, pp. 150–1) or explicitly (Simons, 1948, p. 169; cf. James, 1985, pp. 79–80) linked their proposals to the need for non-par value deposits.

Non-Par-Value Deposits

Mutual Funds Accounts

The concept of non-par-value, return-bearing deposits has found embodiment in US money market mutual funds accounts. These provide cheque-clearing facilities and a deposit whose value fluctuates with the underlying value of a portfolio invested in government bills, bonds and equities. The risk of a variable nominal value has not deterred depositors.[53]

The principal advantage of transactions accounts on a mutual fund basis is their ability to offer a return without the risk of insolvency or illiquidity. Since the fund makes no commitment to guarantee any deposits' nominal value, and holds widely-traded assets whose values are publicly known, there is no 'insolvency' incentive for depositors to engage in a run (King and Goodhart, 1989, p. 6). Stability is enhanced by the probability that if depositors transferred *en masse* between funds, this would simply realing assets between fund managers, avoiding the insolvencies banks would suffer. If depositors deserted fund accounts in favour of cash, through fear of capital losses, the consequent fall in fund asset prices would have the stabilizing effect of raising their probable returns. These properties of mutual funds render DI and LLR functions obsolete and avoid their inherent dilemmas.[54] Such may be the result of a completely deregulated market for transactions media, and possibly would have developed instead of fractional reserve banking if financial asset markets had been sufficiently deep at the time (James, 1985, p. 79).[55]

Investment Accounts

Proposals for interest-free banks to issue equity-type time deposits, and to concentrate on profit-share and rental assets, are an attempt to provide a risky, return-bearing savings medium as an alternative to mutual fund accounts (where equity markets are poorly developed) or as a complement to them. Such banks are also needed to provide the informationally-intensive PLS funds required by borrowers otherwise unable to raise funds through equity flotation. The bank can better take such asset risks because no fixed commitments have been made on the liabilities side. Hence, such banks should be more akin to venture capital investment trusts because they are not exposed to insolvency risk.

PLS savings deposits should ensure that an interest-free bank is less prone to instability. The absence of guaranteed nominal value savings should eliminate any incentive for depositors to 'run' through fear of insolvency (e.g. M.S. Khan, 1986, p. 19), whilst the emphasis on profit-share assets ought to eliminate interlocking bank deposits – so reducing 'contagion' potential (Chapra, 1988, p. 35). However, a PLS bank, unlike a mutual fund, still faces the risk of a run from depositors who suspect liquidity problems. Such a bank holds some non-marketable assets of uncertain value. If faced with a high withdrawal demand, it could find itself illiquid and unable to repay creditors until its assets matured, or forced to sell reserve assets at low prices. Hence, depositors may still try to withdraw before the bank sustains such losses and the possibility of a 'self-fulfilling prophecy' remains. Therefore, to mitigate liquidity risk, a PLS bank will continue to hold substantial reserves and marketable assets (e.g. equities) in addition to imposing minimum notice periods for time deposit withdrawals. The central bank may still need to organise an interest-free emergency loan fund for PLS banks or offer LLR facilities on an equity basis to prevent bank illiquidity (e.g. Chapra, 1985, p. 156; El-Ashker, 1987, pp. 221–2).

A further benefit claimed for PLS deposits comes from their influence on the portfolio choices of bank managements. A conventional bank (with fixed value liabilities, DI coverage *and* limited liability share capital) will maximize equity value by choosing a portfolio with a higher risk–return profile than if shareholder liability was unlimited or depositors shared in residual profit (John et al., 1991).[56] This propensity is exacerbated by banks now engaging in 'liability management', so making their profit on the differential between variable borrowing and lending rates. Hence, profits are maximized when the portfolio is expanded to the point where the interest rate margin equals expected default losses (e.g. Kaufman, 1977, p. 185; Wojnilower, 1980, p. 295). The incentive for banks to overinvest in risky projects should be reduced by PLS depositors sharing in the benefits of successful risk-taking, while the emphasis upon profit-share assets and the absence of an inter-bank loan market will force PLS banks to engage in 'asset management'. Their profit will then depend on the quality of their assets rather than the size of their portfolio.

Finally, non-par-value deposits are essential if a non-interest financial system is to contribute to greater stability in the macroeconomy.[57] During upswings, PLS banks share in rising corporate profits, so reducing the retained profits available for further real investment, and passing them on to depositors. Conversely, during downswings, a fall in the profitability of real assets is reflected in a decline in the nominal value of firms' monetary liabilities. The subsequent reduction in monetary claims (through the declining values of bank deposits and shares) occurs automatically, whereas an interest-based economy requires costly bankruptcies, bank failures or inflation to achieve the corresponding adjustment of monetary claims to real asset values (M.S. Khan, 1986, pp. 15–19).

Hence, PLS deposits can be expected to contribute to banking system robustness, less risky bank portfolios and macroeconomic stability. They enable monetary authorities to dispense with DI when complemented by 100 per cent reserve and mutual fund transactions accounts.

Assessment

These proposals face several serious objections. First, separating transactions and intermediary banking would forfeit the monitoring advantages that a bank enjoys as lender from handling transactions accounts
(Fama, 1985). This implies that a non-interest, 100 per cent reserve
bank should continue both activities but maintain a rigorous separation of reserves and capital to preserve confidence in the absolute
security of its transactions accounts.

Secondly, whereas a mutual fund invests in liquid assets whose
values are established publicly and minute-by-minute in secondary
markets, many of a PLS bank's assets would be information-intensive,
non-tradable and so opaque. This problem also besets a conventional
bank, but its fixed-value liabilities reduce the moral hazard faced by
depositors (e.g. Diamond, 1984; Bernanke and Gertler, 1987, p. 91ff).
However, the increased potential for a non-interest bank to exploit its
depositors should be limited by the relative ease of deposit withdrawal,
increased depositor monitoring, the possible development of a secondary market in PLS bank deposits and competition for savings amongst
non-interest banks and with other savings outlets.[58]

Finally, the elimination of interest-bearing demand deposits will result
in welfare losses for risk averse savers wanting a return-bearing, capital-
certain asset providing insurance against illiquidity risk (e.g. Bhattacharya and Gale, 1987, p. 69). The probable results are a rise in the cost
of intermediation, a reduction in intermediated savings and an increase in
cash hoards. These are the main costs of a non-interest banking system
and will only be partially mitigated by the provision of equity mutual
funds. However, it is the very desire to offer a capital-certain, return-
bearing, liquid deposit contract that is the root cause of bank instability,
with its attendant externality costs. If such costs could not be passed on to
others, banks would be unable to offer such contracts.[59]

Utilising the terminology of Knight (1921), an interest-based, fractional reserve banking system operates on the assumption that its
environment is 'risky'. Deposit withdrawals and default rates are
assumed to be independent and predictable (cf. Minsky, 1976,
pp. 128–9). Unfortunately, such events are characterised by 'uncertainty', making the conventional bank inherently vulnerable to failure
by its very structure. That such institutions survive is largely due to
governmental regulation, assistance (LLR facilities) and underwriting
(DI guarantees). Without them, a conventional bank would have
difficulty operating (e.g. Hayek, 1976, p. 95; Qureshi, 1985, p. 8).

Thus far, state intervention has largely succeeded in preventing system-wide bank collapses at the expense of subsidising banks to take risks; favouring large banks over small, and banks in general over other financial intermediaries; incurring high costs to taxpayers through bank rescues and nationalisations (e.g. US, Sweden, Norway); adding to the inflationary bias of capitalist economies; and perpetuating a banking system that amplifies the economic cycle. Interest-based banking has survived thus far by persuading the monetary authorities to underwrite many of its liabilities.

The options facing monetary authorities are either to 'paper over the cracks' (e.g. by tinkering with DI liabilities) and risk the costly support or collapse of the edifice in the future; or to rebuild the financial structure on firmer foundations, rendering external support unnecessary. If some preconditions are met, a non-interest banking system should not only be feasible, but also be more stable and less costly to the rest of the economy.

PUBLIC FINANCE AND GOVERNMENT BORROWING

Islamic public finance indicates that, for non-revenue-making government investment projects and consumption expenditures, there are no satisfactory non-interest alternatives to full tax funding. Consequently, many Islamic economists advocate that the Muslim state aim for a balanced budget, or small surplus, over the cycle, with PLS bonds or equities floated to finance investment by revenue-raising state enterprises (e.g. Metwally, 1983, pp. 74–5; Siddiqi, 1983b, pp. 132–42). Counter-cyclical alterations in fiscal stance could be achieved by reducing the aggregate government surplus, or the government's stock of real and financial assets.

The elimination of interest-bearing government debt has serious welfare disadvantages. In particular, investment projects yielding non-pecuniary benefits far into the future (e.g. a road network) would have to be paid for by current taxpayers, seemingly inequitably and inefficiently. However, the long-term economic and moral advantages should outweigh these costs. Notwithstanding the disputed potential for government deficit financing to raise real interest rates and 'crowd-out' private investment,[60] the accumulation of a significant public debt and interest commitments imposes various economic costs.[61] The high taxes needed to fund the debts of the past often exacerbate disincentives to work and to save, the expansion of the 'black' economy, the erosion of the legitimacy of taxation, the inflexibility of fiscal policy (e.g. Ratchford, 1942, p. 464) and the flight of capital and labour abroad (e.g. Ricardo, 1951, I, pp. 247–8). Not only must taxpayers bear the costs of making a market in government debt, but also those of a tax bureaucracy that transfers funds to and from largely the same group of citizens (Congdon, 1985).

In addition, the existence of interest-bearing government debt has other undesirable consequences. Heavy government indebtedness tempts the monetary authorities to ease disinflationary pressures in order to reduce the real burden of debt servicing (e.g. Ruebling, 1978). Alternatively, the existence of safe, return-bearing government bonds encourages a rentier class and mentality (e.g. Hume, 1970, pp. 94–6), and risk aversion in financial intermediaries forced to compete for funds (Veseth, 1990, pp. 68, 74, 124–5).[62] The discretion to borrow permits the executive to be less zealous in cost-cutting than would otherwise be necessary (e.g. Chapra, 1985, pp. 136–7).

However, perhaps the most important effect of government borrowing is that it permits current taxpayers to impose unwarranted burdens upon future generations by postponing taxation to fund consumption expenditure.[63] Again, the existence of interest encourages the current generation to use its temporal position to avoid the full costs of its actions.[64] Perhaps the most startling assertion of those wishing to eliminate the state's ability to borrow is that there would be fewer wars as a result (*sic*). If a populace were to bear the immediate consequences of war, in higher taxation, capital levies or inflation, then countries would be less willing to initiate and sustain a war effort.[65]

Consequently, although short-term welfare losses would result from restricting deficit financing, an argument can be made that an economy would benefit in the long run.

Mortgage and Consumer Debt

The most widely-felt impact of a non-interest financial system would be the elimination of interest-bearing mortgage and consumer debt. Again, this would have immediate welfare costs. Interest-bearing consumer 'credit' facilitates welfare-augmenting intertemporal trades by permitting agents to transfer consumption to those periods when relative expenditure needs are greatest (e.g. Baltensperger, 1989, p. 948). It enables the less well-off to enjoy a higher standard of living and is, in one sense, egalitarian (e.g. Galbraith, 1975a, pp. 70–1;

George, 1988, p. 11). Modern life would be immeasurably less convenient without ready easy access to personal loans.

This ignores the high social and economic costs paid for relying heavily on interest-based consumer loans, and the potential of non-interest alternatives. Notwithstanding paternalistic arguments for credit restrictions, high levels of household indebtedness can prove economically divisive – as the well-off enjoy better terms and access to credit – and socially destructive.[66] Further detrimental consequences can include depressed aggregate savings propensities and more volatile consumer durables demand (e.g. Steindl, 1989). High levels of household leverage yield a more fragile macroeconomy, vulnerable to rises in real interest rates.[67] These effects are amplified by a housing sector dependent on mortgage finance to fund house purchases. Recent UK and US experience has been marked by volatile property prices, having a destabilizing impact on the wider economy, and a rising trend of repossessions and loan arrears (Miles, 1992).

Clearly, the current reliance upon interest-bearing mortgage and consumer credit is not without its costs. Consequently, there are practical reasons for advocating its replacement (e.g. Siddiqi, 1983b, pp. 157–64). Once the legitimacy of rental charges is accepted, then interest-bearing credit for purchasing durables (especially housing) can be emulated by variations on the 'hire-purchase' theme.[68] These have the advantages of not committing the borrower to acquiring full ownership in the house, but permitting part-rent part-ownership arrangements, and never placing the 'borrower' 'in debt' unless servicing payments are defaulted upon. In addition, the cost paid for housing services ought to become more reflective of prevailing housing market conditions (through rental levels) rather then being directly dictated by the volatile, and often contrary, movements in the cost of borrowing. Other non-interest alternatives to conventional mortgages include PLS 'endowment' arrangements (whereby the property is rented whilst a lump-sum is accumulated in a bank investment account or unit trust) and 'salary-linked mortgages' (whereby borrowers pay a fixed proportion of their pre-tax income to the financier for the duration of the 'loan').[69]

A potential difficulty for a non-interest financial system is the provision of credit needed for immediate consumption or liquidity purposes. The only feasible substitutes, apart from charitable or state-run interest-free loans funds, are non-interest mutual credit arrangements[70] and time-multiple overdraft facilities.

8 The Prohibition of Interest in Western Literature

INTRODUCTION

Moneylenders have never been popular – condemned for their laxity in good times and for their parsimony and greed in bad. Bankers, and orthodox economists, dismiss such feelings as the result of irrational cultural prejudice. Given a competitive supply of credit, any belief that lenders are exploiting their borrowers is thought irrational.

However, the Western belief in the benign results of interest-based financial operations is historically relatively novel. More typical has been the attitude of the English Puritan, Henry Smith, expressed four centuries ago, to the effect that lending at interest is *inherently* exploitative and socially divisive:

> The Usurer loveth the borrower, as the Ivy loveth the Oak: The Ivy loveth the Oak to grow up by it, so the Usurer loveth the borrower to grow rich by him. The Ivy claspeth the Oak like a lover, but it claspeth out all the juice and sap, that the Oak can not thrive after: So the Usurer lendeth like a friend, but he covenanteth like an enemy, for he claspeth the borrower with such bands, that ever after he diminisheth, as fast as the other increaseth. (Smith, 1591, p. 14)

Indeed, the Puritan anti-usury polemicists made great play of the surprising degree of consensus in the opposition of monotheistic religion and classical thought to the very existence of interest, to reinforce their case.

Islam therefore has not had a monopoly in advocating the prohibition of interest. Admittedly the moral, religious and pragmatic arguments traditionally espoused by the opponents of interest now claim few Western adherents due to the divorce of ethical debate from economic theorizing. However, there was far more economic sense in the historic opposition to interest than is currently assumed. This chapter will give a brief overview of the history of the hostility to interest in Western thought and summarize the recurring arguments made by its adversaries.

A NECESSARY CLARIFICATION

The contemporary meanings of the terms 'interest' and 'usury' differ from their original usage. Currently, interest has the connotation of a legitimate payment for a monetary loan, whereas usury has that of extortion through rates of interest that exceed the bounds of law or justice.

The original meanings of the two terms were substantially different. 'Usury' initially referred non-pejoratively to the charge made for the use of any form of property, but came to be applied solely to that made for a money loan. Hence, usury referred to what would now be termed interest.

'Interest' derives from the Latin *interesse*, meaning 'to come in between'. From the thirteenth century in Europe it referred to payments made on a monetary loan that compensate the lender for any loss suffered as a result of the transaction. Interest was originally intended to indemnify the lender, rather than provide a financial return. The number of instances when such payments were deemed legal was gradually increased until most loan charges were legitimized under the guise of 'compensation'. Lenders persisted with the euphemism 'interest' in order to avoid the unwelcome associations of 'usury'.

Hence, the historical opposition to usury was aimed at what we now call interest. Its arguments were aimed predominantly at the charge made for a monetary loan, rather than the return on financial and real capital *per se* (e.g. partnership profits, dividends and rent). Consequently, it is to be distinguished from the socialist attack upon all profit (as the unwarranted extraction of surplus value), and from simple 'anti-banker' populism.

A SUMMARY OF THE WESTERN OPPOSITION TO INTEREST

Whilst ancient law codes, such as the Babylonian Code of Hammurabi, contained restrictions on the maximum interest rates payable and the compounding of interest, the first instance of an outright prohibition of interest is found in Deuteronomy:

> Do not charge your brother interest, whether on money or food or anything else that may earn interest. You may charge a foreigner interest, but not a brother Israelite.[1]

This prohibition was reinforced elsewhere in the Old Testament by injunctions not to lend to the poor at interest and denunciations of the unrighteous usurer.[2] There is, however, no explicit rationale for the prohibition given within the texts themselves. Consequently, Jewish rabbinical teaching explained the prohibition largely in terms of encouraging charity and community feeling, rather than declaring interest to be inherently unjust. Jewish communities have tended to observe the prohibition of interest amongst themselves but charged interest on loans made to Gentiles (following the brother/foreigner distinction of Deuteronomy).

Whilst interest-free lending to family and friends was greatly esteemed within ancient Greek societies, interest was regarded as legitimate if charged on an impersonal or business loan. After rioting by Athenian debtors in 594 BC, Solon ameliorated their position by cancelling debts and proscribing debt slavery and the compounding of interest. However, restrictions on interest rates were not imposed. Only Plato and Aristotle voiced outright opposition to the very existence of interest within Greek thought.

The early Roman authorities were far more interventionist, however, as the perpetual indebtedness of peasant farmers, and the severe penalties for default, resulted in periodic debtor revolts. The maximum interest rate was set at 10 per cent in 450 BC but eventually lowered to zero in 342 BC. This outright prohibition quickly became obsolete in practice, but was periodically revived during debt crises. Sulla eventually adopted the customary rate of 12 per cent as the legal maximum in 88 BC, which continued until the fall of the Western Empire.

The New Testament makes only passing reference to interest. Most relevant is Jesus' teaching to his disciples on lending:

> If you lend to those from whom you hope to receive, what credit is that to you? Even sinners lend to sinners in order that they may receive in return the equal amount. But love your enemies, and do good and lend, despairing of nobody.[3]

An idiomatic rendering of the final phrase would be 'lend, without hoping for any return'. Whilst Jesus is clearly advocating a radically liberal approach to lending, it is not clear what is to be forgone – interest, principal or the hope of reciprocal favours. Nevertheless, this text was often used to justify a prohibition of interest within Christian circles. The only explicit New Testament references to interest come in the parables of the talents and the ten minas.[4] By implication, these references describe interest as 'reaping where one has not sown'.

The biblical material gave sufficient grounds for the proscription of interest within the Church – first enacted at the Council of Elvira (306 AD). The Church Fathers were unanimous in their condemnation of usury on the grounds of greed and uncharitableness. Only Augustine ventured further by declaring usury to be a variant of theft, and so inherently immoral. Interest was first proscribed for all citizens by a Christian legislature in 789 under Charlemagne.

Until approximately 1050, interest-taking was considered by the Church to be a sin of greed and lack of charity. However, the commercial revival of the late eleventh century, and the ensuing increase in demand for business loans, forced Church lawyers and theologians to reclassify usury as a sin of injustice. In the succeeding centuries, these scholastics developed various arguments from natural law, to reinforce those from scripture and authority, to 'prove' interest-taking to be immoral. Ultimately, the harshest anti-usury Church legislation was passed by the Council of Vienna (1317). This not only called for the excommunication of usurers but also that of any ruler who sanctioned usury. To declare that interest-taking was not a sin was classed as heresy.

The force of the medieval Church's prohibition of interest was lessened by royal exemptions granted to certain groups (notably the Jews and Lombards) for purposes of state borrowing and taxation; the gradual widening of the legal grounds on which 'compensation' could be paid; and the diversion of business finance into 'licit' contractual forms (e.g. foreign currency loans at a mark-up and secured annuities). Nevertheless, the proscription had a marked, and probably beneficial, impact on the forms of financial intermediation within Medieval economies (eg. Postan, 1928; Lane, 1966) and sanctified the popular suspicion of moneylenders.

Within Catholic Europe, the usury prohibition continued to have some practical force until the late eighteenth century. (The Vatican only formally recognising the legitimacy of interest in 1917.[5]) However, Protestant Europe vehemently debated the interest question for most of the sixteenth century. Ultimately, Calvin's grudging acceptance that usury was not inherently unjust when charged to the rich at a moderate rate, proved to be the crucial concession. In England, the last Act condemning all interest as contrary to God's law was passed in 1571. However, the punishments enacted were far more severe for loans yielding over 10 per cent interest, so setting the *de facto* maximum rate of interest at that level. From 1600 onwards, the debate was transformed from whether to proscribe interest altogether, to which rate was most expedient to have as the legal maximum. Bowing to agrarian interests, Parliament periodically reduced the legal maximum to 5 per cent by 1714.

Ultimately, the debate shifted to whether a legal maximum could be justified at all. For instance, Adam Smith supported the restriction of interest rates to just above the normal market rate. Otherwise:

> the greater part of the money which was to be lent, would be lent to prodigals and projectors, who alone would be willing to give this high interest. Sober people...would not venture into the competition. (A. Smith, 1776, II, iv, 15)

In effect, Smith argued for a usury law to improve the efficiency of credit allocation. Such reasoning was rejected by Jeremy Bentham. He argued that a cap on interest rates subsidised wealthy borrowers, raised black market rates of interest and constituted a paternalistic restriction on economic freedom:

> No man of ripe years and sound mind, acting freely, and with his eyes open, ought to be hindered,...from making such bargain, in the way of obtaining money, as he thinks fit. (Bentham, 1787, I, p. 129)

Bentham's arguments eventually carried the day. In Britain, the 1854 Moneylenders Act abolished the 5 per cent usury law and allowed lenders to charge any rate. A limit of 48 per cent was reimposed in 1927 in an attempt to protect vulnerable borrowers. However, since the passage of the Consumer Credit Act (1974), no such restriction exists – borrowers must instead demonstrate exploitation to a court, given their circumstances.

COMMON GROUNDS FOR CRITICISM

Interest, Charity and Social Divisions

Interest has been most frequently attacked for the potential it affords for exploitation of the needy. Indeed, from one perspective this occurs automatically because a loan is 'by nature' without interest, and a borrower is 'needy', by definition:

> Now lending on interest is a blameworthy action, for a person who borrows is not living on a superabundance of means, but is obviously in need, and since he is compelled to pay the interest as well as the capital, he must necessarily be in the utmost straits. (Philo, *De specialibus legibus*, 2.74–77; cited in Maloney, 1971, p. 105)

Throughout history, usurers have been condemned for seeming to profit from the misfortune of others. Plutarch believed moneylenders to be more oppressive than foreign invaders (*Moralia*, 829), whilst the medieval Church placed usurers in the same moral category as prostitutes, for their overt greed and lack of charity (Le Goff, 1979, pp. 35–6). Dante consigned moneylenders to the end of the seventh circle of hell in a rain of fire (*Divina Comedia*, Inferno, Canto XVII), whilst usurers from Shylock to Harpagon (in Molière's *The Miser*) have been the butt of literary ridicule for their archetypical miserliness.

Such universal condemnation stems from the prevalence of localised monopolies in the supply of credit, the high risk premia charged on small, unsecured loans and the potential for compound interest to render debt traps ineluctable. Hence, 'exploitation' has been widespread despite the borrowers' seeming 'freedom of choice' in the matter.

A related theme is that of the potential divisiveness and inequality that interest can create in society by favouring a rentier class and generating an impoverished debtor class.

Permitting loans to attract 'unearned income' entrenches initial inequalities of wealth and the resulting social divisions. Interest *tends* to accrue to those with surplus wealth and come from those without, whilst the existing maldistribution of wealth can be shielded from the uncertainties of actual production and trade by being invested in interest- bearing debt, especially riskless government bonds. When borrowing, the rich receive more favourable terms due to their access to collateral (Mishan, 1971, p. 205). Consequently, critics have regarded usury as a socially divisive institution.

For instance, Plato regarded usury as incompatible with the most desirable organisation of the city state. Although Plato highlighted the unethical nature of compound interest (*Laws*, 842d) and noted that money was barren (*Republic*, 556a), his opposition was based on the observation that interest-bearing debt divided society into antagonistic camps. On the one hand are the unpropertied, usually owing money and eager for revolution:

> On the other hand, the men of business, stooping as they walk and pretending not even to see those whom they have already ruined, insert their string – that is, their money – into someone else . . . and recover the parent sum many times over multiplied into a family of children: and so they make drone and pauper of them. (*Republic*, 556a)

Moneylenders hasten the decay of the polis by dividing society into rentiers and paupers, whereas legislation ought to reduce the conflict between rich and poor (Lowry, 1979). Hence, Plato would not have obliged a debtor to repay an interest- bearing loan, nor provided legal protection to the lender in a credit sale (*Laws*, 742c and 850). Interest was only permissible as compensation for late repayment of a debt (ibid., 921).

Interest and Relationships

A related theme is that lending at interest disavows economic solidarity and a close relationship between borrower and lender. At a personal level, interest charges signal to the borrower that the loan is on a 'commercial' rather than reciprocal-favour basis. Hence, the interest-free loan is foundational to economic 'brotherhood', particularly in tribal societies, and became influential in Judaeo-Christian thought through the Deuteronomic 'brother–foreigner' distinction. This prompted the belief that interest charges are inappropriate between co-religionists, and that usury should only be taken from one's enemies.[6] Christ's teaching upon the 'love of enemies' then inspired the Christian universalisation of the interest prohibition.

On a wider level, interest economises on the information transfer needed between lender and borrower, particularly in investment loans. It promotes the development of financial intermediaries and an 'anonymous' loan market, in which the ultimate lender and borrower need not know each other. This expands the supply of loanable funds, but also facilitates the migration of financial capital from depressed communities, the funding of businesses that savers might deem 'unethical' and the separation of the interests of lenders from the circumstances of borrowers.

Interest and Work

A recurring observation is that interest is financial gain without effort. Often the lender makes no sacrifice and faces minimal risk, yet is permitted to derive income from the work of others. The medieval Church condemned usurers in the same breath as sluggards, whilst socialists regard interest, rent and pure profit as the common fruits of worker exploitation. Even defenders of interest have admitted to unease about its role as unearned income.[7] Calvin disapproved of moneylending as an occupation whilst Proudhon, Keynes and Harrod eagerly anticipated the 'euthanasia of the rentier'.

Interest and Risk

For those critics who have accepted the legitimacy of rent and profit, the unacceptable feature of interest is its allocation of risk. If profit was always certain, the 'productivity' justification of interest would hold. Lenders would merely share in the profit that their financial capital had definitely procured for the borrower. However, to state the obvious, profit is rarely 'certain' and it is presumptuous or naïve to believe otherwise.[8] Hence, the Jewish and Christian emphasis upon profit-sharing partnerships comes from recognising the uncertain nature of profit. If the providers of finance are to share in the rewards, it is only fair that they share in the risks. Indeed, a return to capital is only legitimate if ownership responsibilities and risks are retained by the supplier, as in a partnership or rental agreement. Their transfer in a loan contract renders interest illegitimate.

Two corollaries flow from this. First, if profit is uncertain, interest cannot be justified on opportunity cost grounds (e.g. Benvenisti, 1937, p. 30n). Aquinas and Luther resisted the extension of the title to 'compensation' from a loan from its outset by observing that if lenders have alternative investment opportunities, then they should be exploited, rather than expecting the borrower to provide a certain return instead. Secondly, interest cannot be justified by the risk of lending, since both parties to the contract face risks. Why should the lender's risk-bearing be compensated and not the borrower's, especially when the loan is secured and/or repayable on demand?

Interest and Money

Interest has perennially been attacked for contravening the original intentions behind the institution of money – that it should act primarily as a medium of exchange rather than as a source of gain or store of value. Notably, Aristotle regarded usury as the ultimate abuse of money by treating it as a means of profit rather than as a facilitator of exchange.

In Aristotle's view, making money in exchange for produced commodities is a legitimate aspect of household management. Money is being used to facilitate exchange – the primary reason for its existence (*Nichomachean Ethics*, 1133a). The problem for Aristotle is that the accumulation of money through the exchange process is all too often made the goal of economic activity. This occurs in retail trade when the sale of goods is solely motivated by the desire for profit. The 'abuse' of money is most pronounced, however, in lending at interest:

> There are two sorts of wealth-getting...; one is part of household management, the other is retail trade: the former necessary and honourable, while that which consists in exchange is justly censured; for it is unnatural, and a mode by which men gain from one another. The most hated sort, and with good reason, is usury, which makes a gain out of money itself, and not from the natural object of it. For money was intended to be used in exchange, but not to increase at interest. And this term usury (*tokos*), which means the birth of money from money, is applied to the breeding of money because the offspring resembles the parent. Wherefore, of all modes of getting wealth, this is the most unnatural. (*Politics*, 1258a; 1952, p. 452)

Much of the subsequent discussion of Aristotle's position is based on the misconception that the philosopher thought that since money was 'barren', it could not naturally reproduce. Interest made it do so and therefore contravened the sexual laws of nature (e.g. Böhm-Bawerk, 1959, I, p. 11).[9] Of course, this 'barren metal' approach can naïvely be controverted by pointing out that money *can* be 'productive' and fruitful in certain circumstances.

However, this is a parody of Aristotle's views. Instead of claiming that money is barren and that therefore interest contravenes natural law and is immoral, Aristotle's argument is that money *can* be made fruitful but that this subverts the original purpose for which money was brought into existence – namely to act as a medium of exchange. The affront to nature comes in the use of money for a purpose for which it was not intended. Whilst Aristotle readily conceded that it was not necessarily wrong to use an object (such as a shoe) for a purpose other than its primary one (*Politics*, 1257a), it was because lending at interest *had* to be motivated by the desire to profit from an exchange of money that made it unnatural, and therefore immoral (Cannan et al., 1922; Spiegel, 1983, p. 26).[10]

But Aristotle was not alone in his views on money. Aquinas believed that interest undermined the stability of money as a measure of value – by ascribing different, time-dependent values to a given quantity of money it 'diversified the measure'. Finally, the monetary radicals (Proudhon, Gesell and Douglas) each ascribed the existence of interest to the creators or hoarders of money. These kept the circulating medium in artificially short supply to extort a monopoly tax (interest) from the exchange process. This results in an unstable velocity of circulation and price level and frequently inadequate aggregate demand.

Interest and Time

Interest embodies various 'undesirable' attitudes towards the passage of time. For many scholastics, usury involved the illicit 'sale of time', forcing capital to work all of the time, irrespective of divinely ordained Sabbaths. Also, the exponential growth of compound interest over time has commonly been regarded as 'unnatural' (e.g. the prohibition of compound interest in Babylonian, Hindu and Byzantine law codes, despite their admission of simple interest).

A further, time-related critique of interest is raised by the presumptive attitude towards future profitability and income contained in commercial and consumption borrowing decisions. Profits and purchasing power are anticipated and 'brought forward' by means of interest-bearing debt. In the process, borrowers are made vulnerable to unexpected changes in circumstances, and the interests of future generations are discounted relative to our own (e.g. by burdening future taxpayers with government debt interest payments). Monotheists have been more circumspect in acquiescing to such financial commitments, and have argued for greater cognizance of stewardship responsibilities with regard to future generations.

Essentially, the whole usury debate turns on our attitude towards time. The justification of interest entails the claim that, quite literally, 'time is money'. Since the mere passage of time supposedly alters the value of assets, money and satisfaction automatically, their forfeiture over time (through a loan) automatically justifies interest as compensation. The opponents of interest would dissent. Since nothing is certain in time, we ought not act as though it is. Contingent profit-share and rental contracts allow for positive returns to be made, and the services of durables to be enjoyed, over time. But they do not presume that the mere passage of time necessarily affects anything. Hence, it is unwarranted to justify discounting through positive time preference.

SUMMARY

It appears that a strong case has been made against the existence of interest through the centuries of Western thought aimed at its abolition. On biblical grounds, the antipathy to usury is more robust than is commonly realised. The prohibition does not just apply to excessive rates, or interest from the poor, or from co-religionists, or on consumption loans, but to interest from those considered as 'brothers' or 'fellow countrymen'. If anything, Jesus universalized the application of the prohibition for his followers.

On ethical grounds, if one accepts that the use, as well as the acquisition, of wealth ought to be subject to moral scrutiny, there are a number of bases from which to attack usury. For instance, if wealth is to be used primarily to help others, there is no scope for interest to be charged – for interest should not be taken from the poor and, if taken from the rich, the original loan was misallocated in the first place. Also, interest liabilities are not contingent upon the circumstances of the borrower. They can therefore lead to borrower immiseration or insolvency inconsistent with the ethical use of wealth. Often, the ultimate lender may be unaware of these immoral outcomes due to the assistance interest has given to the development of an anonymous, intermediated financial market. In a way, the usurer provides nothing of service to the borrower, since ownership passes to the borrower in a loan. Hence, interest rewards nothing and constitutes pure exploitation of the borrower's labour. Initial inequalities of wealth are then entrenched by the operations of interest.

On legal grounds, the existence of interest can be justifiably challenged. For in a rental or partnership contract, ownership rights, risks and responsibilities for the transferred asset are retained by the original owner. Yet in a loan, these are transferred to the borrower, who is then under a legal obligation to return the original asset, or its equivalent, at the specified time. Hence, if the ownership of property is relinquished by the lender, why should interest reward the absentee owner? It is no coincidence that interest was not intrinsic to loan contracts under Roman law but had to be contracted for separately.

On economic grounds, the case against interest is often compelling. The availability of interest-bearing assets has mitigated against the supply of risk capital and encouraged a rentier mentality. Interest facilitates the divorce of the processes of saving from investment, so creating the potential for an unemployment equilibrium. The non-contingency of interest payments encourages borrowing for specula-tion and exacerbates the amplitude of the economic cycle.

Whilst this accumulation of evidence against interest might seem compelling to some, unfortunately the case for the prosecution has one major flaw. Most of its arguments are predicated upon initial premises – be they religious, ethical, or legal – that are not universally held. If usury could easily be equated with an obviously immoral act, such as theft, then the case for prohibition would be clear. But this is not the case. In most instances, interest-bearing loans are contracted voluntarily. Bor-rowers are not forced to incur such liabilities, they frequently enjoy the advantages of competition amongst lenders and receive obvious benefits from loans. The borrower and lender simply agree to exchange the principal now for the promise of its return at a premium in the future. The anticipated value of the services rendered to the borrower must equal or exceed the interest paid or the exchange would not occur. Hence, it has not been automatically apparent to societies uncommitted to monotheistic revelation that there is anything sufficiently immoral about interest to warrant its outright prohibition.

This is not to say that there are no practical drawbacks to interest. But these must be weighed against the pragmatic disadvantages of its prohibition. In particular, the proscription of interest in a society uncommitted to the underlying requisite religious or ethical ethos will merely result in a thriving black-market for loans – with suitably adjusted risk premia – and the proliferation of contractual devices that disguise interest as profit, rent or unconnected favours.

Hence, on the ethical and legal grounds that have featured in the Western debate over interest, the case would appear to be 'not pro-ven'. Whilst compelling grounds can be given for the rationalization of the Biblical prohibition of interest, their acceptance depends on prior commitment to particular religious or ethical norms. In this sense, the scholastics failed in their quest to provide an all-embracing, convin-cing critique of interest on the basis of natural law.

Without moral pre-commitments, the usury debate becomes a prag-matic one. Whilst there are many practical disadvantages to a free market in interest-bearing loans, these are now thought at least in non-Islamic economies to be too obscure, amorphous or inconsequential to outweigh the practical benefits of such a market combined with the difficulties of maintaining an interest ban. Western societies have been stripped of the religious and ethical presuppositions conducive to the proscription of interest. Consequently, if the legitimacy of interest is to be seriously questioned again, the debate must hinge on the feasibility and practical benefits of a non-interest financial system, which have been examined in the preceding chapters.

9 Conclusions

THE PROGRESS OF NON-INTEREST FINANCE

Given the novelty and radical nature of the concept, interest-free financial theory and practice have developed surprisingly far. Interest-free banks have proved to be durable institutions enjoying substantial deposit growth. Pakistan and Iran operate a technically non-interest financial sector. Theoretically, profit-share, mutual fund and rental contracts can perform many of the functions of debt finance and their *exclusive* use offers many potential benefits. These include the more efficient allocation of loanable funds; a banking sector that can more readily supply long-term risk capital; a greater emphasis on productive investment *vis-à-vis* consumption and speculation; and a stable and stabilizing financial sector.[1] Interest-free theory has developed sufficiently to counter the allegations that the elimination of interest would significantly reduce savings propensities, that monetary policy would be impotent without an interest rate to influence and that such an economy would be rendered unworkable by moral hazard problems.

REMAINING DIFFICULTIES

Serious practical and theoretical shortcomings remain, however (M. F. Khan, 1989; Cobham, 1992b). Existing Islamic banks continue to concentrate on mark-up trade credit rather than profit-share investment finance. This can be explained through various features of their operating environment (e.g. the artificial advantages granted to conventional banks, the continued existence of government debt). However, existing non-interest banks have not yet demonstrated that the concept has significant developmental potential. In addition, Islamic theorists have generally failed to address the difficult practical issues of the repayment of existing government debt; the impact of non-interest operations on foreign exchange rate determination and international capital flows; and the precise accounting definition of 'profit' that is to be shared with capital suppliers.

The most serious theoretical questions still to be satisfactorily answered concern the increases in depositor information-gathering and entrepreneurial disincentives attendant upon PLS operations; the potential for rent-yielding property to replace conventional bank deposits as *the* liquid, return-bearing asset; and the possibility that high-quality borrowers will avoid PLS finance and raise debt finance either in a domestic 'black' market or from international sources. This is, of course, assuming that the preconditions necessary for a non-interest financial system to be effective are fulfilled.[2]

THE EXTERNALITY CASE AGAINST INTEREST

The discussion thus far has centred on the advantages and disadvantages of a non-interest financial system and its theoretical feasibility. However, establishing feasibility and possible benefits is insufficient to sway the argument in favour of proscribing interest. As has been already established, the critics of interest have been unable to devise a universally accepted legal or moral argument that proves usury to be inherently unjust (akin to theft, for instance). Given contractual freedom, lenders and borrowers will willingly enter into interest-bearing contracts, and will seek to do so even if interest is proscribed. Notwithstanding overt economic paternalism, those who wish to assert that interest 'should not exist' must produce a strong externality case against interest. That is, interest-based contracting must impose sufficient costs on the wider community to warrant abrogating individuals' economic freedoms.

The externality case against interest is founded on the shifting of risk to third parties that widespread debt-financing entails. Interest-bearing contracts are entered into by borrowers and lenders on the grounds that their operating environments are characterised by risks with quantifiable probabilities. Hence, non-contingent liabilities are incurred with the expected risks catered for through risk premia on interest rates, collateral and residual equity. However, economic conditions are often 'uncertain' in that outcomes fall outside the range of variation allowed for on the basis of historical experience. Consequently, individual, corporate and bank insolvencies ensue when cash-flows are inadequate to validate debt service commitments.

Such outcomes impose negative externalities on many levels. First, limited liability, personal bankruptcy limitations and deposit insurance ensure that the failure of leveraged borrowers imposes direct costs on creditors and taxpayers. Legal obligations to meet all debt commitments are waived in straitened circumstances, transforming debt into a contingent liability *ex post*. The risk premium element in the cost of capital rises as a result. Secondly, the abrupt failure of firms and banks, and the distress sale of their assets, forfeits managerial experience, investment opportunities and firm-specific capital (White, 1989).

However, the externality costs of the widespread use of debt finance are felt more widely yet. The amplitude of the economic cycle is magnified by the interaction of credit conditions and asset values. The insolvency risks faced by interest-based banks necessitates their underwriting by the tax-raising and money-issuing authorities, with the concomitant regulatory burdens raising the cost of financial inter-mediation. Finally, the leveraging of firms and households provides an inflationary bias to the inflation/output trade-off, since the productive economy is benefited in the short run by unanticipated inflation (which also helps to maintain bank solvency).[3] Heavy reliance on debt finance also requires the state to act as 'borrower of last resort' during recessions in order to validate the debt service commitments of the private sector (Minsky, 1992/3, p. 81). Hence, not only does interest-based finance entail direct costs to the unsatisfied creditors of bankrupt borrowers, but it also imposes less obvious but far more burdensome costs on the wider economy.

THE DOMINANCE OF DEBT OVER EQUITY FINANCE

Negative economic externalities are conventionally addressed by adjusting relative prices through the tax system, so that the marginal cost faced by the individual is equated to the marginal cost to society. Such a solution would indicate that, rather than the proscription of interest, debt finance ought to be penalized, relative to equity, via the tax system. It is somewhat ironic, therefore, that personal and corporate indebtedness has invariably been encouraged via the treatment of interest as a cost rather than a return to capital.

However, notwithstanding the practical difficulties of establishing the level to which debt finance ought to be penalized and applying this to a deregulated financial system, merely changing the relative costs of debt and equity will not yield the full theoretical advantages of a non-interest financial system. For instance, PLS banks will face difficulties in competing with conventional banks due to the adverse selection of potential borrowers. If an interest-based alternative is available, appli-cants for PLS finance will self-select towards those with extremely risky projects or those with high expected non-pecuniary benefits relative to profit. Conversely, conventional banks will receive applicants who believe their projects to be of high quality and who therefore do not wish to dilute control. In addition, the costs of project appraisal and monitoring will be higher for PLS banks than their competitors, due to the contingency of their return, and will be reflected in a higher expected cost of capital from PLS banks. As with Weitzman's profit-share and flat rate wages, the two systems are probably unable to co-exist successfully.

This conclusion also applies on a wider scale. The very existence of interest on financial assets, irrespective of tax treatment, would still leave scope for the money rate of interest to dictate the returns on other assets and lead to an unemployment equilibrium. Similarly, due to the importance of the timing of project cash-flow resulting from debt servicing commitments, firms would continue to assess projects inefficiently on the basis of payback period rather than total net present value.[4] The existence of conventional banks will necessitate the continuation of state guarantees whilst the persistence of debt finance will preserve inflationary bias in the system.

Consequently, there are various reasons why PLS and conventional systems cannot easily co-exist, even if debt finance were penalized through the tax system. Outright prohibition of interest,[5] rather than tax penalties, is the only means to achieve the benefits of a non-interest financial system.

> [C]ompound interest is compound sin: it lets loose in a finite economic world exponential growth causing great injustice and making debts unpayable. It was not abstract theology, but thousands of years of sad experience of concentration of wealth in a few hands and of debt slavery, that caused all the ancient books of wisdom: the Bible, the Koran, the Greek philosophers to condemn interest ... In a world where neither per capita nor total real output is growing, and money is metallic and cannot be increased readily, the charging of any positive rate of interest very quickly leads to over-concentration of wealth in the hands of a few rentiers, and economic breakdown. (Hotson, 1991, p. xvii)

THE SCHOOLS OF THOUGHT

In the history of economic thought concerned with interest and moneylending, four relatively distinct positions emerge. At one end of the spectrum is the belief that the terms of loan contracts should not be restricted by legislation because individual agents are the best judges of their own interests. If interest rates are restricted, welfare-enhancing exchanges will be prevented and an unregulated market with usurious rates becomes probable. Bentham's contribution (1787) was the earliest pure expression of this belief, but it has since become the prevailing orthodoxy.

Historically, the more prevalent view has been that localised credit markets are insufficiently competitive, or borrowers insufficiently informed or self-controlled, that society is benefited by the imposition of interest rate controls. This desire to limit borrower exploitation guided the legislatures of many ancient civilisations, was the primary concern of the early Church, prevailed in post-Reformation Protestant Europe and still survives in support for 'usury laws' to cap consumer credit charges in many societies.

The most radical anti-interest position is that which ascribes its existence to some form of exploitation or maldistribution of wealth. Clearly, the socialist categorization of interest, with rent and profits, as surplus value extracted from labour, condemns it by association. Within this category one can also include Proudhon, Gesell and Douglas for attributing the existence of interest to the artificial short-age of capital produced by a defective monetary system.

Between the latter positions lies that of early medieval scholasticism (reiterated by the English Puritans and interwar Catholic radicals), and most rigorous Islamic thought. Both schools believe the interest-bearing loan to be prohibited by scripture, an illicit contractual form, exploitative of the poor borrower, a corruption of the function of money and an unjust method of financing commercial enterprise. The recommended alternatives are interest-free, charitable loans or profit-share variants, with hire and rental charges deemed permissible.[6]

SHOULD INTEREST EXIST?

Which of these schools of thought is correct? Certainly, the last has many tenuous features; it admits the legitimacy of deriving a return (albeit risk-related) from property or financial capital, yet objects to an interest return derived from a loan. It generally accepts a compet-itive market determination of profit and prices and yet maintains that the market for loans should not be permitted to generate a competit-ively-determined price. Such a position is extremely inconvenient in that useful financial arrangements (e.g. short-term trade credit; overdrafts) become difficult to provide on a commercial basis. It is understandable that conventional wisdom dismisses the idea of a non-interest financial system as untenable and impractical.

From the contemporary standpoint, one can understand why theologians, moralists and philosophers sought to prohibit usury. In circumstances where most debt was incurred for emergency consumption needs, where economic growth was low and faltering, where loan supply was uncompetitive and collateral excessive, one can readily envisage the social division, exploitation and economic damage that a free loan market would have clearly manifested. However, where these conditions do not prevail, it is not apparent to the contemporary observer that individuals' economic freedom of contract ought always to be restricted in this area. Accepting the rationalisations of the theologians and philosophers entails the adoption of moral presuppositions alien to contemporary Western society.

And yet, as this book has attempted to demonstrate, a surprisingly diverse collection of undesirable features of market economies can be attributed to the existence of interest, *vis-à-vis* a non-interest 'PLS' economy. These range from DC debt problems to an unjust intergenerational distribution of resources and tax burdens; from destabilizing speculation to the inflationary bias of indebted economies; and from fragile banking systems to the misallocation of loanable funds. These are all damaging consequences that flow from the existence of interest, but which cannot unequivocally be ascribed to it. Consequently, these problems each have their proposed palliatives but few economic physicians see beyond each symptom to the underlying malady.

The case against interest in an economy with a competitive loan supply thus turns on the costs imposed on the wider society through interest-based contracting, rather than the criticism of obvious borrower exploitation.[7] Although difficult to quantify, these are significant, not just in the direct costs of creditor losses in bankruptcies, but mainly in the greater instability imparted to the real economy and financial system, and the unanticipated inflation required as a palliative. Although these detriments would be mollified if the tax bias in favour of debt finance were reversed, it is difficult to envisage how a non-interest banking system could survive whilst conventional banks persisted. To reap the full theoretical benefits of a non-interest financial system, legislative action would need to be taken against the charging of interest.

This is not to say that interest should be prohibited now in Western societies. The case for a non-interest financial system requires more proof. Major theoretical lacunae remain to be closed. Practical experiments have been insufficiently long-lived, wide-ranging or successful to demonstrate anything more than the viability of a certain brand of Islamic banking. The world financial system is now so flexible that restrictions within one country could be easily circumvented. Many of the benefits sought, could be achieved by tax penalties against debt finance. Nevertheless, there are sufficient grounds to wish that, in hindsight, the prohibition of usury had not been undermined in Europe in the sixteenth century. More practical wisdom was embodied in the moral stand against usury than was then realised.

Notes

CHAPTER 1 ISLAMIC ECONOMICS AND BANKING

1. The corpus of Islamic law (*Shari'ah*) comprises the Qu'ran, the pattern of Mohammed's behaviour (*Sunnah*), his attributed sayings (*hadiths*), the consensus rulings of Islamic scholars and jurists (*ijuni*) and, sometimes, analogous teachings drawn from these sources (*qiyas*).
2. This approach turns on two beliefs concerning the Qu'ran; first, that it is the ultimate knowledge revealed to mankind which, when applied to economic structures, should balance equity and efficiency so as to 'automatically generate maximum social felicity' (Choudhury, 1989, p. 36); second, that it is applicable to all societies and times (Ariff, 1982a, p. 2).
3. For instance, some Islamic economists base their models of consumption behaviour or the social welfare function upon the presumed preferences of *Homo Islamicus*. In contrast to the insatiable, hedonistic *Homo economicus* of Western thought, 'Islamic man' is motivated by ultimate ethical values, rather than immediate material gain, and voluntarily adheres to the teachings of *Shari'ah* by avoiding gambling and conspicuous consumption, working diligently, giving alms and trading honestly (e.g. Choudhury, 1986).
4. Islamic economists tend to advocate a system of distribution in which incomes and wealth-holdings are not equal, but in which wide divergences of income are not encouraged and large wealth-holdings are difficult to preserve. This is achieved by a combination of a wealth tax (*zakat*), the enforced division of estates between family members (Wilson, 1983b, pp. 121–3) and the prohibition of interest.
5. Islamic law makes a strong distinction between contracts that seek to create or exploit risk, and those which seek to share existing risk (e.g. mutual insurance) (Wilson, 1985, pp. 53–4). The latter are sanctioned and believed to be socially beneficial (e.g. Choudhury, 1983).

CHAPTER 2 THE ISLAMIC CRITIQUE OF INTEREST

1. Mohammed's opposition to interest may have resulted from familiarity with the Old Testament's anti-usury position (e.g. Stein, 1956, p. 142; Schacht, 1964, p. 13; Anin, 1986, p. 25). Neither text rationalises the prohibition.
2. Quotations from the Qu'ran are taken from Chapra (1985, pp. 235–6).
3. Detailed discussions of textual interpretation are found in Homoud (1985), Saleh (1986) and Mallat (1988).
4. See especially Udovitch (1970, p. 86; 1979, p. 257), Mannan (1970, p. 160ff), Chapra (1985, p. 62) and Baeck (1991, p. 6).

5.   For instance, the Saudi Arabian banking system operates by levying 'service charges' on a fixed, percentage basis (e.g. R. Wilson, 1983b, p. 125; P. Wilson, 1991).
6.   *Riba* generally means any unwarranted excess but, in the context of a money loan, is defined as 'a monetary advantage without countervalue which has been stipulated in favour of one of the two contracting parties in an exchange of two monetary values' (Schacht, 1964, p. 145; cf. Rodinson, 1978, p. 18).
7.   S. M. Ahmad (1969, p. 189). A full discussion of the hire/interest distinction is given by Udovitch (1970, p. 107ff) and Saleh (1986, pp. 35–47).
8.   An interest-bearing commercial loan is essentially a 'Heads I win, Tails you lose' scam (Qureshi, 1946, p. 204).
9.   Detailed criticisms of an interest-based economy will be given when the attributes of the Islamic and conventional financial systems are compared in later chapters. See also Chapter 8.
10.   M. Ahmad (1967) cites examples from Smith, Ricardo, Say, Böhm-Bawerk and Fisher, and speculates whether the confusion of interest with profit and rent was a deliberate ploy to justify 'unjust' interest by association with 'legitimate' profit and rent (pp. 177–8).
11.   See Uzair (1978, p. 5), Ariff (1982b, p. 295), Zaidi (1986, p. 38) and Presley and Sessions (1994, p. 586).
12.   The Islamic position parallels the attribution of the existence of profit to the exercising of managerial responsibility and risk-bearing in uncertain trading conditions by Knight (1921) and Schumpeter (1934) (S. R. Khan, 1987, pp. 95–8).
13.   'The theory of interest has for a long time been a weak spot in the science of Economics, and the explanation and the determination of the interest rate still gives rise to more disagreement amongst economists than any other branch of general theory' (Haberler, 1937, p. 195).
14.   See Qureshi (1946, pp. 19–20), Ariff (1982b, p. 294) and Anwar (1987b, pp. 74–5); cf. Kierstead (1959, pp. 12–13).
15.   By including the speculative demand for money in his demand for money function, Islamic writers repeat Dennis Robertson's allegation that Keynes has the rate of interest 'pull itself up by its own bootstraps'. This makes an element of 'liquidity preference' the effect and not the cause of interest (e.g. Siddiqi, 1982, p. 26).
16.   Uzair (1980, p. 41); Presley (1988, p. 68); cf. Somerville (1932, p. 321).

CHAPTER 3   THE INTEREST-FREE FINANCIAL SYSTEM

1.   See Siddiqi (1985), Saleh (1986) and El-Ashker (1987, ch. 5) for detailed discussion of permitted contractual variations within Islamic law.
2.   Islamic jurists usually insist on the sharing of the net, rather than the gross, crop since otherwise the landlord faces no risk of loss (S.R. Khan, 1987, p. 123). Haque points out that if absentee landlords are permitted to extract fixed rents, land would replace the interest-bearing loan as

the safe, return-bearing, liquid asset of an Islamic economy (1980b, pp. 14–18).

3. Although the basic concept of interest-free banking on a PLS basis was suggested in the 1940s, the theoretical model most frequently referred to is that of Siddiqi (1983b; originally 1969).

4. For instance, maintaining an average balance of £1000 interest-free for two years could entitle a depositor to a £2000 overdraft for one year (e.g. El-Ashker, 1987, p. 93).

5. See especially Qureshi (1946, p. 214), Siddiqi (1983a, pp. 76–7), and PAID (1989).

6. E.g. Uzair (1982, pp. 225–6); Karsten (1982, p. 127); and Kazi (1984, pp. 15).

7. The range of policy options is detailed in Siddiqi (1983, pp. 100–2), CII (1983), Chapra (1985, pp. 202–5) and Khan and Mirakhor (1987c). Their efficacy depends upon the control of government borrowing.

8. Throughout this chapter, the conventional debt–equity division will be taken to symbolize that between interest-based and PLS contracts in Islamic thought.

9. Whilst the principal may measure performance *ex post*, the results are often ambiguous since they depend both on factors under the agent's control (e.g. effort) and on stochastic exogenous influences (e.g. macroeconomic conditions). Hence, a 'poor' result might be the fault of the agent or external circumstances (Harris and Raviv, 1979; Barnea *et al.*, 1985, p. 29).

10. Such considerations apply only to capital users who benefit directly from the maximization of declared profits (e.g. owner-farmers, entrepreneurs or managers with profit-related pay).

11. Debt can be equated to rental in the case of agricultural land, whilst PLS or equity is mirrored by sharecropping. It is often assumed that the latter is inefficient because the tenant will not work as hard:

> Under ... [sharecropping], ... schemes the tenants will equate their marginal disutility of effort with their share of their marginal product rather than their total marginal product. Therefore, too little effort will be forthcoming from agents. (Stiglitz and Weiss, 1981, p. 407)

Despite the existence of futures markets and the damage done to work incentives, crop-sharing still survives because it shares the idiosyncratic risk of crop failure between landlord and tenant (Stiglitz, 1974; Hirshleifer and Subrahmanyan, 1993).

12. 'Equity is soft, debt hard. Equity is forgiving, debt insistent. Equity is a pillow, debt a sword' – G. B. Stewart and D. M. Glassman, quoted by Jensen (1989, p. 67).

13. It is no coincidence that the theoretical models which find debt to be the optimal financial contract do so under the assumption of universal risk neutrality (e.g. Diamond, 1984). Once the capital user is assumed to be risk averse, the result becomes either indeterminate (e.g. Gale and Hellwig, 1985) or one where the optimal contract has a profit-related return (e.g. Terlizzesse, 1989).

14. With a risk neutral bank and risk averse borrower, a contract that
     relates the bank's return to project outcome, so sharing risk, will always
     dominate the conventional debt contract *if* the reported project outcome
     is the same (W. M. Khan, 1985, ch. 3).
15. E.g. Siddiqi (1983c, p. 181); Stiglitz (1988, pp. 314–15). Firms with the
     lowest debt – equity ratios are usually those with high levels of profit
     volatility, high industry failure rates and large sunk costs (e.g. Casta-
     nias, 1983; Bradley et al., 1984). All-equity firms tend to be small, with
     managers attempting to reduce the risk associated with large undiver-
     sifiable investments of personal wealth (Agrawal and Nagarajan, 1990).
     Leveraged firms demonstrate more volatility in employment, investment
     and stock-building (Cantor, 1990).
16. The incentive for excessive risk-taking arises from the limited liability of
     shareholders. This effectively permits them to gamble with creditors'
     capital and receive all the pay-out, whilst putting up only a proportion
     of the stake (Orhnial, 1982, pp. 182–3).
17. Kim and Maksinovic (1990) discovered that, for the US passenger air
     transport sector (1970–81), increases in the level of debt finance were
     associated with significant rises in variable costs and excess capacity.
     Also, the greater preponderance of bankruptcy produced by corporate
     leverage leads to the inefficient reassignment of asset ownership through
     distress sales (Shleifer and Vishny, 1992) and under-investment in firm-
     specific human capital.
18. Highly profitable firms will have an incentive to disintermediate under a
     non-interest financial system by offering bonds directly to the public.
     Hence, the potential for a 'black market' in interest-bearing commercial
     loans would exist (M. A. Khan, 1991, pp. 49–50).
19. Proportional income and corporation taxes are preferred over lump
     sum taxes, for their risk-sharing benefits, despite the large monitoring
     and disincentive costs arising (W. M. Khan, 1985).
20. See Siddiqi (1983a, p. 31) and W. M. Khan (1985, pp. 59–64). In some
     models, where the penalties for cheating are severe enough, PLS con-
     tracts with random monitoring can dominate the standard debt con-
     tract, even on moral hazard grounds (Mookerjee and Png, 1989).
21. The Faisal Islamic Bank of Sudan introduced a comprehensive system
     of follow-up for PLS borrowers, involving inspection and management
     advice. The reported returns on investment projects rose from 5–6 per
     cent to 15 per cent (O. Ahmed, 1990, p. 80).
22. See especially W. M. Khan (1987, p. 104) and Bashir (1990). Game
     theoretic explanations of economic 'morality', and adherence to cooperat-
     ive conventions, rely upon repeated interactions to explain the absence of
     cheating when monitoring and punishment are costly (e.g. Sugden, 1986).
23. 'When the ... [agency relationship] ... repeats itself over time, the
     effects of uncertainty tend to be reduced and dysfunctional behaviour
     is more accurately revealed, thus alleviating the problem' (Holmstrom,
     1979, p. 90; see also Townsend, 1982, p. 1168).
24. E.g. Radner (1981); Pratt and Zechauser (1985); Webb (1989). The
     robustness of this result depends on the agent acting as though the
     time horizon were infinite, and not discounting future benefits too

severely, otherwise the current valuation of the gains from cheating will exceed those of continued cooperation (Townsend, 1982; Radner, 1985).

25.   In interviews, Holland (1994) discovered that large UK firms benefited from cultivating a number of 'relationship' banks. Credit rationing and collateral requirements are eased by the development of long-term relationships in which the bank receives a secure flow of high-quality loan requests and non-credit custom, at slightly beneficial rates, in return for a better quality and priority of service and 'understanding' during recessions. Informal agreements to share sensitive information are bolstered by the sustained flow of transactions business and close social ties between the personnel involved.

26.   E.g. Nakatani (1984); Hoshi et al. (1990a); Corbett (1994).

27.   See Morishima (1982) and Dore (1983). The traditional arrangement disintegrated somewhat when Japanese companies replaced bank finance with bonds, retained profits and equity issues (Hoshi et al., 1990b; *Economist*, 1991c).

28.   The connection is more obvious to Christian economists developing the implications of the ban on interest against the background of the whole Old Testament economic system (Schluter and Lee, 1993, pp. 198–206). The Qu'ranic prohibition is not set within a similar context of economic laws designed to maintain stable, local communities.

29.   For instance, Porteous (1993a) found evidence that the national banking systems of Australia and Canada have imposed tougher credit conditions on peripheral regions relative to the core, particularly in small business lending. Data limitations prevent the UK experience being similarly tested. However, the supply of venture capital in the UK is disproportionately concentrated in those areas where venture capital suppliers are located (Mason, 1987).

30.   The feasibility of localized, regional banking is reinforced by US evidence that operating economies of scale run out at a relatively low level of deposits (around \$25m – e.g. Benston et al., 1982). Goldberg and Hanweck (1988) failed to find any operating advantages for bank holding companies from branching interstate whilst Rhoades and Savage (1991) report that whilst small banks earned returns on assets comparable to large banks, medium-sized operations (with assets of \$100m–\$1bn) were the most profitable. Large US banks hold more diversified assets but are more highly leveraged and fail more frequently (Boyd and Runkle, 1993).

31.   Porteous (1993b, pp. 25–9). This dual banking system operates well in Germany where small, regional banks supply the majority of loans to 'Mittelstand' companies. These banking arrangements are a major contributor to the strength and stability of the 'Mittelstand' (Harm, 1992).

32.   E.g. Black (1975); Fama (1985); Pecchenino (1988).

CHAPTER 4   MODELLING PROFIT-AND-LOSS SHARING

1.   This result relies upon the *ex post* remuneration of every other worker falling when employment is expanded, due to realised profit being divided between more workers.

2. This result depends upon numerous assumptions concerning borrower decision-making (e.g. constant returns, risk neutrality).

3. For instance, firms will always want to revert to paying wages in a profit-share economy so as to attract risk averse, high quality workers and regain the discretion to make lay-offs. A bank in a non-interest system will wish to offer interest-bearing loans to attract high quality borrowers and reduce monitoring costs.

4. Firms with profit-share schemes tend to report relatively higher productivity, profits and growth (e.g. Fitzroy and Kraft, 1987; Wadhwani and Wall, 1990). Chelius and Smith (1990) found that firms with profit-share schemes enjoy greater employment stability during demand contractions than 'pure wage' firms.

5. This chapter is adapted from 'Islamic Economics: The Emergence of a New Paradigm', *Economic Journal*, May 1994, 104 (424), 584–97.

6. The following model is a simplified, uni-variable screening application of the analyses set out in Holmstrom and Weiss (1985) and Meyer (1986).

7. In what follows we will use the term 'syndicate' to denote the group of investors within a particular project.

8. The 'outcome' of a project is interpreted in terms of its monetary value.

9. In what follows we use the notation $g_k^i(.)$ to define the partial derivative of a function $g^i(.)$ with respect to the argument k in state i.

10. It is, of course, permissible for a *riba* contract to relate s to both I and y (and, indeed, in a more general setting, any other observable variables as well). Such a multivariate screening problem is examined in detail by HW. In this paper we restrict our attention to a 'pure' *riba* contract in which s is related to I only. Such an assumption greatly eases the analytical exposition of our results without compromising unduly their generality.

11. Note the term *mudarabah* is used to indicate that the outcome of the project is an explicit argument of the loan agreement. It is important to note, however, that a *riba* contract need not be one that specifies a fixed payment in all states; payments may fluctuate with a variety of arguments.

12. It could also be assumed that the *mudarabah* contract related s to the 'gross' outcome of the project, z.

13. Note that $s_i, i = 1,$ 2, represents the payment to the syndicate net of the repayment of I, which has already been included as a cost term. Thus the syndicate actually receives $I + s_i$.

14. For instance, Kennedy (1988, p. 55) believes that interest flows are the major reason for the perpetuation of German wealth inequalities since only the top 20 per cent of households are *net* recipients.

CHAPTER 5   NON-INTEREST BANKING IN PRACTICE

1. 'In the past, Arab countries have been geared to the motto "lending money is easier than investing it" ... This view, along with ensuring an absence of risk capital, has kept the Arab world in a state of economic decline since many investment outlets were not being used to their full capacity. As such, liquidity and safety have been the two principal

determinants of most Arab oil-surplus countries' investment policies' (Abdul-Hadi, 1988, p. 108).

2. An 'Islamic' bank not only operates without resorting to interest, but also employs a *Shari'ah* advisory board to certify adherence to other Qu'ranic proscriptions (of *gharar*, alcohol and pork) and administer a *zakat* fund.

3. Islamic banks must be strongly distinguished from Islamic 'investment houses' which also operate on a non-interest basis, but which have tended to speculate in property, foreign currency, precious metals and shares. Unsurprisingly, several have collapsed (see Edge, 1988, pp. 49–51; Wilson, 1990b, p. 4). Although BCCI offered variants of Islamic savings and investment contracts, it was predominantly an interest-based bank.

4. For instance, by the end of their second year of operation (1987) the two Turkish Islamic finance houses had attracted 1.16 per cent of total bank deposits (Baldwin, 1990, p. 47).

5. Kuwait (20 per cent), Egypt (17 per cent) and Bahrain (16 per cent) (Wilson, 1990b, pp. 7–8). By 1986, six Islamic banks were amongst the hundred largest Arab banks (Nienhaus, 1988, p. 136).

6. Impressive early 'dividends' were paid to depositors by the Faisal Islamic Bank of Egypt (FIBE) and Sudan (FIBS) (Bashir, 1984; El-Ashker, 1987, p. 130), whilst the Islamic banks in the Gulf states have consistently outperformed the conventional competition (Nassief, 1990). However, the subsequent performance of Arab Islamic banks has been disappointing due to their over-exposure to trade finance (depressed by the Gulf War) and BCCI (Moore, 1990).

7. 'The alternative to Islamic banking in many countries . . . is not conventional banking, but a void, with savings merely hoarded as idle cash or held as precious metals and other commodities. Many devout Muslims would only put even more funds into housing and real estate, causing rising prices but no real development' (Wilson, 1990a, p. 5).

8. This contravenes the theoretical prediction that Islamic banks need to hold minimal reserves against their investment deposits due to the denial of instant access, and the payment of profit-related returns (El-Ashker, 1987, pp. 220–1).

9. Pakistan's Council of Islamic Ideology described such arrangements as 'no more than a second best solution from the viewpoint of an ideal Islamic economic system'. It also warned, 'there is a danger that they could eventually be misused as a means for opening a back-door for interest along with its attendant evils. It is, therefore, imperative that the use of these methods should be kept to a minimum . . . and that their use as general techniques of financing must never be allowed' (CII, 1983, p. 110). These fears have been realised. Islamic banks have adapted mark-up contracts to ensure their equivalence to interest-based alternatives (M. A. Khan, 1991, p. 53) and offer Western multinationals trade credit on mark-up terms which vary with LIBOR (Ireland, 1990).

10. Trade finance as a percentage of invested assets has ranged from 60–70 per cent for FIBE (1979–84), 80 per cent for the Jordan Islamic Bank (1984–7), 82.5 per cent for Bank Islam Malaysia (1988) and 90 per cent of the Turkish Islamic Bank (1987) (see El-Ashker, 1987, p. 136; Shallah, 1990, p. 117; Naughton and Shanmugan, 1990, p. 27; Baldwin, 1990, p. 50).

11.   The discrepancy between theory and practice is apparent to Western
       observers (e.g. Cooper, 1981, p. 55; Nienhaus, 1988, p. 159) and
       acknowledged by Islamic theorists (e.g. M. A. Khan, 1991, p. 51–3)
       and bankers (see Baldwin, 1990, pp. 53, 57).

12.   The need for a return-bearing, liquid reserve asset for non-interest
       banks has prompted the Islamic Development Bank – a Muslim coun-
       terpart to the World Bank – to float CDs in its investment portfolio,
       which could be traded between Islamic banks to provide emergency
       liquidity (Wilson, 1990d, pp. 206–7). 13.

       The Jordan Islamic Bank ascribes its relative neglect of PLS finance
       to the low level of morality in the Jordanian business community
       (Shallah, 1990, p. 128; cf. Wilson, 1987, p. 223).

14.   Where Islamic banks compete with conventional rivals, their chances of
       survival are greatest in plural Muslim societies. They can then exploit
       the segmentation of society into moderate and fundamentalist constitu-
       encies, enjoy a stable deposit base and invest funds more easily (Moore,
       1990).

15.   In January 1992, Pakistan's federal *Shari'ah* court prohibited all forms
       of interest in the country. This includes interest on government debt,
       foreign currency deposits and international loans, which were excluded
       from the original Islamization process (Hussain, 1992). The government
       successfully appealed against the decision in the Supreme Court (*Eco-
       nomist*, 1992b; Parker, 1993).

16.   Centralised direction of capital will weaken, however, with the gradual
       privatisation of Pakistan's banking system, initiated in 1991.

17.   The authorities' commitment does not stretch to implementing true PLS
       banking. Not only are the nominal values of investment deposits guar-
       anteed, but minimum and maximum PLS ratios and uniform deposit
       returns have been imposed to deter deposit switching.

18.   See Mirakhor (1988, pp. 99–105), Aryan (1990, pp. 169–170) and Khan
       and Mirakhor (1990, pp. 362–3).

19.   Malaysia is Islamizing its banking system in a different manner.
       Islamic and conventional banks currently operate under the same regu-
       latory and capital adequacy structure. The central bank has established
       its own *Shari'ah* council to standardize acceptable operating procedures
       for Islamic banks and avoid duplication. The explicit aim is to bring
       zealous Muslims into the banking system (Parker, 1993; *Economist*,
       1993a).

20.   Islamic literature is silent on the issue of how to service existing govern-
       ment debt in a non-interest economy since, in most cases, its amortisa-
       tion would take decades without inflation or repudiation.

CHAPTER 6   NON-INTEREST FINANCE AND
MACROECONOMIC STABILITY

1.   It is to be distinguished from the 'pure monetary' theory of Hawtrey
       (1926, 1927). He attributed fluctuations in effective demand solely to

the variability of monetary expenditure resulting from hoarding and an 'inherently unstable' banking system (see Haberler, 1937, ch. 2).

2. Bank margins will also rise to cover the increased default risk.

3. The experience of developing countries in response to the debt overhang exemplifies the Fisher Paradox. IMF Structural Adjustment Programmes have entailed devaluation and a switch in production to cash crop exports:

> the efforts of each developing country acting independently to meet debt service obligations has, by reducing export earnings for all exporters of these commodities, collectively made it more difficult for developing primary producers as a group to meet their obligations. (Gilbert, 1989, pp. 783–4; see also Sarkar, 1991)

4. E.g. (1963), (1976), (1977), (1982) and (1985). Similar analyses are given by Robinson (1977, p. 1331), Sinai (1977), Knodell and Levine (1985) and Kindleberger (1989).

5. Whenever asset prices are rising strongly, leveraged Ponzi schemes will almost always appear profitable, whatever the interest rate, because the cost of capital is invariant with speculative returns (Wray, 1992).

6. With a fragile financial structure, Minsky believes that full employment can only be achieved at the expense of high inflation rates to erode the real value of debts (1976, pp. 140–1).

7. New equity flotations are interpreted as management attempts to reduce bankruptcy risk, due to adverse inside information (e.g. Ross, 1977); as existing shareholders passing off low quality assets (e.g. Myers and Majluf, 1984); as managers attempting to avoid the disciplines of debt financing (e.g. Harris and Raviv, 1990); or as a sign that banks with inside information have already refused the request for funding (Greenwald and Stiglitz, 1988b, p. 146). Many of these effects rely on the existence of debt finance for an equity issue to signal adverse inside information and would disappear in a non-interest financial system.

8. E.g. Fazzari et al. (1988); Greenwald and Stiglitz (1990, p. 21); and Bond and Meghir (1994).

9. Indeed, bank lending to small firms is significantly more procyclical than for large ones due to the importance of asset values in determining entrepreneurs' access to and cost of capital (Gertler and Gilchrist, 1993).

10. Kiyotaki and Moore (1993) show, in a complete dynamic model, how technology shocks, leading to asset price fluctuations, produce cycles in real output through the use of assets as loan collateral.

11. The one possible exception could be the return on land-holdings, which may not fall in line with returns in the productive economy due to population growth.

12. Declines in US bank capital (due to defaults and property losses), combined with higher statutory capital requirements, produced a 'capital crunch' in the early 1990s (Bernanke and Lown, 1991). This added significantly to the US credit contraction which was concentrated on

business lending, particularly to small firms, by banks with the weakest capital positions. Despite the relaxed US monetary stance, banks charged record loan margins and tightened non-price lending conditions. Supply constraints were significant in reducing total lending (Akhtar, 1993/4).

Llewellyn and Drake (1994) also find UK evidence of a 'credit crunch' in 1990–1. In particular, they cite the widening of bank margins on business lending, whilst wholesale spreads narrowed, as evidence of an independent supply constraint.

13.   Webb (1993) develops a model in which, because banks use debt contracts for monitoring and discipline reasons, the health of their balance sheets will be positively correlated with the prospects of borrowers, leading to destabilizing lending flows.

14.   E.g. Angell (1935, pp. 4–5); Kindleberger (1989, pp. 18, 59).

15.   Under a theoretical PLS system.

> credit would be created only to the extent that there exist genuine possibilities of creating additional social wealth through productive enterprise. Demand for profit-sharing advances will be limited to the extent of the available resources and banks' ability to create credit will be called into action only to the extent of this demand, subject to the constraint imposed by profit expectations. (Siddiqi, 1977, p. 10)

16.   Bernanke and James (1991) compared the experiences of 24 countries in 1930–3. Those which experienced banking panics suffered significantly more serious falls in output than those that did not.

17.   E.g. M. S. Khan (1986, p. 19); Khan and Mirakhor (1990, p. 357).

18.   Shleifer and Vishny (1992) analyse the interaction of asset values and corporate debt on the assumption that many commercial assets are most valuable when sold as 'going concerns' to experienced operators in the same business. In an upswing, markets in such assets are both high and liquid because strong cash-flows enable industry buyers to finance asset acquisitions and induce favourable expectations of future asset returns. Liquidity and willingness to lend are self-reinforcing:

> People borrow and banks lend in liquid markets because resale is attractive. But resale is made attractive by the ability of future buyers to borrow. So the ability to borrow increases liquidity, which in turn raises the ability to borrow. (ibid., p. 1362)

However, during industry- or economy-wide recessions, when such assets may need to be sold to meet debt service payments, 'insider' firms most likely to value the assets highly are also facing cash-flow constraints and credit rationing. The assets of distressed firms are therefore likely to be bought at depressed prices by outside, 'deep pocket' investors who will use the resources less efficiently. The ultimate effects of leverage are to exaggerate swings in corporate asset values and to misallocate their ownership.

19. Islamic theorists assert that a bank governed by *Shari'ah* would not finance purely speculative ventures. Zarqa (1983c) and Siddiqi (1991, p. 3) also believe that exchange rate speculation will be reduced dramatically by eliminating interest.

20. King (1994), however, points out that creditor households will not necessarily increase consumption, as their real wealth rises, sufficiently to offset the retrenchment of debtor households, because the redistribution occurs amid increased macroeconomic uncertainty. Indeed, creditors may increase savings for precautionary reasons.

21. The debt service: national income ratio rose from 9 per cent to 19.8 per cent (1929–33). By then, 45 per cent of all farmers had defaulted (Bernanke, 1983, p. 260; cf. Hamilton, 1987; Calomiris, 1993).

22. 'The financial factor has affected the length, depth, amplitude and intensity of the cyclical process. Indeed,... the post-war experience suggests that the financial factor is a critical ingredient in the business cycle' (Eckstein and Sinai, 1986, p. 62; see also Wojnilower, 1980; 1985; and B. M. Friedman, 1986a). Wolfson (1990) finds Minsky-type relationships to have held in post-war US business cycles.

23. Bernanke et al. (1990) simulated the 1973–4 US recession, using the 1988 corporate capital structure. By year two, 25 per cent of firms were insolvent. 'In other words, these firms have equity cushions in 1988 that are less than the decline in their market value during the 1973–4 recession' (p. 269).

24. E.g. Liebling (1980, p. 76); B. M. Friedman (1986b); Kaufman (1986).

25. E.g. Fisher (1933b, p. 118); Simons (1948, p. 165); Gertler and Hubbard (1990, p. 52).

26. See especially, Chapra (1985, pp. 117–22), M. S. Khan (1986, p. 15ff) and Siddiqi and Zaman (1989, pp. 46–7). The robustness of the Japanese economy to external shocks has been attributed to its profit-and risk-sharing financial system (e.g. Nakatani, 1984, pp. 243–5).

27. Sargent (1991) and Milne (1993) describe the growth in UK private sector indebtedness. Davis (1992) and IMF (1992) offer international comparisons.

28. These include: the loss of firm-specific investments by workers and suppliers; the loss of synergies from the distress sale of assets; the increased risk premia similar borrowers subsequently pay; and the knock-on insolvencies of creditors.

CHAPTER 7 SOME KEY ISSUES IN THE ISLAMIC FINANCIAL SYSTEM

1. For a fuller discussion see, for example, the various works of Dr M. V. Chapra cited in the bibliography.

2. Many Islamic theorists express scepticism concerning the significance of the interest elasticity of savings (e.g. Mannan, 1970, pp. 168–9; Ariff, 1982b, p. 294; Siddiqi, 1983b, pp. 168–9; cf. Kurihara, 1955, p. 272).

3. Theoretical models and empirical studies confirm this prediction (e.g. Leland, 1968; Ishikawa and Ueda, 1984).
4. See Tobin (1958) and Fama and Miller (1972, ch. 7).
5. In addition, El-Din (1991) contends that the analysis of mean-variance portfolio theory is dependent upon the convexity of investors' risk–return indifference curves. However, if asset returns are imperfectly correlated (as seems likely), investors' indifference curves need not be convex and the analysis loses its critical implication for non-interest banking (*contra* S. Ahmed, 1989, p. 161).
6. E.g. Phelps (1967); Sandmo (1970); Hanson and Menezes (1978). These models do predict, however, that desired savings will fall *if* greater return variance is combined with a lower expected mean return. However, the average return paid on PLS investment accounts should exceed their interest-bearing equivalents *because* of their risk-sharing properties (El- Ashker, 1987, p. 52) and because PLS banks ought to be more efficient allocators of loanable funds (see below).
7. Some proponents even claim that PLS deposits could become good inflation hedges (El-Ashker, 1987, p. 219), and reduce hoarding and capital flight in economies prone to hyperinflation (Anwar, 1987b, pp. 61–71).
8. In practice, these monitoring requirements are 'artificially' reduced by government regulation and deposit insurance (Iqbal and Mirakhor, 1987, p. 30 n. 60).
9. In a non-interest economy, banks would face more competition for investors' funds from equities than they do in a conventional economy. Not only will companies, banks and investors be forced to make greater use of the share market (due to the absence of debt finance), so reducing transactions costs, but the risk of holding equities should also be reduced by the deeper market, the absence of loan-financed speculative share purchases and the reduction in corporate gearing. (Lower gearing ratios reduce the coefficient of variation of net corporate profits, leading to more stable share prices and dividends; Baumol, 1977, p. 627).
10. Monitoring costs and moral hazard considerations have not prevented Islamic banks from successfully attracting depositors in practice (El-Din, 1991, p. 64).
11. e.g., 'The market rate of interest . . . rations out, into the uses with the highest net productivities, society's scarce supply of capital goods.' (Samuelson, 1976, p. 602).
12. e.g. Malinvaud (1965, p. 221); De Meza and Webb (1987, p. 284).
13. Credit rationing theorists openly acknowledge that, in the presence of asymmetric information concerning borrowers' attributes and actions, interest-based intermediation *cannot* achieve the first-best allocation of loanable funds (e.g. Mankiw, 1986, p. 460). In the most frequently cited model (Stiglitz and Weiss, 1981), the interest-bearing debt contract gives borrowers an incentive to choose projects with a higher risk–return trade-off than lenders desire. If the rate of interest increases beyond some point, loan applicants self-select towards those with highly risky projects, and take greater risks in their production decisions. However, the inability of lenders easily to identify and monitor

risky borrowers means that their total revenue may be maximized at a rate of interest below its market-clearing level. In such circumstances:

> there is no presumption that the market equilibrium allocates credit to those for whom the expected return on their investments is highest. (ibid., p. 407)

Competing lenders cannot profitably satisfy unfulfilled loan demand by supplying more credit at a higher rate of interest because they will tend to attract the more risky and optimistic borrowers, with a high likelihood of default. Consequently, in circumstances of asymmetric information and costly monitoring, interest-based credit allocation is systematically biased *against* those projects with maximum expected returns (e.g. Jaffee and Stiglitz, 1990, p. 868) and too few projects are financed. With equity or PLS contracts, capital suppliers will wish to fund these projects, but will face the alternative problems of moral hazard and adverse selection discussed beforehand.

14. 'Since banks mainly hold debt claims, they receive little of the up-side from unusually good firm performance... shareholders, in contrast, care only about maximising the up-side. This conflict may result in excessively conservative investment policies if banks control corporate investment decisions' (Hoshi et al., 1990b, p. 122; cf. Jaffee and Stiglitz, 1990, p. 842).

15. See Siddiqi (1983a, pp. 69–70; 1991, p. 30), Nassief (1990, p. 57) and Stiglitz (1985, p. 146).

16. Currently, the British banking system is reluctant to fund small business expansion adequately due to the risks involved and the probable dearth of profit in their initial period of operation. The funding gap is rarely filled by venture capital (VC) suppliers due to high risks and appraisal costs, meaning that project quality must be extremely high to attract funding. Also, VC suppliers dilute control of the business and eventually require the public flotation of shares to realise their investment (Lorenz, 1989, pp. 150–3). PLS banks could fill this VC gap by economizing on monitoring costs and not necessarily requiring that the borrower 'go public'.

17. High collateral requirements (and non-contingent debt service obligations) may dissuade the risk averse entrepreneur from even applying for bank finance, despite having a potentially lucrative project (Ordover and Weiss, 1981). Alternatively, profitable investments may be postponed until sufficient collateral has been accumulated (Zhou, 1992).

18. Even Christian analysis of the 'debt crisis' fails to identify interest as the root of the problem (e.g. Pontifical Commission, 1986; Christian Aid, 1991). Many decry the irresponsibility of bank lending (e.g. Elliott, 1987, p. 32; Mahoney, 1991, pp. 56–7; Higginson, 1993, pp. 107–12) without realising that interest-based financing gives few direct incentives for banks to lend responsibly (see subsequent discussion).

19. For instance, in the period 1983–90, Brazil made interest payments of $65.76 bn and amortisation payments of $43.51 bn, yet its total external

debt rose from \$98.27 bn to \$116.17 bn through accruing interest and supplementary loans (World Bank, 1991, II, p. 38).

20.   e.g. Griffiths-Jones and Sunkel (1986, p. 67, 107); George (1988, pp. 14–29); Vallely (1990, pp. 149–58).

21.   PLS banks should not be so feckless because they would have to be confident that the financed project would yield a return/dividend realisable in foreign exchange (e.g. Siddiqi, 1983a, pp. 78–81; Chapra, 1985, p. 74; cf. Ballantyre, 1988, p. 8).

22.   The DC debt overhang has prompted an examination of development loans with the return contingent on the borrowing country's commodity output or revenue, rather than interest. Revenue-sharing contacts dominate interest-bearing and commodity price-indexed loans by smoothing borrower net income. However, restrictive covenants would still be necessary to attenuate moral hazard (O'Hara, 1990; see also Froot et al., 1989).

23.   e.g. Snowden (1987); World Bank (1991, pp. 48–9); cf. Kubarych (1982).

24.   Overt government subsidy has taken the form of tax relief on bank provisions against bad DC debts which have not, as yet, been written-off (e.g. Vallely, 1990, p. 194). Less obvious support includes government deposit insurance, regulatory leeway on when provisions were to be taken on balance sheet, and emergency IMF loans to service outstanding debts to the banks, with their attendant 'disciplines'. The multilateral agencies have, effectively, acted as debt collectors for the commercial banking system (Dornbusch, 1986, p. 63).

25.   'Our painful experience has demonstrated that private banks are incapable of making reliable judgements about risks involved in financing economic development. Nor do we have even the slightest chance of influencing how or to what use the proceeds of the loans we make are put, ... The disastrous record of private financing for economic development shows that this is no place for banks' (anonymous international banker, 'Bad Business for All Concerned', *International Herald Tribune*, 16 Oct. 1985; quoted in George, 1988, p. 34).

26.   Non-interest banks should be less risk averse in their allocation of funds than conventional counterparts because they would not have issued liabilities whose value and return they have guaranteed (Albach, 1982; Mohsin, 1982, p. 190).

27.   This is not to claim, however, that such banks would not insist on some collateral to reduce lending risk, and to maintain entrepreneurial incentives for effort.

28.   This feature should be most beneficial in a developing economy where managerial skills and experience are rare (Abdeen and Shook, 1984, p. 187).

29.   For instance, discounting would continue in investment project appraisal on opportunity cost grounds. The discount rate applied would be some appropriate proxy for the expected profitability of alternative investments, such as the rate of return on a firm's equity capital, or that on a PLS bank deposit (e.g. Mannan, 1982; Zarqa, 1983a; Tomkins and Karim, 1987; M. F. Khan, 1991).

30. Under Islamic law, a partnership contract must specify a *fixed* PLS ratio for its duration. This can be altered only when the partnership is recontracted.
31. This discussion is predicated upon the strong assumption that a borrower's declared profits are invariant with the PLS ratio contracted with the bank. If, however, a high ratio prompts lower borrower effort or greater moral hazard, a non-interest bank may profit maximize by offering PLS ratios below the market-clearing level – the PLS equivalent of credit rationing.
32. e.g. Haque and Mirakhor (1987). Bashir et al. (1993) found that these predictions were fulfilled in the Kuwait Finance House's investment experience (1978–88).
33. e.g. Uzair (1978, p. 49); Siddiqi (1983a, pp. 102–10); S. R. Khan (1984).
34. Greenwald et al. (1984, p. 194) find Keynes' analysis lacking in contemporary relevance because the 'liquidity trap' relies too heavily upon the speculative demand for money, and investment has been found to be generally interest rate inelastic.
35. For instance, Amsler (1993) tested Keynes' idea that the Gold Standard could force interest rates to levels incompatible with full employment in order to attract specie inflows. She found that the US and UK engaged in bank rate competition (1925–31) to the detriment of mutual employment levels.
36. The incentive to on-lend on a fractional reserve basis exists whenever some return is available from the committal of funds (e.g. dividends). Consequently, interest is not a *sine qua non* of the process, and fractional reserve PLS banks exist in both theory and practice (e.g. Siddiqi, 1983b, p. 89).
37. Bryant (1980) and Diamond and Dyvbig (1983) explain the existence of interest-bearing demand deposits as an optimal solution to the need of depositors to insure themselves against liquidity risk whilst providing a positive return (which monetary hoards fail to do).
38. Extreme maturity mismatch is intrinsic to highly-leveraged, interest-based banks. It is only the ability of depositors to withdraw rapidly that protects them from exploitation in favour of bank shareholders (Flannery, 1994).
39. The banks' predicament is illustrated by the demand of one depositor during a run in the 1930s: 'If you have my money, I don't want it. If you don't, I do.'
40. In addition, the sequential servicing of depositor withdrawals contributes to runs (e.g. Bryant, 1980; James, 1985, p. 80). If position in the queue did not affect the probability of repayment, depositors would not rush to be the first to withdraw.
41. 'The situation is analogous to the problem of a communal good... [W]ith par-valued deposits, depositors have a fixed claim on a pool of assets. When the value of the assets is less than the value of the fixed claims, depositors have an incentive to convert the communal pool of assets to private assets by withdrawing funds' (Furlong and Keeley, 1985, p. 223). This is a sub-optimal outcome because the bank may be solvent, but illiquid, and embodies informational capital as a going

concern. An analogous, sub-optimal 'run' equilibrium exists when a firm is suspected of insolvency and creditors rush to secure repayment, resulting in premature bankruptcy.

42. It is 'as bad as could be devised' (Simons, 1948, p. 55) and 'inherently unstable' (King and Goodhart, 1989, p. 5). See also Goodhart, 1987, p. 83.

43. When investment decision quality cannot be assessed *ex post*, due to the potential for exogenous stochastic shocks, the managerial labour market will evaluate performance relative to that of other managers. Hence, it is rational for risk averse decision-makers to 'follow the crowd' rather than risk idiosyncratic mistakes (Scharfstein and Stein, 1990). Hence,

> 'A "sound" banker, alas! is not one who foresees danger and avoids it, but one who, when he is ruined, is ruined in a conventional way along with his fellows, so that no-one can really blame him'. (Keynes, 1931, p. 156; cf. Lavington, 1922, pp. 32–3).

44. See Kindleberger and Laffargue (1982, p. 10) and Goodhart (1988, pp. 53–5).

45. 'While the precedent created of assisting an insolvent bank may pose greater future hazards by dulling market discipline, when confronted with a clear and present danger of an impending crisis, concerns about the potential benefits of greater discipline seem invariably to give way' (Guttentag and Herring, 1987, p. 165; cf. Kindleberger, 1989, p. 182).

46. Boyd and Gertler (1993) attribute the exceptionally poor performance of large US banks in the 1980s to the 'too-big-to-fail' doctrine embodied in DI and LLR facilities. Banks with assets in excess of $10 bn had the riskiest liability structures and asset portfolios of all bank size classes, resulting in the worst provisions: assets and income: assets ratios (1984–91). If they had performed as well as banks with assets of 0.25–1 bn, they would have made $45 bn fewer provisions (ibid., p. 23).

47. Guaranteeing deposits permits banks to pay a lower rate of return and take greater risks (Karekan and Wallace, 1978). Indeed, insured banks that do not avail themselves of this risk-taking subsidy face shareholder revolt and take over (Kane, 1985, p. 115). This was the predicted outcome from the outset of DI (e.g. Emerson, 1934; Fisher, 1935b; cf. Hugins, 1960, p. 175).

48. In the same week in 1991, the FDIC allowed a community bank in Harlem, the Freedom National, to fail with a minimum deposit pay-out, whilst extending 100 per cent coverage to the much larger Bank of New England (*Economist*, 1991a).

49. These criticisms of current practice are common to the advocates of 'free banking' and interest-free banking. For instance, bank instability is blamed entirely on government intervention depriving banks of the incentive to be prudent (Hayek, 1976, p. 95; Karekan and Wallace, 1978; Karekan, 1985, pp. 647; Dowd, 1989, pp. 35–7). The 'free banking' solution – to permit anyone to issue notes and demand liabilities that the public will willingly hold – is designed to discipline banks to restrict monetary growth to preserve their seigniorage rents (e.g. White, 1984a; cf. Gorton, 1985). This, however, ignores the potential for bank

contagion (Baltensperger and Dermine, 1987, p. 71) and the inherent incentive to take excessive risks given to bank managers by the limited liability of shareholders, irrespective of DI (John et al., 1991). Fundamentally, it is the issuing of fixed claims against a variable-value portfolio that makes banks unstable (cf. Rolnick and Weber, 1984).

50. There is no intrinsic reason why these functions should be performed by the same institution, let alone with the same funds (Karekan, 1985, p. 74; Tobin, 1985, p. 25). Consequently, some advocate the separation of US commercial banks. The 'narrow', transactions side would be completely insured but restricted to holding safe and liquid assets (e.g. government debt and high quality bonds). The intermediary side would accept uninsured deposits and acquire risky assets (e.g. Litan, 1987; Bryan, 1991; *Economist*, 1991a & b; Pierce, 1991).

51. The boom in 100 per cent reserve proposals came in the 1934–7 period when the banking system was widely held responsible for the Depression (e.g. Currie, 1934; Simons, 1934; Angell, 1935; Fisher, 1935b; Graham, 1936; Benvenisti, 1937; cf. Soddy, 1926, pp. 197–8, 297; Mints, 1945, p. 270ff; Allen, 1993). Friedman (1948) flirted with 100 per cent reserves due to their potential for non-discretionary monetary control, but became disillusioned (e.g. 1969) due to his faith in the efficacy of open market operations. The proposal has been resuscitated by Tobin (1985), Golembe and Mingo (1985), Karekan (1985), Hotson (1985), Hixson (1991) and some Islamic theorists (see previous discussion).

52. 'Interest should not be paid on money or on any money contracts that one may purchase without sacrifice of liquidity; and this proposition is certainly as valid for interest paid in banking services (to demand depositors) as for interest paid in cash (to savings depositors). It is anomalous... that customers should be left without financial incentives to economize their use of such services' (Simons, 1948, pp. 235–6). See also Johnson (1968); Darrat (1985, p. 102); M.S. Khan (1986, p. 20).

53. Mutual funds have continued to be popular in the US despite the lifting of demand deposits interest rate restrictions (which prompted their initiation), and having no DI cover. They accounted for $2.0 trillion of assets in June 1994, exceeding the value of retail bank deposits, and were owned by 27 per cent of US households.

54. e.g. Pierce (1985); Goodhart (1987); *Economist* (1991b). Mutual funds can survive without central bank intervention. However the authorities might deem it desirable for funds to have more stability than volatile asset markets provide. Hence, they might engage in stabilizing open market operations (King and Goodhart, 1989).

55. White (1984b) dissents. He believes that it is no mere happenstance that banking was *not* established on a mutual funds basis. He claims that mutual funds are impractical as the sole transactions medium due to high trading costs, computational complexities and the necessity of having fund units convertible into bank or fiat money. White is correct in believing that mutual funds could not act as the *only* exchange medium, but this is not the point. Mutual funds offer a way in which a return-bearing demand deposit *can* by fashioned on an equity basis, if a sufficiently liquid securities market exists. In a non-interest economy,

for instance, such funds would need to be supplemented by cash and 100 per cent reserve deposits to produce a complete transactions system. (However, moves are afoot in the US to establish a central clearing fund so that debits from mutual fund accounts would not require the sale of underlying assets and could be cleared outside the banking system – Ferguson, 1993).

Goodhart (1993, p. 283) raises two further difficulties of an equity mutual funds payments system – both of which are answered within a non-interest environment. First, the volatility of equities, which would otherwise lead to sharp fluctuations in the nominal values of mutual funds accounts, will be dampened by the sharp reduction in corporate gearing and leveraged speculation in shares. Secondly, the financing needs of small firms, without access to the equity market, will continue to be met by local PLS banks.

56. In previous chapters, conventional banks have been criticised for not taking enough risks (e.g. long-term investment finance; venture capital). In this, they are blamed for taking too much (e.g. junk bonds, property speculation). The inconsistency is explained by the supposed social benefits of risk-taking varying from activity to activity.

57. This claim is examined more fully in the following chapter.

58. The increased scope for depositor exploitation may mean that PLS banking is feasible only with accreditation by an external banking supervisor. The religious context of Islamic banking, with the requirement of a *Shari'ah* supervisory board, also reduces the monitoring costs of Muslim depositors (Gambling et al., 1993).

59. 'The major source of trouble...is the contract to deliver on demand large fixed sums of money out of non-monetary assets. The idea of having money generally available...and of earning on it as well, should be relegated to the realm of exploded magic' (Graham, 1936, p. 439).

60. Conflicting evidence is presented by Evans (1985) and Lal and Wijnbergen (1986).

61. The stock of Italy's public debt was equivalent to 112.6 per cent of GDP in 1993. Interest payments accounted for 10.9 per cent of GDP (BIS, 1994, p. 29).

62. It is doubtful, however, whether conventional banks could survive without the return-bearing, highly liquid reserve assets that government bonds provide. If they did not exist, they would have to be created.

63. This statement explicitly denies those theories that posit either that government debt is not a burden on future generations because 'we owe it to ourselves' (e.g. Kahn, 1931, p. 193; Lerner, 1964, p. 17), or that savings automatically increase to offset the future tax liability implied by bond-finance (e.g. Barro, 1974). See Ferguson (1964) and Buchanan et al. (1987) for discussion.

64. B.M. Friedman describes the recent penchant of US federal governments for deficit-financing as a violation of the moral principle of providing for the interests of future generations:

   We have broken with that tradition by pursuing a policy that amounts to living not just in, but for, the present. We are living well by running up our debt and selling off our assets. America has thrown itself a party and billed the tab to the future. (1989, p. 4)

65.   The expenses of a war are the moral check which it has pleased the Almighty to impose upon the ambition and the lust of conquest that are inherent in so many nations... The necessity of meeting from year to year the expenditure it entails is a salutary and wholesome check. (William Gladstone, *Hansard*, 6 March 1854; quoted by Bastable, 1903, p. 675 n. 1; cf. Smith, 1776, pp. 919–20)

       A central tenet of Islamic public finance is that capital, as well as labour, is to be conscripted in wartime through compulsory interest-free loans to the state (e.g. Qureshi, 1946, pp. 191–5; Metwally, 1983, pp. 73–4). 'If wars had to be financed by capital levies, the rich would be our most effective pacifists' (Dennis, 1932, p. 316).

66.   Following the UK lending boom of the mid-to-late 1980s, it is estimated that 11 per cent plus of households are in some form of default (Jubilee Centre Policy Group, 1991, p. 12). The pressures of indebtedness result in social isolation, divorce and suicide (Hanna, 1988).

67.   Lenders claim that high levels of aggregate household income gearing are sustainable due to off-setting increases in asset values (e.g. Browne, 1991). This ignores the illiquidity of most personal assets and the concentration of debt on those with low current net worth and high propensities to consume (e.g. Troelstrup, 1961, p. 552; Schluter, 1990; Sargent, 1991).

68.   Syedain (1989) describes how Islamic banks in the UK finance house purchase through leasing agreements. Naturally, the payments do not qualify for mortgage interest tax relief.

69.   See Asher (1991). A South African pension fund has considered investing in salary-linked mortgages to provide it with secured assets indexed to earnings growth.

70.   These include mutual and friendly societies, credit unions and rotating savings and credit associations that charge borrowers only administration costs. These institutions have been, and are, significant sources of liquidity in economies where the supply of commercial credit is non-existent or uncompetitive (e.g. Firth and Yamey, 1964, pp. 31–2: Besley et al., 1990).

       Although it works on a low-interest basis, the Grameen Bank of Bangladesh has 1.3 million members and has lent Taka 16.1 bn (£283m) to poor borrowers to finance housing, farms and enterprises. Its extremely high rate of loan recovery (98 per cent) results from 'peer monitoring' – loans are granted to groups of borrowers who agree to monitor each other; if one defaults, the whole group loses its access to credit (Wahid, 1994).

CHAPTER 8   THE PROHIBITION OF INTEREST IN WESTERN LITERATURE

1.   Deuteronomy 23: 19, 20; quoted from the New International Version.
2.   Exodus 22: 25; Leviticus 25:36,37; Psalms 15:3,5; Proverbs 28:8; Ezekiel 18:13; 22:11, 12; and Nehemiah 5:1–13.

3. Luke 6: 34, 35.
4. Matthew 25: 14–30; Luke 19: 11–26.
5. Codex iuris canonici, *c*.1735.
6. Shakespeare expressed the thought thus:

> If thou wilt lend this money, lend it not
> As to thy friends, – for when did friendship take
> A breed of barren metal of his friend? –
> But lend it rather to thine enemy;
> Who if he break, thou mayst with better face
> Exact the penalty.
> (Antonio to Shylock, *The Merchant of Venice*, Act I, Sc. III, 133–7)

7. 'Thanks to the institution of interest it is possible to lead a completely luxurious or parasitical existence ... This taint clings to interest, even when we are obliged to admit that is indispensable in the present economic order' (Brunner, 1937, p. 435).
8. It is no coincidence that Böhm-Bawerk describes the production process as present goods inexorably 'ripening' into future goods of greater value (1959, II, p. 301). Those in business would be surprised to learn that 'adding value' was as certain as fruit ripening.
9. Bentham (1787, p. 158) ridiculed the position by imagining that Aristotle examined coins for reproductive organs and, finding none, declared interest to be unnatural.
10. The background moralising behind Aristotle's position is that trade is virtuous if pursued within rational limits to fulfil moderate desires. The use of money in exchange can, however, be motivated by unlimited and irrational desires. This is assumed always to be the case with a loan at interest (see especially Lewis, 1978; Langholm, 1984, p. 65; Grunebaum, 1987, pp. 41–3).

CHAPTER 9   CONCLUSIONS

1. Unsurprisingly, these theoretical properties have attracted interest, and some support for the concept, from non-Muslim commentators (e.g. Karsten, 1982; Taylor and Evans, 1987, pp. 21–2; Wilson, 1990b, p. 17).
2. These include a liquid and stable equity market (to provide PLS banks with return-bearing reserve assets), well-defined legal and accounting standards, and sufficient competition in product and financial markets to ensure that profit levels are, in some sense, 'fair'.
3. Significantly reliance on debt to finance production and consumption is incompatible with strict adherence to hard currency systems that attempt to impose an external discipline on the price level (e.g. Gold Standard; ERM). Sooner or later, either the discipline will have to be released or debt deflation is threatened (Polanyi, 1944, pp. 193–4; Hixson, 1991, pp. 47–8).
4. The very existence of interest can also force the users of equity finance to offer a more certain return by analogy. For instance, institutional

investors do not look favourably on companies whose dividend payout rates vary with profitability through the cycle, since dividend cuts are interpreted as a signal of managerial pessimism. An M&G fund manager explicitly compared the institution's equity investments to a building society account on which regular interest is paid – 'the same principle arises in equity investment' (House of Commons, 1993/4, p. 75). Similar thinking also explains why commercial landlords invariably seek to increase the certainty of their rental income by including 'upward-only rent review' clauses in tenancy agreements.

5. The proscription of interest need not necessarily take the form of a positive ban. Rather, one could simply make loan contracts legally unenforceable if interest were present. This would still permit individuals to contract on an interest-basis, so avoiding much of the 'black market' problem, whilst garnering most of the positive institutional benefits of a non-interest financial system, and *ex post* profit-sharing in downturns, when borrowers could default without risking bankruptcy.

6. The similarities are not surprising considering the Old Testament's influence upon the Qu'ran, the widespread use of partnership arrangements in medieval Christendom and Islam and the cross-fertilization of economic ideas between the two faiths in the twelfth and thirteenth centuries (Mirakhor, 1987b).

7. In its transformation from a religious issue to one over the costs imposed on wider society, the usury debate prefigured the contemporary question of Sunday trading in the UK. With the religious presuppositions that originally prompted the restrictions on Sunday trading largely eroded, advocates of individual economic freedom can see no justification for the continuation of laws restricting the days and times when people can shop.

    The simple libertarian case, however, ignores the externalities imposed by indulging such desires. Complete freedom of shopping hours theoretically leads to too few shops remaining in business, but opening for longer hours and at higher prices than is socially beneficial (de Meza, 1984; Ferris, 1990). In addition, Sunday trading imposes externality costs through the forced employment of support workers and the erosion of family structures (e.g. Townsend and Schluter, 1985; John Lewis Partnership, 1993).

References

S. M. Abbasi, K. W. Hollman and J. H. Murray, 'Islamic Economics; Foundations and Practices', *International Journal of Social Economics*, 16(5) (1989) 5–17.

A. Abdallah, 'Islamic Banking', *Journal of Islamic Banking and Finance*, 4(1) (1987) 31–56.

A. M. Abdeen, and D. M. Shook, *The Saudi Financial System* (Chichester: John Wiley, 1984).

A. Abdouli, 'Access to Finance and Collaterals: Islamic versus Western Banking', *Journal of King Abdulaziz University: Islamic Economics*, 4 (1991) 56–64.

A. S. F. Abdul-Hadi, *Stock Markets of the Arab World* (London: Routledge, 1988).

A. Agrawal, and N. J. Nagarajan, 'Corporate Capital Structure, Agency Costs, and Ownership Control: the Case of All-Equity Firms', *Journal of Finance*, 45 (1990) 1325–31.

K. Ahmad (ed.), *Studies in Islamic Economics* (Leicester: Islamic Foundation, 1980).

M. Ahmad, 'Semantics of the Theory of Interest', *Islamic Studies*, June (1967) 171–96.

S. M. Ahmad, *The Economics of Islam: a Comparative Study* (Lahore: Muhammed Ashraf, 1947).

——, 'Interest and Unemployment', *Islamic Studies*, March (1969) 9–46.

O. Ahmed, 'Sudan: The Role of the Faisal Islamic Bank', in Wilson, R. (ed.), *Islamic Financial Markets* (London: Routledge, 1990), pp. 76–99.

S. Ahmed, 'Islamic Banking and Finance: a Review Essay', *Journal of Monetary Economics*, 24 (1989) 157–67.

Z. Ahmed, P. Iqbal and M. F. Khan, 'Introduction', in *Money and Banking in Islam* (Islamabad: Institute of Policy Studies, 1983a), pp. 1–25.

——, —— and ——, 'Introduction', in *Fiscal Policy and Resource Allocation in Islam* (Islamabad: Institute of Policy Studies, 1983b), pp. 1–25.

M. A. Akhtar, 'Causes and Consequences of the 1989–92 Credit Slowdown: Overview and Perspective', *Federal Reserve Bank of New York Quarterly Review*, Winter (1993/4) 1–23.

M. A. Al-' Arabi, 'Contemporary Bank Transactions and Islam's Views Thereon', *Islamic Review*, May (1966) 10–16.

H. Albach, 'Risk Capital, Business Investment and Economic Cooperation', in Ali, M. (ed.), *Islamic Banks and Strategies of Economic Cooperation* (London: New Century, 1982).

S. A. Ali, 'Risk-sharing and Profit-sharing in an Islamic Framework: Some Allocational Considerations', in Ahmed, Z., Iqbal, M. and Khan, M. F. (eds), *Fiscal Policy and Resource Allocation in Islam* (Islamabad: Institute of Policy Studies, 1983), pp. 253–70.

M. A. Al-Jarhi, 'A Monetary and Financial Structure for an Interest-Free Economy: Institutions, Mechanisms and Policy', in Ahmed, Z., Iqbal, M.

and Khan, M. F. (eds), *Money and Banking in Islam* (Islamabad: Institute of Policy Studies, 1983), pp. 69–87.

W. R. Allen, 'Irving Fisher and the 100 Percent Reserve Proposal', *Journal of Law and Economics*, 36 (1993) 703–17.

C. Amsler, 'Keynes and the Bank Rate Policy: Interest Rates Inconsistent With Full Employment', *Journal of Post-Keynesian Economics*, Spring (1993) 409–25.

J. W. Angell, 'The 100 Per Cent Reserve Plan', *Quarterly Journal of Economics*, November (1935) 1–35.

S. H. Anin, *Islamic Banking and Finance: The Experience of Iran* (Tehran: Vahid Publications, 1986).

M. Anwar, 'Reorganisation of Islamic Banking: a New Proposal', *American Journal of Islamic Social Science*, 4(2) (1987a) 295–304.

——, *Modelling an Interest-Free Economy* (Washington: The International Institute of Islamic Thought 1987b).

M. Ariff (ed.), 'Introduction', in *Monetary and Fiscal Economics of Islam* (Jeddah: International Centre for Research in Islamic Economics, 1982a), pp. 1–23.

——, 'Monetary Policy in an Interest-free Islamic Economy – Nature and Scope', in *Monetary and Fiscal Economics of Islam* (Jeddah: International Centre for Research in Islamic Economics, 1982b), pp. 287–309.

Aristotle, *Works*, Jowett, B. trans. (Chicago: William Benton 1952).

K. J. Arrow, *Essays in the Theory of Risk-Bearing* (Amsterdam: North-Holland 1971).

H. Aryan, 'Iran: The Impact of Islamization on the Financial System', in Wilson, R. (ed.), *Islamic Financial Markets* (London: Routledge, 1990), pp. 155–70.

A. Asher, 'Salary-Linked Mortgages: an Outline' (University of Witswatersrand, mimeo, 1991).

P. Asquith and D. W. Mullins, 'Equity Issues and Offering Dilution', in Edwards, J., Franks, J., Mayer, C. and Schaefer, S. (eds), *Recent Developments in Corporate Finance* (Cambridge: Cambridge University Press, 1986), pp. 257–76.

G. L. Bach, *Economics* (Englewood Cliffs, NJ: Prentice-Hall, 1977).

L. Baeck, 'The Economic Theory of Classical Islam', in Barker, W. J. (ed.), *Perspectives on the History of Economic Theory*, Vol. V (Aldershot: Edward Elgar, 1991), pp. 3–20.

D. Baldwin, 'Turkey: Islamic Banking in a Secularist Context', in Wilson, R. (ed.), *Islamic Financial Markets* (London: Routledge, 1990), pp. 33–58.

W. Ballantyre, 'Islamic Law and Financial Transactions in Contemporary Perspective', in Mallat, C. (ed.), *Islamic Law and Finance* (London: Graham and Trotman, 1988).

E. Baltensperger, 'Credit', in Eatwell, J., Milgate, M. and Newman, P. (eds), *The New Palgrave – Money* (London: Macmillan, 1989), pp. 97–102.

E. Baltensperger and J. Dermine, 'The Role of Public Policy in Ensuring Financial Stability: a Cross-Country, Comparative Approach', in Portes, R. and Swoboda, A. K. (eds), *Threats to International Financial Stability* (Cambridge: Cambridge University Press, 1987).

A. Barnea, R. A. Haugen and L. W. Senbet, *Agency Problems and Financial Contracting* (Englewood Cliffs, NJ: Prentice-Hall, 1985).

R. J. Barro, 'Are Government Bonds Net Wealth?', *Journal of Political Economy*, 82 (1974) 1095–1117.

Y. Barroux, 'Comments', *European Economic Review*, 32 (1988) 1187–9.

A. Bashir, 'Profit-Sharing Contracts with Moral Hazard and Adverse Selection', *American Journal of Islamic Social Science*, 7(3) (1990) 357–84.

——, A. F. Darrat and M. O. Suliman, 'Equity Capital, Profit Sharing Contracts and Investment: Theory and Evidence', *Journal of Business Finance and Accounting*, 20(5) (1993) 639–51.

B. A. Bashir, 'Portfolio Management of Islamic Banks; "Certainty Model"', *Journal of Banking and Finance*, 7(3) (1983) 339–54.

——, 'Successful Development of Islamic Banks', *Journal of Research into Islamic Economics*, Winter (1984) 63–71.

C. F. Bastable, *Public Finance*, 3rd edn (London: Macmillan, 1903).

W. J. Baumol, *Economic Theory and Operations Analysis*, 4th edn (Englewood Cliffs, NJ: Prentice-Hall, 1977).

R. Beckman, *Crashes: Why They Happen – What to Do* (London: Sidgwick and Jackson, 1988).

D. Bell, *The Cultural Contradictions of Capitalism* (London: Heinemann, 1976).

G. J. Benston, G. Hanweck and D. B. Humphrey, 'Scale Economies in Banking', *Journal of Money, Credit and Banking*, 14 (1982) 435–56.

J. Bentham, 'Defence of Usury', and 'Letter to Dr. Smith', in Stark, W. (ed.), *Jeremy Bentham's Economic Writings*, vol. I (London: George Allen and Unwin, 1787, repr. 1952), pp. 123–87.

J. L. Benvenisti, *The Iniquitous Contract* (London: Burns, Oates and Washbourne, 1937).

A. N. Berger, K. K. King, and J. M. O'Brien, 'The Limitations of Market Value Accounting and a More Realistic Alternative', *Journal of Banking and Finance*, 15 (1991) 753–83.

M. Berlin, A. Saunders, and G. F. Udell, 'Deposit Insurance Reform: What are the Issues and What Needs to be Fixed?', *Journal of Banking and Finance*, 15 (1991) 735–52.

B. S. Bernanke, 'Non-monetary Effects of the Financial Crisis in the Propagation of the Great Depression', *American Economic Review*, 73 (1983) 257–76.

——, 'Credit in the Macroeconomy', *Federal Reserve Bank of New York Quarterly Review*, Spring (1992/3), 50–70.

B. S. Bernanke, J. Y. Campbell and T. M. Whited, 'US Corporate Leverage: Developments in 1987 and 1988', *Brookings Papers on Economic Activity*, vol. I (1990) 255–78.

B. S. Bernanke and M. Gertler, 'Banking and MacroEquilibrium', in Barnett, W. A. and Singleton, K. J. (eds), *New Approaches to Monetary Economics* (Cambridge: Cambridge University Press, 1987), pp. 89–111.

—— and ——'Agency Costs, Net Worth, and Business Fluctuations', *American Economic Review*, 79 (1989) 14–31.

—— and ——, 'Financial Fragility and Economic Performance', *Quarterly Journal of Economics*, 105 (1990) 87–114.

B. S. Bernanke, and H. James, 'The Gold Standard, Deflation and Financial Crisis in the Great Depression: an International Comparison', in Hubbard,

R. G. (ed.), *Financial Markets and Financial Crises* (Chicago: University of Chicago Press, 1991).

B. S. Bernanke, and C. S. Lown, 'The Credit Crunch', *Brookings Papers on Economic Activity*, vol. II (1991) 205–239.

T. Besley, S. Coate and G. Loury, 'The Economics of Rotating Savings and Credit Associations', mimeo (1990).

A. Bhadhuri, 'On the Formation of Usurious Interest Rates in Backwards Agriculture', *Cambridge Journal of Economics*, 1 (1977) 341–52.

S. Bhattacharya, 'Aspects of Monetary and Banking Theory and Moral Hazard', *Journal of Finance*, 37 (1982) 371–84.

S. Bhattacharya and D. Gale, 'Preference Shocks, Liquidity and Central Bank Policy', in Barnett, W. A. and Singleton, K. J. (eds), *New Approaches to Monetary Economics* (Cambridge: Cambridge University Press, 1987), pp. 69–88.

BIS, *Bank of International Settlements Annual Report* (Basle: June 1994).

F. Black, 'Bank Funds Management in an Efficient Market', *Journal of Financial Economics*, 2 (1975) 325–39.

O. J. Blanchard, and M. W. Watson, 'Bubbles, Rational Expectations and Financial Markets', in Wachtel, P. (ed.), *Crisis in the Economic and Financial Structure* (Lexington, Mass.: Lexington Books, 1982), pp. 295–316.

E. von Böhm-Bawerk, *Capital and Interest*, Huncke, G. D. and Sennholz, H. F. trans., (South Holland, Ill.: Libertarian Press, orig. 1884, 1889; 1959).

S. Bond and C. Meghir, 'Financial Constraints and Company Investment', *Fiscal Studies*, 15(2) (1994) 1–18.

C. Bordes and J. Melitz, 'Business Debt and Default in France', *Discussion Paper 333*, Centre for Economic Policy Research (1989).

K. E. Boulding, *Economic Analysis*, I, 4th edn (New York: Harper and Row, 1966).

J. H. Boyd and M. Gertler, 'US Commercial Banking: Trends, Cycles and Policy', *NBER Working Paper 4404* (Cambridge, Mass: National Bureau of Economic Research, 1993).

J. H. Boyd and D. E. Runkle, 'Size and Performance of Banking Firms: Testing the Predictions of Theory', *Journal of Monetary Economics*, 31 (1993) 47–67.

M. Bradley, G. A. Jarrel and E. H. Kim, 'On the Existence of an Optimal Capital Structure: Theory and Evidence', *Journal of Finance*, 39 (1984) 857–78.

A. H. Browne, 'The Banks and Personal Credit', *Banking World*, January (1991) 17–19.

E. Brunner, *The Divine Imperative*, O. Wyon trans. (London: Lutterworth Press, 1937).

L. Bryan, *Bankrupt* (New York: Harper Business Books, 1991).

J. Bryant, 'A Model of Reserves, Bank Runs and Deposit Insurance', *Journal of Banking and Finance*, 4(4) (1980) 335–44.

——, 'Bank Collapse and Depression', *Journal of Money, Credit and Banking*, 13 (1981) 454–64.

J. M. Buchanan, 'Budgetary Bias in Post-Keynesian Politics', in Buchanan, J. M., Rowley, C. K. and Tollison, R. D. (eds), *Deficits* (Oxford: Blackwell, 1987), pp. 180–95.

C. W. Calomiris, 'Financial Factors in the Great Depression', *Journal of Economic Perspectives*, Spring (1993) 61–85.

C. W. Cameron, 'Household Debt Problems; Towards a Micro–Macro Linkage', *Review of Political Economy*, 5 (1993) 205–20.

E. Cannan, W. D. Ross, J. Bonar and J. P. Wicksteed, 'Who Said "Barren Metal"?', *Economica*, 1 (1922) 105–11.

R. Cantor, 'The Effects of Leverage on Investment and Employment', *Federal Reserve Bank of New York Quarterly Review*, Summer (1990) 31–41.

G. Cassel, *The Nature and Necessity of Interest* (London: Macmillan, 1903).

R. Castanias, 'Bankruptcy Risk and Optimal Capital Structure', *Journal of Finance*, 38 (1983) 1617–35.

M. V. Chapra, 'The Islamic Welfare State', in Donohue, J. J. and Esposito, J. L. (eds), *Islam in Transition* (New York: Oxford University Press, 1982), pp. 223–9.

——, *Towards a Just Monetary System* (Leicester: The Islamic Foundation, 1985).

——, 'Mechanics and Operations of an Islamic Financial Market', *Journal of Islamic Banking and Finance*, 5(3) (1988) 31–6.

——, 'The Need for a New Economic System', *Review of Islamic Economics*, 1(1) (1991) 9–47.

J. Chelius and R. S. Smith, 'Profit Sharing and Employment Stability', *Industrial and Labour Relations Review*, February (1990) 256–73.

V. Chick and S. C. Dow, 'A Post-Keynesian Perspective on the Relationship Between Banking and Regional Development', in Arestis, P. (ed.), *Post-Keynesian Monetary Economics* (Aldershot: Edward Elgar, 1988), pp. 219–50.

M. A. Choudhury, 'Investment and Insurance in Islamic Perspective', *International Journal of Social Economics*, 10 (1983) 14–26.

——, *Contributions to Islamic Economic Theory* (Basingstoke: Macmillan, 1986).

——, 'The Blending of Religious and Social Orders in Islam', *International Journal of Social Economics*, 16(2) (1989) 13–45.

Christian Aid, *Banking on the Poor: the Ethics of Third World Debt* (London: 1991).

CII (Council of Islamic Ideology), 'Elimination of Interest from the Economy', in Ahmed, Z., Iqbal, M. and Khan, M. F. (eds), *Money and Banking in Islam* (Islamabad: Institute of Policy Studies, 1983), pp. 103–200.

D. Cobham, 'Islamic Banking: Perspectives from the Theory of Financial Intermediation', mimeo, Department of Economics, University of St. Andrews, December (1992).

T. Congdon, 'Heresy of Worshipping the National Debt', *Financial Weekly*, 26 July (1985) 4.

——, *The Debt Threat* (Oxford: Blackwell, 1988).

R. Cooper, 'A Calculator in One Hand and the Koran in the Other', *Euromoney*, November (1981) 44–64.

J. Corbett, 'An Overview of the Japanese Financial System', in Dimsdale, N. and Prevezer, M. (eds), *Capital Markets and Corporate Governance* (Oxford: Clarendon Press, 1994), pp. 306–24.

L. Currie, *The Supply and Control of Money in the United States* (Cambridge, Mass.: Harvard University Press, 1934).

A. F. Darrat, 'Are Checking Accounts in American Banks Permissible Under Islamic Law?', *American Journal of Islamic Social Science*, (1985) 101–3.

P. Dasgupta, P. Hammond and E. Maskin, 'The implementation of social choice rules: some general results on incentive compatibility', *Review of Economics Studies*, 46 (1979) 185–216.

E. P. Davis, *Debt, Financial Fragility and Systemic Risk* (Oxford: Clarendon Press, 1992).

D. de Meza, 'The Fourth Commandment: Is It Pareto Efficient?', *Economic Journal*, 94 (1984) 379–83.

——and D. C. Webb, 'Too Much Investment: a Problem of Asymmetric Information', *Quarterly Journal of Economics*, 102 (1987) 281–92.

L. Dennis, 'Usury', *Economic Journal*, 42 (1932) 312–18.

D. W. Diamond, 'Financial Intermediation and Delegated Monitoring', *Review of Economic Studies*, 51 (1984) 393–414.

——and P. H. Dyvbig, 'Bank Runs, Deposit Insurance and Liquidity', *Journal of Political Economy*, 91 (1983) 401–19.

R. Dore, 'Goodwill and the Spirit of Market Capitalism', *British Journal of Sociology*, 34 (1983) 459–82.

R. Dornbusch, 'International Debt and Economic Instability', in *Debt, Financial Stability, and Public Policy* (Kansas City: Federal Reserve Bank of Kansas City 1986), pp. 63–86.

K. Dowd, *The State and the Monetary System* (Hemel Hempstead: Philip Allan, 1989).

——,'Optimal Financial Contracts', *Oxford Economic Papers* (1992) 672–93.

A. Duncan, *An End to Illusions* (London: Demos, 1993).

G. A. Dymski, 'A Keynesian Theory of Bank Behaviour', *Journal of Post-Keynesian Economics*, Summer (1988) 499–526.

O. Eckstein and A. Sinai, 'The Mechanisms of the Business Cycle in the Postwar Era', in Gordon, R. J. (ed.), *The American Business Cycle* (Chicago: University of Chicago Press, 1986), pp. 39–105.

Economist, The, 'A Brave New World for America's Banks', 12 January (1991a) 87–8.

——, 'The Case for Run-Resistant Money', 12 January (1991b) 89.

——, 'The New State of Corporate Japan', 27 April (1991c) 36–9.

——, 'Banking Behind the Veil', 4 April (1992a) 76.

——, 'Nearer My God, to Theocracy', 5 September (1992b) 74–7.

——, 'For God and GDP', 7 August (1993a) 56–7.

I. D. Edge, '*Shari'a* and Commerce in Contemporary Egypt', in Mallat, C. (ed.), *Islamic Law and Finance* (London: Graham and Trotman, 1988), pp. 31–55.

B. Eichengreen and R. Portes, 'The Anatomy of Financial Crises', in Portes, D. and Swoboda, A. K. (eds), *Threats to International Financial Stability* (Cambridge: Cambridge University Press, 1987), pp. 10–58.

A. A.-F. El-Ashker, *The Islamic Business Enterprise* (London: Croom Helm, 1987).

S. I. T. El-Din, 'Risk Aversion, Moral Hazard and Financial Islamization Policy', *Review of Islamic Economics*, 1(1) (1991) 49–66.

C. Elliott, 'The Ethics of International Debt', in Centre for Theology and Public Issues, Finance and Ethics, *Occasion Paper 11* (Edinburgh: University of Edinburgh, 1987), pp. 27–36.

G. Emerson, 'Guaranty of Deposits Under the Banking Act of 1933', *Quarterly Journal of Economics*, 48 (1934) 229–44.

S. Estrin, P. Grout and S. Wadhwani, 'Profit Sharing and Employee Share Ownership: an Assessment' *Economic Policy*, 4 (1987) 1–60.

P. Evans, 'Do Large Deficits Produce High Interest Rates?', *American Economic Review*, 75 (1985) 68–87.

E. F. Fama, 'What's Different about Banks?', *Journal of Monetary Economics*, 15 (1985) 29–39.

—— and M. H. Miller, *The Theory of Finance* (New York: Holt, Richart and Winston, 1972).

S. M. Fazzari and J. Caskey, 'Debt Commitments and Aggregate Demand: A Critique of the Neo-Classical Synthesis and Policy', in Semmler, W. (ed.), *Financial Dynamics and Business Cycles: New Perspectives* (Armonk, NY: M. E. Sharpe, 1989), pp. 188–99.

—— R. G. Hubbard and B. C. Petersen, 'Financing Constraints and Corporate Investment', *Brookings Papers on Economic Activity*, I (1988) 141–95.

J. M. Ferguson (ed.), *Public Debt and Future Generations* (Chapel Hill, Va.: University of North Carolina Press, 1964).

T. W. Ferguson, 'Gordon Getty's Plan to Replace the US Banking System', *Wall Street Journal*, 4 March (1993).

J. S. Ferris, 'Time, Space, and Shopping: the Regulation of Shopping Hours', *Journal of Law, Economics and Organization*, (1990) 171–87.

R. Firth and B. S. Yamey (eds), *Capital, Saving and Credit in Peasant Societies* (London: George Allen and Unwin, 1964).

I. Fisher, *The Theory of Interest* (New York: Macmillan, 1930).

——, 'The Debt-Deflation Theory of Great Depressions', *Econometrica*, 1 (1933a) 337–57.

——, *Booms and Depressions* (London: George Allen and Unwin, 1933b).

——, *100 per cent Money* (New York: Adelphi 1935).

F. R. Fitzroy and K. Kraft, 'Cooperation, Productivity and Profit-Sharing', *Quarterly Journal of Economics*, 102 (1987) 23–35.

M. J. Flannery, 'Debt Maturity and the Deadweight Cost of Leverage: Optimally Financing Banking Firms', *American Economic Review*, 84 (1994) 320–31.

J. S. Fleming, 'Comment', in Kindleberger, C. P. and Laffargue, J.-P. (eds), *Financial Crises: Theory, History and Policy* (Cambridge: Cambridge University Press, 1982).

A. B. Frankel and J. D. Montgomery, 'Financial Structure: an International Perspective', *Brookings Papers on Economic Activity*, 1 (1991) 257–97.

P. Frazer, 'Decline and Fall: Is There Time to Save the US Banking System?', *Banking World*, April (1991), 23–5.

C. Freedman, 'Discussion', in Portes, R. and Swoboda, A. K. (eds), *Threats to International Financial Stability* (Cambridge: Cambridge University Press, 1987), pp. 189–94.

B. M. Friedman, 'Money, Credit, and Interest Rates in the Business Cycle', in Gordon, R. J. (ed.), *The American Business Cycle* (Chicago: Chicago University Press, 1986a), pp. 395–458.

——, 'Increasing Indebtedness and Financial Instability in the United States', in *Debt, Financial Stability and Public Policy* (Kansas City: Federal Reserve Bank of Kansas City, 1986b), pp. 27–53.

——, *Day of Reckoning* (London: Pan Books 1989).

——, 'Implications of Corporate Indebtedness for Monetary Policy', *NBER Working Paper 3266* (Cambridge, Mass.: National Bureau of Economic Research, 1990).

——, 'Comments', *Brookings Papers on Economic Activity*, 2 (1991) 240–4.

M. Friedman, 'A Monetary and Fiscal Framework for Economic Stability', *American Economic Review*, 38 (1948) 245–64.

K. A. Froot, D. S. Scharfstein and J. C. Stein, 'LDC Debt: Forgiveness, Indexation and Investment Incentives', *Journal of Finance*, 44 (1989) 1335–50.

F. T. Furlong and M. C. Keeley, 'The Search for Financial Stability', in Federal Reserve Bank of San Francisco, *The Search for Financial Stability: the Past Fifty Years* (San Francisco: Federal Reserve Bank, 1985) pp. 125–146.

J. K. Galbraith, *Money: Whence it Came, Where it Went* (London: Andre Deutsch 1975a).

——, *Economics and the Public Purpose* (New York: New American Library, 1975b).

D. Gale and M. Hellwig, 'Incentive-Compatible Debt Contracts: the One-Period Problem', *Review of Economic Studies*, 52 (1985) 647–63.

T. Gambling, R. Jones and R. A. A. Karim, 'Credible Organizations: Self-Regulation v. External Standard-Setting in Islamic Banks and British Charities', *Financial Accountability and Management*, August (1993) 195–207.

S. George, *A Fate Worse Than Debt* (London: Penguin Books, 1988).

M. Gertler, 'Financial Structure and Aggregate Economic Activity: an Overview', *Journal of Money, Credit and Banking*, 20 (1988) 559–88.

—— and S. Gilchrist, 'The Cyclical Behaviour of Short-term Business Lending: Implications for Financial Propagation Mechanisms', *European Economic Review*, 37 (1993) 623–31.

—— and R. G. Hubbard, 'Taxation, Corporate Capital Structure and Financial Distress', in Summers, L. H., (ed.), *Tax Policy and the Economy*, NBER, vol. 4 (Cambridge, Mass.: MIT Press, 1990), pp. 43–71.

—— and ——, 'Corporate Financial Policy, Taxation, and Macroeconomic Risk', *RAND Journal of Economics*, 24 (1993) 286–305.

C. Gieraths, 'Pakistan: Main Participants and Final Financial Products of the Islamization Process', in Wilson, R. (ed.), *Islamic Financial Markets* (London: Routledge, 1990), pp. 171–95.

C. L. Gilbert, 'The Impact of Exchange Rates and Developing Country Debt on Commodity Prices', *Economic Journal*, September (1989) 773–84.

L. G. Goldberg and G. A. Hanweck, 'What We Can Expect from Interstate Banking', *Journal of Banking and Finance*, 12(1) (1988) 51–67.

R. W. Goldsmith, *Financial Structure and Development* (New Haven: Yale University Press, 1969).

C. H. Golembe and J. J. Mingo, 'Can Supervision and Regulation Ensure Financial Stability?', in Federal Reserve Bank of San Francisco, *The Search for Financial Stability: The Past Fifty Years* (San Francisco: Federal Reserve Bank, 1985), pp. 125–46.

C. A. E. Goodhart, 'Why do Banks Need a Central Bank?', *Oxford Economic Papers*, 39 (1987) 75–89.

——, 'Bank Insolvency and Deposit Insurance: a Proposal', in Arestis, P. (ed.), *Contemporary Issues in Money and Banking* (Basingstoke: Macmillan, 1988), pp. 49–69.

——, 'Are Central Banks Necessary?', *Special Paper No. 16* (London: London School of Economics, Financial Markets Group, 1989).

——, 'Can We Improve the Structure of Financial Systems?', *European Economic Review*, 37 (1993) 269–91.

G. Gorton, 'Banking Theory and Free Banking History', *Journal of Monetary Economics*, 16 (1985) 267–76.

F. D. Graham, 'Partial Reserve Money and the 100 Per Cent Proposal', *American Economic Review*, 26 (1936) 428–40.

B. C. Greenwald and J. E. Stiglitz, 'Imperfect Information, Finance Constraints and Business Fluctuations', in Kohn, M. and Tsiang, S.-C. (eds), *Finance Constraints, Expectations and Macroeconomics* (Oxford: Clarendon Press, 1988a), pp. 103–40.

——and——, 'Money, Imperfect Information and Economic Fluctuations', in Kohn, M. and Tsiang, S.-C. (eds), *Finance Constraints, Expectations and Macroeconomics* (Oxford: Clarendon Press, 1988b), pp. 141–65.

——and——, 'Macroeconomic Models with Equity and Credit Rationing', in Hubbard, R. G. (ed.), *Asymmetric Information, Corporate Finance and Investment* (Chicago: University of Chicago Press, 1990), pp. 15–42.

——, ——and A. Weiss, 'Informational Imperfections in the Capital Market and Macroeconomic Fluctuations', *American Economic Review (Papers and Proceedings)* (1984) 194–9.

S. Griffith-Jones and O. Sunkel, *Debt and Development Crises in Latin America: the End of an Illusion* (Oxford: Clarendon Press, 1986).

S. Grossman and O. Hart, 'Implicit Contracts, Moral Hazard, and Unemployment' *American Economic Review, (Papers and Proceedings)*, 71 (1981) 301–18.

——and——, 'Corporate Finance Structure and Managerial Incentives', in McCall, J. J. (ed.), *The Economics of Information and Uncertainty* (Chicago: University of Chicago Press, 1982), pp. 107–37.

J. O. Grunebaum, *Private Ownership* (London: Routledge and Kegan Paul, 1987).

J. Guttentag and R. Herring, 'The Insolvency of Financial Institutions: Assessment and Regulatory Disposition', in Wachtel, P. (ed.), *Crises in the Economic and Financial Structure* (Lexington, Mass.: Lexington Books, 1982), pp. 99–126.

——and——, 'Disaster Myopia in International Banking', *Essays in International Finance No. 164* (Princeton: Princeton University Department of Economics, 1986).

——and——, 'Emergency Liquidity Assistance for International Banks', in Portes, R. and Swoboda, A. K. (eds), *Threats to International Financial Stability* (Cambridge: Cambridge University Press, 1987), pp. 150–86.

G. Haberler, *Prosperity and Depression* (London: George Allen and Unwin, 1937).

J. D. Hamilton, 'Monetary Factors in the Great Depression', *Journal of Monetary Economics*, 19 (1987) 145–69.

R. Hanna, 'Families in Debt: the People and Their Money Problems', in Hartropp, A. (ed.), *Families in Debt* (Cambridge: Jubilee Centre Publications, 1988), pp. 41–60.

D. L. Hanson and C. F. Menezes, 'The Effect of Capital Risk on Optimal Savings Decisions', *Quarterly Journal of Economics*, 92 (1978) 653–70.

N. Haque and A. Mirakhor, 'Optimal Profit-Sharing Contracts and Investment in an Interest-Free Islamic Economy', in Khan, M. S. and Mirakhor, A. (eds), *Theoretical Studies in Islamic Banking and Finance* (Houston: Institute for Research and Islamic Studies, 1987), pp. 141–61.

——— and ———, 'Saving Behaviour in a Economy without Fixed Interest', *Journal of Islamic Banking and Finance*, 6(3) (1989) 24–38.

Z. Haque, '*Riba*, Interest and Profit', *Pakistan Economist*, 24 May (1980a) 14–35.

———, '*Riba*, Interest and Profit', *Pakistan Economist*, 31 May (1980b) 13–30.

M. J. Harm, 'The Financing of Small Firms in Germany', *Financial and Policy System Working Papers WPS 899* (Washington, DC: World Bank, 1992).

M. Harris and A. Raviv, 'Optimal Incentive Contracts with Imperfect Information', *Journal of Economic Theory*, 20 (1979) 231–59.

——— and ———, 'Capital Structure and the Informational Role of Debt', *Journal of Finance*, 45 (1990) 231–349.

R. F. Harrod, *Towards a Dynamic Economics* (London: Macmillan, 1948, repr. 1969).

A. G. Hart and C. H. Walker 'The "Chicago Plan" of Banking Reform', *Review of Economic Studies*, 2 (1934/5) 104–21.

O. Hart, 'Optimal Labour Contracts under Asymmetric Information: an Introduction' *Review of Economic Studies*, 50 (1983) 3–35.

O. Hart and B. Holmstrom, 'The Theory of Contracts', in Bewley, T. F. (ed.), *Advances in Economic Theory* (Cambridge: Cambridge University Press, 1987).

J. Haubrich, 'Financial Intermediation – Delegated Monitoring and Long-Term Relationships', *Journal of Banking and Finance*, (1989) 9–20.

R. G. Hawtrey, 'The Trade Cycle', in *Readings in Business Cycle Theory* (Homewood, Ill.: Irwin, 1926, repr. 1951), pp. 330–49.

———, 'The Monetary Theory of the Trade Cycle and Its Statistical Test', *Quarterly Journal of Economics*, XLI (1927) 471–86.

F. A. von Hayek, *Monetary Theory and the Trade Cycle*, Kaldor, N. and Croome, H. M. trans. (London: Jonathan Cape, 1933).

———, *Denationalization of Money* (London: Institute for Economic Affairs, 1976).

M. Hellwig, 'Banking, Financial Intermediation and Corporate Finance', in Giovanni, A. and Mayer, C. (eds), *European Financial Integration* (Cambridge: Cambridge University Press, 1991), pp. 35–63.

J. Hicks, 'Limited Liability: the Pros and Cons', in Orhnial, T. (ed.), *Limited Liability and the Corporation* (London: Croom Helm, 1982), pp. 11–21.

R. Higginson, *Called to Account* (Guildford: Eagle, 1993).

F. Hirsch, 'The Bagehot Problem', *The Manchester School* (1977) 241–57.

D. Hirschleifer and A. Subrahmanyam, 'Futures Versus Share Contracting as Means of Diversifying Output Risk', *Economic Journal*, 103 (1993) 620–38.

W. F. Hixson, *A Matter of Interest: Reexamining Money, Debt and Real Economic Growth* (New York: Praeger, 1991).

J. Holland, 'Banking Lending Relationships and the Complex Nature of Bank–Corporate Relations', *Journal of Business Finance and Accounting*, April (1994) 367–93.

R. C. Holland, 'The Problem of Financial Stability', in *The Search for Financial Stability: the Past Fifty Years* (San Francisco: Federal Reserve Bank of San Francisco, 1985), pp. 1–6.

B. Holmstrom, 'Moral Hazard and Observability', *Bell Journal of Economics*, 10 (1979) 74–91.

—— and L. Weiss, 'Managerial Incentives, Investment, and Aggregate Implications: Scale Effects', *Review of Economic Studies*, 52 (1985) 403–26.

S. H. Homoud, *Islamic Banking* (London: Arabian Information, 1985).

T. Hoshi, A. Kashyap and D. Scharfstein, 'The Role of Banks in Reducing the Costs of Financial Distress in Japan', *Journal of Financial Economics*, September (1990a) 67–88.

——, —— and ——, 'Bank Monitoring and Investment: Evidence from the Changing Structure of Japanese Corporate Banking Relationships', in Hubbard, R. G. (ed.), *Asymmetric Information, Corporate Finance and Investment* (Chicago: University of Chicago Press, 1990b), pp. 105–26.

J. H. Hotson, 'Ending the Debt–Money System', *Challenge*, March–April (1985) 48–50.

——, 'Foreword', in Hixson, W. F., *A Matter of Interest: Reexamining Money, Debt and Real Economic Growth* (New York: Praeger, 1991), pp. xv–xxiv.

House of Commons, *Competitiveness of UK Manufacturing Industry*, Trade and Industry Select Committee, Report 41–I, I (1993/4).

W. Hugins, *Jacksonian Democracy and the Working Class – the Banking Question* (Stanford: Stanford University Press, 1960).

D. Hume, *Writings on Economics*, Rotwein, E. (ed.) (Madison: University of Wisconsin Press, 1970).

Z. Hussain, 'Court Rules Out Bank Interest in Pakistan', *The Times*, 22 January (1992).

IFS, *Equity for Corporations: a Corporation Tax for the 1990s* (London: Institute for Fiscal Studies, 1991).

IMF, 'Asset Price Deflation, Balance Sheet Adjustment and Financial Fragility', *IMF World Economic Outlook*, October (1992) 57–68.

Z. Iqbal and A. Mirakhor, 'Islamic Banking', *IMF Occasional Paper 49*, (Washington: IMF, 1987).

L. Ireland, 'In Good Faith: Dealing with Islam', *Corporate Finance*, April (1990) 21–2.

M. Ishfaq, 'Anatomy of *Riba* and Interest', *Journal of Islamic Banking and Finance*, 8(3) (1991) 58–64.

T. Ishikawa and K. Ueda, 'The Bonus Payment System and Japanese Personal Savings', in Aoki, M. (ed.), *The Economic Analysis of the Japanese Firm* (Amsterdam: North-Holland, 1984), pp. 133–92.

M. T. Jacobs, *Short-Term America: the Causes and Consequences of Our Business Myopia* (Boston: Harvard Business School, 1991).

D. Jaffee and J. Stiglitz, 'Credit Rationing', in Friedman, B. M. and Hahn, F. H. (eds), *Handbook of Monetary Economics* (Amsterdam: North-Holland, 1990), pp 837–88.

C. M. James, 'Discussion', in *The Search for Financial Stability: the Past Fifty Years* (San Francisco: Federal Reserve Bank of San Francisco, 1985), pp. 79–82.

P. N. Jefferson, 'Nominal Debt, Default Costs and Output', *Journal of Macroeconomics*, Winter (1994) 37–54.

M. C. Jensen, 'Agency Costs of Free Cash Flow, Corporate Finance and Takeovers', *American Economic Review (Papers And Proceedings)*, May (1986) 323–9.

——, 'The Eclipse of the Public Corporation', *Harvard Business Review*, September/October (1989) 61–74.

—— and W. Meckling, 'Theory of the Firm: Managerial Behaviour, Agency Costs and Ownership Structure', *Journal of Financial Economics*, October (1976) 305–60.

K. John, T. A. John and L. W. Senbet, 'Risk-Shifting Incentives of Depository Institutions: a New Perspective on Federal Deposit Insurance Reform', *Journal of Banking and Finance*, 15 (4, 5) (1991) 895–915.

—— L. W. Senbet and A. K. Sundaram, 'Corporate Limited Liability and the Design of Corporate Taxation', (1993) mimeo.

John Lewis Partnership, *A Decision for Parliament: the Future of Sunday Trading* (London: October 1993).

H. G. Johnson, 'Efficiency in Monetary Management', *Journal of Political Economy*, 76 (1968) 971–91.

R. Jolly, 'The Human Dimensions of International Debt', in Hewitt, A. and Wells, B. (eds), *Growing Out of Debt* (London: Overseas Development Institute, 1989).

M. Joyce and J. Lomax, 'Patterns of Default in the Non-Financial Private Sector', *Bank of England Quarterly Bulletin*, November (1991) 534–7.

Jubilee Centre Policy Group, *Escaping the Debt Trap: the Problems of Consumer Credit and Debt in Britain Today* (Cambridge: Jubilee Centre Publications, 1991).

M. Kahf, *The Islamic Economy* (Plainfield, Ind.: The Muslim Students' Association of the US and Canada, 1978).

R. F. Kahn, 'The Relation of Home Investment to Unemployment', *Economic Journal*, 41(1) (1931) 173–98.

S. M. A. Kalam, 'The Basic Principles of Islamic Economics', *Journal of Islamic Banking and Finance*, 8(3) (1991) 16–24.

E. J. Kane, *The Gathering Crisis in Federal Deposit Insurance* (Cambridge: Mass.: MIT Press, 1985).

J. H. Karekan, 'Ensuring Financial Stability', in *The Search for Financial Stability: the Past Fifty Years* (San Francisco: Federal Reserve Bank of San Francisco, 1985), pp. 53–77.

—— and N. Wallace, 'Deposit Insurance and Bank Regulation: a Partial Equilibrium Exposition', *Journal of Business*, 51(3) (1978) 413–38.

R. A. A. Karim and A. E. -T. Ali, 'Towards and Understanding of the Use of Financing Mechanisms of Islamic Banks', *Arab Journal of the Social Sciences*, April (1988) 55–67.

I. Karsten, 'Islam and Financial Intermediation', *IMF Staff Papers*, March (1982) 108–48.

H. Kaufman, 'Financial Crises: Market Impact, Consequences and Adapt-ability', in Altman, E. I. and Sametz, A. W. (eds), *Financial Crises* (New York: John Wiley, 1977), pp. 153–9.

——, 'Debt: the Threat to Economic and Financial Stability', in *Debt, Financial Stability and Public Policy* (Kansas City: Federal Reserve Bank of Kansas City, 1986), pp. 15–26.

A. G. N. Kazi, 'Islamic Banking in Perspective', *Journal of Islamic Banking and Finance*, 1(3) (1984) 7–21.

M. Kennedy, *Interest and Inflation-Free Money* (Steyerburg: Permaculture Institute, 1988).

J. M. Keynes, 'Consequences to the Banks of the Collapse of Money Values', in *Essays in Persuasion* (1931 repr.), in *The Collected Writings of J. M. Keynes*, vol. IX (London: Macmillan, 1972).

——, *The General Theory of Employment, Interest and Money* (London: Macmillan, 1936).

M. A. Khan, 'A Survey of Critical Literature on Interest-Free Banking', *Journal of Islamic Banking and Finance*, 6(1) (1991) 45–61.

M. F. Khan, 'Time Value of Money and Discounting in Islamic Perspective', *Review of Islamic Economics*, 1(2) (1991) 35–45.

M. S. Khan, 'Islamic Interest-Free Banking: a Theoretical Analysis', *IMF Staff Papers*, (1986) 1–27.

—— and A. Mirakhor (eds), 'Introduction', in *Theoretical Studies in Islamic Banking and Finance* (Houston: Institute for Research and Islamic Studies, 1987a).

—— and——, 'The Framework and Practice of Islamic Banking', in *Theoretical Studies in Islamic Banking and Finance* (Houston: Institute for Research and Islamic Studies, 1987b), pp. 1–13.

—— and——, 'The Financial System and Monetary Policy in an Islamic Economy', in *Theoretical Studies in Islamic Banking and Finance* (Houston: Institute for Research and Islamic Studies, 1987c), pp. 163–84.

—— and——, 'Islamic Banking: Experiences in the Islamic Republic of Iran and in Pakistan', *Economic Development and Cultural Change*, January (1990) 353–75.

S. R. Khan, 'An Economic Analysis of a PLS Model for the Financial Sector', *Pakistan Journal of Applied Economics*, 3(2) (1984) 89–105.

——, *Profit and Loss Sharing: an Islamic Experiment in Finance and Banking* (Karachi: Oxford University Press, 1987).

W. M. Khan, *Towards an Interest-Free Islamic Economic System* (Leicester: The Islamic Foundation, 1985).

——, 'Towards an Interest-Free Islamic Economic System', in Khan, M. S. and Mirakhor, A. (eds), *Theoretical Studies in Islamic Banking and Finance* (Houston: Institute for Research and Islamic Studies, 1987), p. 104.

R. Khouri, 'The Spread of Banking for Believers', *Euromoney*, May (1987) 145–8.

B. S. Kierstead, *Capital, Interest and Profits* (Oxford: Blackwell, 1959).

M. Kim and V. Maksinovic, 'Debt and Input Misallocation', *Journal of Finance*, 45 (1990) 795–816.

C. P. Kindleberger, *Manias, Crashes and Panics*, 2nd edn (New York: Basic Books, 1989).

——and J.-P. Laffargue (eds), 'Introduction', in *Financial Crises: Theory, History and Policy* (Cambridge: Cambridge University Press, 1982), pp. 1–10.

M. King, 'Debt Deflation: Theory and Evidence', *European Economic Review*, 38 (1994) 419–46.

——and C. A. E. Goodhart, 'Financial Stability and the Lender of Last Resort Function: a Note', *Special Paper 2* (London: London School of Economics Financial Markets Group, 1989).

N. Kiyotaki and J. H. Moore, 'Credit Cycles', mimeo (London: London School of Economics, 1993).

F. H. Knight, *Risk, Uncertainty and Profit* (New York: Augustus Kelly, repr. 1964, 1921).

J. Knodell and D. Levine, 'Instability, Crisis and the Limits of Policy-Making', in Jarsulic, M. (ed.), *Money and Macro Policy* (Hingham, Mass.: Kluwer-Nijhoff, 1985), pp. 85–108.

R. A. Korajczyk, D. Lucas and R. L. McDonald, 'Understanding Stock Price Behaviour Around the Time of Equity Issues', in Hubbard, R. G. (ed.), *Asymmetric Information, Corporate Finance and Investment* (Chicago: University of Chicago Press, 1990), pp. 15–42.

R. M. Kubarych, 'Discussion', in Wachtel, P. (ed.), *Crises in the Economic and Financial Structure* (Lexington: Mass.: Lexington Books, 1982), pp. 245–6.

K. K. Kurihara, 'Distribution, Employment and Secular Growth', in *Post-Keynesian Economics* (London: George Allen and Unwin, 1955), pp. 251–72.

D. Lal and S. Wijnbergen, 'Government Deficits, the Real Interest Rate and Developing Country Debt: On Global Crowding Out', in Lal, D. and Wolff, M. (eds), *Stagflation, Savings and the State* (Washington: World Bank, 1986), pp. 182–238.

F. C. Lane, 'Investment and Usury', in *Venice and History: the Collected Papers of F. C. Lane* (Baltimore: John Hopkins Press, 1966).

O. Langholm, *The Aristotelian Theory of Usury* (Bergen: University Press, 1984).

F. Lavington, *The Trade Cycle* (London: P. S. King and Son, 1922).

J. Le Goff, 'The Usurer and Purgatory', *Dawn of Modern Banking* (New Haven: Yale University Press, 1979), pp. 25–52.

H. E. Leland, 'Saving and Uncertainty: the Precautionary Demand for Saving', *Quarterly Journal of Economics*, 82 (1968) 465–73.

A. P. Lerner, 'The New Orthodoxy', in Ferguson, J. M. (ed.), *Public Debt and Future Generations* (Chapel Hill, V.: University of North Carolina Press, 1964), pp. 16–19.

D. Levinthal, 'A Survey of Agency Models of Organisations', *Journal of Economic Behaviour and Organization*, 9(2) (1988) 153–85.

H. Levy and M. Sarnat, *Capital Investment and Financial Decisions* (Englewood Cliffs, NJ: Prentice-Hall, 1978).

T. J. Lewis, 'Acquisition and Anxiety: Aristotle's Case Against the Market', *Canadian Journal of Economics*, 11 (1978) 69–90.

W. A. Lewis, *The Theory of Economic Development* (London: George Allen and Unwin, 1955).

H. I. Liebling, *US Corporate Profitability and Capital Formation: Are Rates of Return Sufficient?* (New York: Pergamon Policy Studies, 1980).

R. E. Litan, *What Should Banks Do?* (Washington, DC: Brookings Institute, 1987).

D. T. Llewellyn, 'Is There a Credit Crunch?', *Banking World*, May (1991) 23–6.

—— and L. Drake, 'Credit Crunch: a British Perspective', mimeo, (Loughborough: Loughborough University Banking Centre, 1994).

T. Lorenz, *Venture Capital Today*, 2nd edn (Cambridge: Woodhead-Faulkener, 1989).

A. Loveday, 'Financial Organisation and the Price Level', in *Economic Essays in Honour of Gustav Cassel* (London: George Allen and Unwin, 1933), pp. 327–42.

S. T. Lowry, 'Recent Literature on Ancient Greek Economic Thought', *Journal of Economic Literature*, 17(1) (1979) 65–86.

J. Mahoney, 'Ethical Aspects of Banking', in *The Banks and Society: the Gilbart Lectures 1990* (London: Bankers' Books, 1991), pp. 49–59.

E. Malinvaud, 'Interest Rates in the Allocation of Resources', in Hahn, F. H. and Brechling, F. P. R. (eds), *The Theory of Interest Rates* (London: Macmillan, 1965), pp. 209–41.

C. Mallat, 'The Debate on *Riba* and Interest in Twentieth Century Jurisprudence', in *Islamic Law and Finance* (London: Graham and Trotman, 1988), pp. 69–88.

R. P. Maloney, 'Usury in Greek, Roman and Rabbinic Thought', *Traditio*, (1971) 79–109.

N. G. Mankiw, 'The Allocation of Credit and Financial Collapse', *Quarterly Journal of Economics*, 101 (1986) 455–70.

M. A. Mannan, 'Islam and Trends in Modern Banking', *Islamic Review*, November–December (1968) 5–10.

——, *Islamic Economics: Theory and Practice* (Lahore: Sh. Muhammed Ashraf, 1970).

——, 'Allocative Efficiency, Decision and Welfare Criteria in an Interest-Free Islamic Economy: a Comparative Policy Approach', in Ariff, M. (ed.), *Monetary and Fiscal Economics of Islam* (Jeddah: International Centre for Research in Islamic Economics, 1982), pp. 43–62.

——, *The Making of Islamic Economic Society* (Cairo: IAIB Press, 1983).

Marshall, A., *Principles of Economics*, 8th edn (London: Macmillan, 1930).

C. Mason, 'Venture Capital in the UK: a Geographical Perspective', *National Westminster Bank Review*, May (1987) 47–59.

C. Mayer, 'New Issues in Corporate Finance', *European Economic Review*, 32 (1988) 1167–89.

T. Mayer, 'Should Large Banks Be Allowed to Fail?', *Journal of Finance and Quantitative Analysis*, 10(4) (1975) 603–10.

I. S. McCarthy, 'Deposit Insurance: Theory and Practice', *IMF Staff Papers*, (1980) 578–600.

R. C. Merton, 'On the Cost of Deposit Insurance when there are Surveillance Costs', *Journal of Banking*, (1978) 439–52.

M. M. Metwally, 'Fiscal Policy in an Islamic Economy', in Ahmed, Z., Iqbal, M. and Khan, M. F. (eds), *Fiscal Policy and Resource Allocation in Islam* (Jeddah: International Centre for Research in Islamic Economics, 1983), pp. 59–81.

M. A. Meyer, 'Profit-sharing, Employment Fluctuations and Entrepreneurial Incentives', mimeo (Oxford: Nuffield College, 1986).

D. Miles, 'Housing and the Wider Economy in the Short and Long Run', *National Institute Economic Review*, February (1992) 64–77.

M. Miller and F. Modigliani, 'The Cost of Capital, Corporation Finance and the Theory of Investment', *American Economic Review*, XLVIII (1958) 261–97.

P. S. Mills, 'Keynes' Belief that the Money Rate of Interest "Rules the Roost"', M.Phil. dissertation (Cambridge University: mimeo, 1989).

A. Milne, 'Financial Problems and Economic Recovery', *London Business School Economic Outlook*, February (1993) 39–47.

H. P. Minsky, 'Can "It" Happen Again?', in Carson, D. (ed.), *Banking and Monetary Studies* (Homewood, Ill.: R. D. Irwin, 1963), pp. 101–11.

——, *John Maynard Keynes* (London: Macmillan, 1976).

——, 'A Theory of Systematic Fragility', in Altman, E. I. and Sametz, A. W. (eds), *Financial Crises – Institutions and Markets in a Fragile Environment* (New York: John Wiley and Sons, 1977).

——, 'The Financial-Instability Hypothesis: Capitalist Processes and the Behaviour of the Economy', in Kindleberger, C. P. and Laffarge, J. -P. (eds), *Financial Crises: Theory, History and Policy* (Cambridge: Cambridge University Press, 1982), pp. 13–39.

——, 'The Financial-Instability Hypothesis: a Restatement', in Arestis, P., and Skouras, T. (eds), *Post-Keynesian Economic Theory* (Brighton: Wheatsheaf Books, 1985), pp. 24–55.

——, 'On the Non-Neutrality of Money', *Federal Reserve Bank of New York Quarterly Review*, Spring (1992/3) 77–85.

——, 'Community Development Banks: an Idea in Search of Substance', *Challenge*, March–April (1993) 33–41.

L. W. Mints, *A History of Banking Theory* (Chicago: University of Chicago Press, 1945).

A. Mirakhor, 'Short-term Asset Concentration and Islamic Banking', in Khan, M. S. and Mirakhor, A. (eds), *Theoretical Studies in Islamic Banking and Finance* (Houston: Institute for Research and Islamic Studies, 1987a), pp. 185–99.

——, 'Muslim Scholars and the History of Economics: a Need for Consideration',*American Journal of Islamic Social Science*, December (1987b) 245–76.

——, 'The Progress of Islamic Banking: the Case of Iran and Pakistan', in Mallat, C. (ed.), *Islamic Law and Finance* (London: Graham and Trotman, 1988), pp. 91–115.

E. S. Mishan, *Cost–Benefit Analysis: an Introduction* (New York: Praeger, 1971).

F. Mishkin, 'The Household Balance Sheet and the Great Depression', *Journal of Economic History*, 38 (1978) 918–37.

M. Mohsin, 'A Profile of *Riba*-Free Banking', in Ariff, M. (ed.), *Monetary and Fiscal Economics of Islam* (Jeddah: International Centre for Research in Islamic Economics, 1982), pp. 187–203.

D. Mookherjee and I. Png, 'Optimal Auditing, Insurance and Redistribution', *Quarterly Journal of Economics*, 104 (1989) 399–415.

C. H. Moore, 'Islamic Banks and Competitive Politics in the Arab World and Turkey', *Middle East Journal*, Spring (1990) 234–55.

M. Morishima, *Why Has Japan 'Succeeded'?* (Cambridge: Cambridge University Press, 1982).

S. C. Myers, 'Determinants of Corporate Borrowing', *Journal of Financial Economics*, 5 (1977) 147–76.

—— and N. S. Majluf, 'Corporate Financing and Investment Decisions when Firms have Information that Investors do Not Have', *Journal of Financial Economics*, 13 (1984) 187–221.

R. B. Myerson, 'Incentive Compatibility and the Bargaining Problem', *Econometrica*, 47 (1979) 61–74.

I. Nakatani, 'The Economic Role of Financial Corporate Grouping', in Aoki, M. (ed.), *The Economic Analysis of the Japanese Firm* (Amsterdam: North-Holland, 1984), pp. 227–46.

S. N. H. Naqvi, *Ethics and Economics – an Islamic Synthesis* (Leicester: The Islamic Foundation, 1981).

M. P. Narayanan, 'Debt Versus Equity Under Asymmetric Information', *Journal of Finance and Quantitative Analysis*, 23(1) (1988) 39–51.

N. Nassief, 'Islamic Banking Around the World', *Journal of Islamic Banking and Finance*, 7(1) (1990) 55–64.

T. Naughton and B. Shanmugan, 'Interest-Free Banking: a Case Study of Malaysia', *National Westminster Bank Quarterly Review*, February (1990) 16–32.

V. Nienhaus, 'Profitability of Islamic PLS Banks Competing with Interest Banks: Problems and Prospects', *Journal of Research into Islamic Economics*, Summer (1983) 37–47.

——, 'Islamic Banking: Microeconomic Instruments and Macroeconomic Implications', *Arab Banker*, 1(6) (1986) 5–7, 29–31.

——, 'The Performance of Islamic Banks: Trends and Causes', in Mallat, C. (ed.), *Islamic Law and Finance* (London: Graham and Trotman, 1988), pp. 129–70.

OECD, *Taxing Profits in a Global Environment* (Paris: Organisation for Economic Co-operation and Development, 1991).

M. O'Hara, 'Financial Contracts and International Lending', *Journal of Banking and Finance*, 14(1) (1990) 11–31.

J. Ordover and A. Weiss, 'Information and the Law: Evaluating Legal Restrictions on Competitive Contracts', *American Economic Review (Papers And Proceedings)*, 71 (1981) 399–404.

T. Orhnial, 'Liability Laws and Company Finance', in *Limited Liability and the Corporation* (London: Croom Helm, 1982), pp. 179–90.

PAID, *Usury: The Root Cause of the Injustices of Our Time* (Norwich: People Against Interest Debt, 1989).

B. M. Parigi, 'Repeated Lending with Limited Liability under Imperfect Monitoring', *Economic Notes*, 21(3) (1992) 468–89.

M. Parker, 'A Point of Interest', *The Banker*, June (1993) 51–2.

R. A. Pecchinino, 'The Loan Contract: Mechanism of Financial Control', *Economic Journal*, 98 (1988) 126–37.

S. Peltzman, 'Capital Investment in Commercial Banking and its Relation to Portfolio Regulation', *Journal of Political Economy*, 78 (1970) 1–26.

M. A. Petersen and R. G. Rajan, 'The Benefits of Lending Relationships: Evidence From Small Business Data', *Journal of Finance*, 49 (1994) 3–37.

E. S. Phelps, 'The Accumulation of Risky Capital: a Sequential Utility Analysis', in Hester, D. D. and Tobin, J. (eds), *Risk Aversion and Portfolio Choice* (New York: John Wiley, 1967), pp. 139–53.

J. L. Pierce, 'Closing Remarks', in *The Search for Financial Stability: the Past Fifty Years* (San Francisco, Federal Reserve Bank of San Francisco, 1985), pp. 191–7.

——, *The Future of Banking* (New Haven: Yale University Press, 1991).

K. Polanyi, *The Great Transformation*, 1957 edn (Boston: Beacon Press, 1944).

Pontifical Commission *'Institia et Pax'*, *International Debt: an Ethical Approach to the Question* (London: Catholic Truth Society, 1986).

D. Porteous, 'The Spatial Dimensions of Intermediary Behaviour', unpublished Ph.D. thesis, Yale University, November (1993a).

——, *The 'Trust' Proposals for Regional Banking in the UK* (Cambridge: Jubilee Policy Group, 1993b).

M. Postan, 'Credit in Medieval Trade', *Economic History Review*, 1 (1928) 234–61.

J. W. Pratt and R. Zeckhauser, *Principals and Agents: the Structure of Business* (Boston: Harvard University Press, 1985).

J. R. Presley, *Directory of Islamic Financial Institutions* (Beckenham: Croom Helm, 1988).

—— and J. G. Sessions, 'Islamic Economics: the Emergence of a New Paradigm', *Economic Journal*, 104 (1994) 584–96.

F. L. Pryor, 'The Islamic Economic System', *Journal of Comparative Economics*, 9(2) (1985) 197–223.

S. M. Qadri, 'The Qu'ranic Approach to the Problem of Interest in the Context of the Islamic Social System', *Islamic Culture*, LV(1) (1981) 35–47.

A. I. Qureshi, *Islam and the Theory of Interest* (Lahore: Muhammed Ashraf, 1946).

——, *The Economic and Social System of Islam* (Lahore: Islamic Book Service, 1979).

R. Radner, 'Monitoring Co-operative Agreements in a Repeated Principal–Agent Relationship', *Econometrica*, 49 (1981) 1127–48.

——, 'Repeated Principal–Agent Games With Discounting', *Econometrica*, 53 (1985) 1173–98.

F. Rahmann, *'Riba* and Interest', *Islamic Studies*, 3 (1) (1964) 1–43.

B. U. Ratchford, 'The Burden of a Domestic Debt', *American Economic Review*, 32 (1942) 451–67.

S. Rhoades and D. T. Savage, 'Post-Deregulation Performance of Large and Small Banks', *Issues in Bank Regulation*, Winter (1991).

D. Ricardo, *The Works and Correspondence of David Ricardo*, Sraffa, P. (ed.) (Cambridge: Cambridge University Press, 1951).

J. Robinson, 'What Are the Questions?', *Journal of Economic Literature*, 15(4) (1977) 1318–39.

M. Rodinson, 'Islam and Capitalism', 3rd edn, trans. B. Pearce (Austin: University of Texas Press, 1978).

A. J. Rolnick and W. E. Weber, 'The Cause of Free Bank Failures: a Detailed Examination', *Journal of Monetary Economics*, 14 (1984) 267–91.

S. Ross, 'The Determination of Financial Structure: the Incentive Signalling Approach', *Bell Journal of Economics*, 8 (1977) 32–40.

C. E. Ruebling, 'Motives Behind Monetary Expansion', in Boulding, K. E. and Wilson, T. F. (eds), *Redistribution through the Financial System* (New York: Praeger, 1978), pp. 59–69.

N. A. Saleh, *Unlawful Gain and Legitimate Profit in Islamic Law* (Cambridge: Cambridge University Press, 1986).

P. A. Samuelson, *Economics*, 10th edn (New York: McGraw-Hill, 1976).

A. Sandmo, 'The Effect of Uncertainty on Savings Decisions', *Review of Economic Studies*, 37 (1970) 353–60.

G. J. Santoni and G. C. Stone, 'Navigating Through the Interest Rate Morass: Some Basic Principles', *Federal Reserve Bank of St Louis Review*, March (1981) 11–18.

M. A. Saqr (ed.), *Al-Iqtisad al-Islami* (Jeddah: International Centre for Research in Islamic Economics, 1980).

J. R. Sargent, 'Debt, Deregulation and Downturn in the UK Economy', *National Institute Economic Review*, August (1991) 75–88.

M. Sarkar, 'Debt Crisis of the Less Developed Countries and the Transfer Debate Once Again', *Journal of Development Studies*, July (1991) 84–101.

M. A. Saud, 'The Economic Order Within the General Conception of the Islamic Way of Life', *Islamic Review*, March (1967) 11–14.

——, 1980, 'Money, Interest and *Qirâd*', in Ahmad, K., *Studies in Islamic Economics* (Leicester: The Islamic Foundation), pp. 59–84.

A. Saunders, 'The Inter-Bank Market, Contagion Effects and International Financial Crises', in Portes, R., and Swoboda, A. K. (eds), *Threats to International Financial Stability* (Cambridge: Cambridge University Press, 1987).

J. Schacht, *An Introduction to Islamic Law* (London: Oxford University Press, 1964).

D. S. Scharfstein and J. C. Stein, 'Herd Behaviour and Investment', *American Economic Review*, 80 (1990) 465–79.

M. G. G. Schluter, contribution to, *Personal Debt – Is It Too Much Encouraged?* (London: Institute of Business Ethics, 1990), pp. 26–31.

—— and D. Lee, *The R Factor* (Seven Oaks: Hodder and Stoughton, 1993).

J. A. Schumpeter, *The Theory of Economic Development* (Harvard: Harvard University Press, 1934).

A. J. Schwartz, 'Real and Pseudo-Financial Crises', in Capie, F. and Wood, G. E. (eds), *Financial Crises and the World Banking System* (Basingstoke: Macmillan, 1986), pp. 11–31.

S. Y. Shah, 'Islam and Productive Credit', *Islamic Review*, March (1959) 34–7.

R. Shallah, 'Jordan: The Experience of the Jordan Islamic Bank', in Wilson, R. (ed.), *Islamic Financial Markets* (London: Routledge, 1990), pp. 100–28.

S. A. Sharpe, 'Asymmetric Information, Bank Lending and Implicit Contracts: a Stylized Model of Customer Relationships', *Journal of Finance*, 45 (1990) 1069–87.

B. A. Sharraf, 'Theories and Facts About Interest Rates', *Arabia*, May (1984) 54–5.

S. M. Sheffrin, *The Making of Economic Policy* (Cambridge, Mass.: Blackwell, 1989).

H. Shirazi, *Islamic Banking* (London: Butterworths, 1990).

A. Shleifer and R. W. Vishny, 'Liquidation Values and Debt Capacity: a Market Equilibrium Approach', *Journal of Finance*, September (1992) 1343–66.

M. N. Siddiqi, 'Economics of Islam', *Islamic Thought*, 14(3) (1971) 22–33.

——, 'Banking in an Islamic Framework', *Islam and the Modern Age*, 8(4) (1977).

——, *Muslim Economic Thinking* (Leicester: The Islamic Foundation, 1981).

——, 'Islamic Approach to Money, Banking and Monetary Policy – a Review', in Ariff, M. (ed.), *Monetary and Fiscal Economics of Islam* (Jeddah: International Centre for Research in Islamic Economics, 1982), pp. 25–42.

——, *Issues in Islamic Banking* (Leicester: The Islamic Foundation, 1983a).

——, *Banking Without Interest* (Leicester: The Islamic Foundation, 1983b).

——, 'Economics of Profit-Sharing', in Ahmed, Z., Iqbal, M. and Khan, M. F. (eds), *Fiscal Policy and Resource Allocation in Islam*, (Islamabad: Institute of Policy Studies, 1983c), pp. 163–85.

——, *Partnership and Profit-Sharing in Islamic Law* (Leicester: The Islamic Foundation, 1985).

——, 'Some Aspects of *Mudarabah*', *Review of Islamic Economics*, 1(2) (1991) 21–33.

S. A. Siddiqi and A. Zaman, 'Investment and Income Distribution Pattern Under *Musharika* Finance: the Uncertainty Case', *Pakistan Journal of Applied Economics*, Summer (1989) 31–71.

H. C. Simons, 'A Positive Program for Laissez-Faire: Some Proposals for a Liberal Economic Society', *Public Policy Pamphlet No. 15* (Chicago: University of Chicago Press, 1934).

——, *Economic Policy for a Free Society* (Chicago: University of Chicago Press, 1948).

H. Simpson, 'Financial Retrenchment in the United States', *Bank of England Quarterly Bulletin*, February (1992) 71–5.

A. Sinai, 'Discussion', in Altman, E. I. and Sametz, A. W. (eds), *Financial Crises* (New York: John Wiley, 1977), pp. 187–203.

A. Smith, *The Wealth of Nations*, Campbell, R. H. and Skinner, A. S. (eds) (Oxford: Clarendon Press; 1776, repr. 1976).

B. D. Smith, 'Private Information, Deposit Interest Rates, and the "Stability" of the Banking System', *Journal of Monetary Economics*, 14 (1984) 293–317.

H. Smith, *The Examination of Usurie in Two Sermons* (London: 1591).

P. N. Snowden, 'International Equity Investment in Less Developed Countries Stockmarkets: the Replacement for Bank Lending?', *National Westminster Bank Quarterly Bulletin*, February (1987) 29–38.

F. Soddy, *Wealth, Virtual Wealth and Debt* (London: George Allen and Unwin, 1926).

H. Somerville, 'Usury and Standstill', *Economic Journal*, 42 (1932a) 318–23.

H. W. Spiegel, *The Growth of Economic Thought* (Durham, NC: Duke University Press, 1983).

S. Stein, 'Interest Taken by Jews from Gentiles', *Journal of Semitic Studies*, (1956) 141–64.

J. Steindl, 'Savings and Debt', in Barrère, A. (ed.), *Money, Credit and Prices in Keynesian Perspective* (Basingstoke: Macmillan, 1989), pp. 71–8.

J. E. Stiglitz, 'Incentives and Risk-Sharing in Sharecropping', *Review of Economic Studies*, 41 (1974) 219–55.

——, 'Credit Markets and the Control of Capital', *Journal of Money, Credit and Banking*, May (1985) 133–52.

——, 'Money, Credit and Business Fluctuations', *Economic Record*, 64 (1988) 307–26.

——, 'Capital Markets and Economic Fluctuations in Capitalist Economies', *European Economic Review*, 36 (1992) 269–306.

J. E. Stiglitz and A. Weiss, 'Credit Rationing in Markets with Imperfect Information', *American Economic Review*, 71 (1981) 393–410.

R. Sugden, *The Economics of Rights, Cooperation and Welfare* (Oxford: Blackwell, 1986).

L. H. Summers, 'Debt Problems and Macroeconomic Policies', in *Debt, Financial Stability and Public Policy* (Kansas City: Federal Reserve Bank of Kansas City, 1986), pp. 15–26.

H. Syedain, 'Survey of Islamic Banking', *Management Today*, May (1989).

T. W. Taylor and J. W. Evans, 'Islamic Banking and the Prohibition of Usury in Western Economic Theory', *National Westminster Bank Quarterly Review*, November (1987) 15–27.

D. Terlizzesse, 'On Incentive-Compatible Sharing Contracts', *Banca D'Italia Discussion Paper No. 121*, June (1989).

J. Tobin, 'Liquidity Preference as Behaviour Towards Risk', *Review of Economic Studies*, (1958) 65–86.

——, *Asset Accumulation and Economic Activity* (Oxford: Blackwell, 1980).

——, 'Financial Innovation and Deregulation in Perspective', *Bank of Japan Monetary and Economic Studies*, September (1985) 19–29.

C. Tomkins and R. A. A. Karim, 'The Shari'ah and its Implications for Islamic Financial Analysis: an Opportunity to Study Interactions Among Society, Organisation and Accounting', *American Journal of Islamic Social Science*, September (1987) 101–15.

C. Townsend and M. G. G. Schluter, *Why Keep Sunday Special* (Cambridge: The Jubilee Centre, 1985).

R. M. Townsend, 'Optimal Contracts and Competitive Markets with Costly State Verification', *Journal of Economic Theory*, October (1979) 265–93.

——, 'Optimal Multiperiod Contracts and the Gain from Enduring Relationships under Private Information', *Journal of Political Economy*, 90 (1982) 1166–86.

A. W. Troelstrup, 'The Influence of Moral and Social Responsibility on Selling Consumer Credit', *American Economic Review*, LI (1961) 549–57.

A. L. Udovitch, *Partnership and Profit in Medieval Islam* (Princeton: Princeton University Press, 1970).

——, 'Bankers Without Banks: Commerce, Banking and Society in the Islamic World of the Middle Ages', in *The Dawn of Modern Banking* (New Haven: Yale University Press, 1979), pp. 255–73.

S. F. Ulgener, 'Monetary Conditions of Economic Growth and the Islamic Concept of Interest', *The Islamic Review*, February (1967) 11–14.

M. Uzair, *Interest-Free Banking* (Karachi: Royal Book Company, 1978).

——, 'Some Conceptual and Practical Aspects of Interest-Free Banking', in Ahmad, K. (ed.), *Studies in Islamic Economics* (Leicester: The Islamic Foundation, 1980), pp. 37–51.

——, 'Central Banking Operations in an Interest-Free Banking System', in Ariff, M. (ed.), *Monetary and Fiscal Economics of Islam* (Jeddah: International Centre for Research in Islamic Economics, 1982), pp. 211–29.

P. Vallely, *Bad Samaritans: First World Ethics and Third World Debt* (Sevenoaks: Hodder and Stoughton, 1990).

T. Veblen, *The Theory of Business Enterprise* (New York: Scribners, 1904, repr. 1932).

M. Veseth, *Mountains of Debt: Crisis and Change in Renaissance Florence, Victorian Britain and Postwar America* (New York: Oxford University Press, 1990).

S. Wadhwani and M. Wall, 'The Effects of Profit-Sharing on Employment, Wages, Stock Returns and Productivity: Evidence from UK Micro-Data', *Economic Journal*, 100 (1990) 1–17.

A. N. M. Wahid, 'The Grameen Bank and Poverty Alleviation in Bangladesh: Theory, Evidence and Limitations', *American Journal of Economics and Sociology*, January (1994) 1–15.

H. C. Wallich, 'Framework for Financial Resiliency', in Altman, E. I. and Sametz, A. W. (eds), *Financial Crises* (New York: John Wiley, 1977), pp. 160–72.

D. C. Webb, 'Long-Term Financial Contracts May Mitigate the Adverse Selection Problem in Project Financing', *Discussion Paper No. 59*, London School of Economics (1989).

——, 'The Procyclical Nature of Bank Lending', mimeo, London School of Economics, 1993.

M. L. Weitzman, 'Some Macroeconomic Implications of Alternative Compensation Schemes', *Economic Journal*, 93 (1983) 763–83.

——, *The Share Economy* (Cambridge, Mass.: Harvard University Press, 1984).

——, 'The Simple Macroeconomics of Profit-Sharing', *American Economic Review*, 75 (1985) 937–53.

——, 'Steady-State Unemployment Under Profit-Sharing', *Economic Journal*, 97 (1987) 86–105.

L. H. White, *Free Banking in Britain* (Cambridge: Cambridge University Press, 1984a).

——, 'Competitive Payments Systems and the Unit of Account', *American Economic Review*, 74 (1984b) 699–712.

M. J. White, 'The Corporate Bankruptcy Decision', *Journal of Economic Perspectives*, 3 (1989) 129–51.

K. Wicksell, *Lectures on Political Economy*, Kahn, R. F. trans. (London: Routledge and Kegan Paul, vol. II, 1935).

——, *Interest and Profits*, Kahn, R. F. trans. (London: Macmillan, 1936).

P. Wilson, *A Question of Interest: the Paralysis of Saudi Banking* (New York: Praeger, 1991).

R. Wilson, *Banking and Finance in the Arab Middle East* (London: Macmillan, 1983a).

——, 'Islam and Economic Development', in MacEoin, D. and Al-Shahi, A. (eds), *Islam in the Modern World* (Beckenham: Croom Helm, 1983b), pp. 119–31.

——, *Islamic Business – Theory and Practice* (London: *Economist* Intelligence Unit, 1985).

——, 'Islamic Banking in Jordan', *Arab Law Quarterly*, 3(2) (1987) 207–29.

——, 'Introduction', *Islamic Financial Markets* (London: Routledge, 1990a), pp. 1–6.

——, 'Competition in Islamic Banking', in *Islamic Financial Markets* (London: Routledge, 1990b), pp. 19–32.

T. F. Wilson, 'Introduction', in Boulding, K. E. and Wilson, T. F. (eds), *Redistribution Through the Financial System* (New York: Praeger, 1978).

T. Wöhlers-Scharf, *Arab and Islamic Banks* (Paris: OECD Development Centre, 1983).

A. M. Wojnilower, 'L'Envoi', in Altman, E. I. and Sametz, A. W. (eds), *Financial Crises* (New York: John Wiley, 1977), pp. 234–7.

——, 'The Central Role of Credit Crunches in Recent Financial History', *Brookings Papers on Economic Activity*, (1980) 277–326.

——, 'Private Credit Demand, Supply and Crunches – How Different Are the 1980s?', *American Economic Review (Papers & Proceedings)* (1985) 351–6.

M. H. Wolfson, 'The Causes of Financial Instability', *Journal of Post-Keynesian Economics*, 12(3) (1990) 333–55.

World Bank, *World Debt Tables 1991–2* (Washington, 1991).

L. R. Wray, 'Commercial Banks, the Central Bank and Endogenous Money', *Journal of Post-Keynesian Economics*, Spring (1992) 285–96.

N. A. Zaidi, 'Interest-Free Banking and Finance in the Economic Paradigm of Islam', *Journal of Islamic Banking and Finance*, 3(3) (1986) 33–41.

——, 'Performance of Banks Under a Non-Interest System', *Journal of Islamic Banking and Finance*, 8(1) (1991) 42–50.

M. A. Zarqa, 'An Islamic Perspective on the Economics of Discounting in Project Evaluation', in Ahmed, Z., Iqbal, M. and Khan, M. F. (eds), *Fiscal Policy and Resource Allocation in Islam* (Islamabad: Institute of Policy Studies, 1983a), pp. 203–34.

——, 'Comments on the Report of the CII', in Ahmed, Z., Iqbal, M. and Khan, M. F. (eds), *Money and Banking in Islam* (Islamabad: Institute of Policy Studies, 1983b), pp. 247–9.

——, 'Stability in an Interest-Free Islamic Economy: a Note', *Pakistan Journal of Applied Economics*, 2(2) (1983c) 181–8.

H. Zhou, 'Bank Credit Allocation, Firm Size and Business Fluctuations', *School of Economics Discussion Paper 134*, November, University of Hong Kong (1992).

Index

Lerner, A.P., 138
Levine, D., 129
Levinthal, D., 29
Levy, H., 22
Lewis, T. J., 46, 140
liabilities, 50, 54
  limited, 26
  non-contingent, 68–70
  variable-return, 26
Litan, R.E., 137
Llewellyn, D.T., 66, 130
Lomax, J., 69
Lorenz, T., 133
Loveday, A., 81
Lown, C.S., 129
Lowry, S.T., 107
Luther, K., 108

Mahoney J., 133
Majluf, N.S., 129
Maksinovic, V., 124
Malinvaud, E., 132
Mallat, C., 121
Maloney, R.P., 106
managers, 35–45
Mankiw, N.G., 64, 132
Mannan, M.A., 4, 14, 16, 19, 76, 121, 131, 134, 130, 132, 135, 141
MaPaysia, 127, 128
markets. bond, 51
Marshall, A., 74
Mason, C., 125
maturity matching, 17, 86, 87
Mayer, C., 30
Mayer, T., 90
McCathy, I.S., 90
Meckling, W., 24, 25
Meghir, C., 129
Melitz, J., 70
Menezes, C.F., 132
Merton, R.C., 91
Metwally, M.M., 98, 139
Meyer, M.A., 126
Miles, D., 100
Miller, M., 22, 132
Milne, A., 131
Minsky, H.P., 61, 62, 64, 68, 97, 116, 129
Mints, L.W., 137
Mirakhor, A., 15, 18, 21, 53, 54, 55, 57, 75, 123, 128
Mishan, E.S., 106
Mishkin, F., 69

Mit Ghamr Bank, 49–50
model
  IS-LM, 21
  Islamic, 2
  Profit-and-loss, 34–39, 125–126
Modigliani, F., 22
Mohsin, M., 134
Molière, 106
money, 11, 12
  illusion, 64
  supply of, 59
  value of, 5
Moneylenders Act, 105
monopoly, 3
Montgomery, J.D., 82
Mookerjee, D., 124
Moore, C.H., 123, 129
morals, 2, 28, 29, 72, 77
Morishima, M., 125
mudarabah (profit-and-loss sharing), 35–37, 40–48, 52, 126
Mullins, D.W., 13
multiplier, Kuhn-Tucker, 42
murabaha (mark-up), 16, 52, 53, 54, 55
mushiharika, 15, 54
mutual funds, accounts, 94–95
Myers, G.C., 26, 129
Myerson, R.B., 41

Nagarayan, N.J., 124
Nakatani, I., 125, 131
Naqvi, S.N.H., 2, 13
Narayanan, M.P., 24
Nasser Social Bank, 50
Nassief, N., 127, 133
Naughton, T., 127
New Testament, see Bible
Nichomachean Ethics, 109
Nienhaus, V., 27, 127, 128
non-par-value deposits, 94–95

O'Hara, M., 134
Old Testament, see Bible
opportunity
  cost, 13
  equal, 3
Ordover, J., 133
Orhnial, T., 124

Pakistan, 49, 53–54, 114, 127, 128
Parigi, B.M., 29
Parker, M., 128
partnership-principle, 6